MW00529474

DAVID EVAN MORSE

RETIRE RICH!

PLANNING A SECURE FINANCIAL FUTURE

A Fireside Book
Published by Simon & Schuster Inc.
New York London Toronto Sydney Tokyo

First Fireside Edition, 1988
Published by Simon & Schuster Inc.
Simon & Schuster Building
Rockefeller Center
1230 Avenue of the Americas
New York, New York 10020
Published by arrangement with Franklin Watts, Inc.
FIRESIDE and colophon are registered trademarks of
Simon & Schuster Inc.
Manufactured in the United States of America
10 9 8 7 6 5 4 3 2 1 Pbk.
Library of Congress Cataloging in Publication Data
Morse, David Evan.
Retire rich!
A Fireside Book.
Originally published: New York: F. Watts, 1987.
Includes index.
1. Aged—United States—Finance, Personal.
2. Retirement income—United States—Planning. I. Title.
[HG179.M67 1988] 332.024'01 88-2006
ISBN 0-671-65687-2 Pbk.

This publication contains the author's opinion on the subject. It must be noted that neither the publisher nor the author is engaged in rendering investment, legal, tax, accounting, or similar professional services. While investment, legal, tax, and accounting issues in this book have been checked with sources believed to be reliable, some material may be affected by changes in the laws or in the interpretations of such laws since the manuscript for this book was completed. Therefore, the accuracy and completeness of such information and the opinions based thereon are not and cannot be guaranteed. In addition, state or local tax laws or procedural rules may have a material impact on the recommendations made by the author, and the strategies outlined in this book may not necessarily be suitable in every case. If legal, accounting, tax, investment, or other expert advice is required, one should obtain the services of a competent practitioner. The publisher and author hereby specifically disclaim any personal liability for loss or risk incurred as a consequence of the advice or information presented in this book.

To my editor and wife,
Michele Block Morse

CONTENTS

PREFACE

People who are able to send their kids to the finest schools, have a comfortable home and retire in luxury are not necessarily tycoons, lottery winners, or corporate moguls. Many of them just developed the simple habit of saving a little money each week, investing wisely and taking advantage of some of America's no-risk tax shelters.

On the other side of the coin are people who spend every penny they earn, no matter how much they have. For every family struggling to get by on $25,000 a year, there seems to be a single person who is barely making it on $50,000. The point is that it's not just your income level that makes it difficult to save, but your outlook.

When it comes to retirement planning, most people have a vague notion that between social security, a company pension and their savings, they'll somehow be okay. But many working Americans will discover too late that they won't be spending their golden years in much style, comfort or financial security. That's because the social security system is in trouble, company pensions are often meager and savings can quickly be eaten up by inflation and taxes. The bottom line is that you've got to plan carefully if you want to retire rich, because nobody else will do it for you.

In days gone by, life was—at least moneywise—simple because there were very few choices. Financial security meant you bought a home with an affordable thirty-year fixed mortgage, protected your family's future through life insurance, and invested any leftover money in a few safe bonds and stocks.

Today, life is anything but simple. In October 1987, the whole economic system teetered on the verge of collapse when Americans lost a collective one trillion dollars in the stock market. To date, no one has been able to explain just why it happened. Two things do seem clear: First, the system *didn't* collapse and, while we may be at the start of a long recession, this isn't 1929 revisited. Unlike the Depression, government stands ready to offer a basic level of protection against anything from bank failures or your company pension running out of money to unemployment and disability insurance; Second, just as no one prophesized the crash, no one knows what's in store for the future. During these uncertain times, people must be extra careful choosing an investment strategy. Even if the right course is simply cutting your personal debt and investing in a money market or insured savings bank account, you still have to do your homework and actively manage your money.

Today's workers also face a bewildering variety of investment options. There are some thirty to forty different kinds of mortgages on the market and even more varieties of life insurance. The investments available for your retirement dollars range from zero coupon bonds and Ginnie Maes to stocks, bonds and the families of mutual funds.

The providers of these products are different, too. Today banks act like brokerage firms and brokerage firms like banks—creating so-called financial supermarkets. The competition for your dollars is keen.

The Tax Reform Act of 1986 has added another layer of confusion (2,000 pages worth) to your retirement plans. The new rules affect every aspect of your finances, from how you spend money to how you save it. You *must* understand the new tax system in order to wisely manage your money. But as dramatic as the new law is, avoiding taxes will still play a big role in your plans to retire rich. And IRAs, or Individual Retirement Accounts, are likely to remain an important part of those plans.

To retire rich you not only have to have money, you must be a savvy financial consumer. It's up to you to educate yourself now so you'll be financially ready for retirement. The time to start planning is while you're still working—and can do something about it—not when you're at the end of your career. This means starting a systematic and conscientious savings plan. It also means protecting your growing retirement nest egg from taxes and inflation, your two greatest financial enemies. Tax shelters such as IRAs, 401(k) plans, Keoghs, your own home and life insurance can protect your savings from taxes—without risk of an IRS audit. And the less you share with Uncle Sam the more you'll have for your own retirement.

If you are already rich, you can hire a financial planner to manage things. But if you want to retire rich you have to plan for yourself. That's what this book is all about.

PART I

BIG BROTHER IS NOT WATCHING

Our social security system is financially ill. It works on a pay-as-you-go basis—today's workers are taxed to pay for today's retirees. But because the nation's birth rate is generally on the decline and people are living longer, there are fewer and fewer workers to pay for each retiree's benefits. Eventually it may reach the point where there won't be enough money coming in to fund even the moderate benefits the system currently dishes out. In that case, social security would become for most people simply a small supplemental retirement cushion or, perhaps, only a government safety net to keep older people from absolute poverty. Chapter 1 discusses what you need to know now about the social security system to wisely plan for retirement.

Chapter 2 takes you through how to protect your interest in a company retirement plan and how it does (or doesn't) fit into your plans to retire rich. The problem with company pensions is that many corporate plans are designed to benefit long-term, highly paid employees. If you stay with your job less than ten years or are not earning a lot, chances are your final pension won't amount to much, if anything. And with today's mobile work force, even highly paid individuals tend not to stick with a company long enough to earn a meaningful pension. To make matters worse, many companies actually reduce the pensions of workers earning in the middle- to low-income range by deducting what they'll get from social security. But on the other hand there is Tax Reform. One result of the new laws will be to make it more likely that even mobile workers get some benefits if they stick around long enough for these laws to take effect.

CHAPTER 1

SOCIAL SECURITY: WHAT WORKING PEOPLE NEED TO KNOW TODAY

Even if you're 21 years old and retirement is the furthest thing from your mind, you need to know something about the social security system.

Why?

First, because most likely more than 7 percent of your wages go toward social security, up to a total tax of $3,379.50. For most workers social security is the biggest tax bite.

Second, the younger you are, the less likely you are to get much benefit from all those taxes when you retire because the system may not survive in its present form until then.

Finally, you should know how much death and disability benefits you and your family eventually will be entitled to, so you can decide now if you also need insurance (probably yes) and how much.

HOW SECURE IS SOCIAL SECURITY?

Not very! Basically, the social security system operates like a giant chain letter in which today's workers are stuck at the bottom. It's a pay-as-you-go setup: the government uses the social security taxes withheld from your own paycheck to pay benefits to people who already are retired.

That means that none of the social security taxes you pay will be used by the government to help fund your benefits when you retire. Your own retirement payments will depend on how much the next generation of workers pays in social security taxes. In other words, social security withholding is a form of income tax used by the government to pay current retirement benefits under the system.

The system has worked reasonably well for more than three decades. But trouble is brewing: America's population is, on average, older than ever before. The number of people over 65 is increasing faster than the number of people under 65, because of longer life expectancy and a declining birth rate. The post-World War II baby boom generation will only worsen the situation: when that large generation—who, on average, are having fewer children—retires around the year 2015, there will not be nearly enough younger workers to support the baby boomers' retirement benefits under the current payment system.

In 1950, there were 16½ workers contributing to the social security system for each retiree. Today there are fewer than 3⅓ workers paying for each beneficiary. By the year 2030, there will be only 2 workers contributing taxes for each person receiving social security benefits.

Think of it this way: Assume that seven people are stranded on a tropical island. They decide that everyone between the ages of 18 and 65 will work to support everyone else. The seven people have the following ages:

Name	*Age*
Robinson Crusoe	65
Friday	50
Monday	30
Tuesday	35
Wednesday	38
Boy	10
Girl	8

Robinson Crusoe is in great shape because he has four people working to support him. By the time Friday retires, there will be five people (because Boy and Girl will be over 18) to support him and Crusoe. But when Monday, Tuesday, and Wednesday decide to retire, there will only be two people left to support them. And what about Boy and Girl? If they want to retire, they have to get busy and produce many more workers who can support them in their old age.

Now you can see the problem with social security. In 1983 the system nearly ran out of money because there were not enough employee taxes coming in to cover the retirement benefits being paid out. To save the system from bankruptcy, Congress decided to gradually increase social security taxes as follows:

	Rate	
Year	*Employees*	*Self-employed*
1983	6.70%	9.35%
1984	7.00	11.30
1985	7.05	11.80
1986–1987	7.15	12.30
1988–1989	7.51	13.02
1990 and later	7.65	15.30

In a roundabout way, Congress also reduced social security benefits at the same time. The minimum social security retirement age gradually will be increased from age 65 to age 67 by the year 2027. There was no cost-of-living increase given to social security recipients between March and September of 1982 and future cost-of-living increases are to be reduced. And, for the first time, Congress voted to tax a retiree's social security benefits if his other income exceeds a certain amount—$25,000 for single individuals and $32,000 for married couples.

Unfortunately, the combined tax increase and reduction in benefits are only a temporary solution. Social security is solvent for now, but the financial crisis is expected to return—possibly within the next several years, according to some economists.

In terms of retiring rich, that means that social security cannot be relied upon to provide anything in the way of adequate retirement income—especially for people under age 50. By the time those younger workers retire, Congress may not be willing to continue raising social security taxes and may reduce benefits even further. The best approach in planning for your retirement is to think of social security as a potential supplement to your own income, in the same category as gifts from a rich and eccentric uncle—nice, but not to be depended upon.

WHAT'S THE TAX?

Both you and your employer pay a certain amount into social security—for 1988, the tax bite is 7.51 percent of your wages. Just to set the record straight, the 7.51 percent tax is actually two taxes. The first is a 6.06 percent tax for Old-Age Survivor and Disability Insurance (cleverly called "OASDI"), which goes for monthly benefits when you retire, become disabled or die. The second is a 1.45 percent tax for Hospital Insurance (you guessed it, "HI"), which goes to pay for Medicare benefits. However, you are not taxed on all your wages, only on a certain level called the "Maximum Taxable Amount." After your wages reach that limit, you are exempt from social security taxes.

The maximum taxable amount changes each year, based on the average increase in earnings of all U.S. workers the previous year. By way of comparison, while in 1965 the maximum taxable amount was only $4,800, for 1988 that amount is $45,000. So if your salary today is $30,000, you'll have $2,253 withheld from your paycheck—that's 7.51 percent—and your employer will have to kick in an additional $2,253. If you earned $45,000, you'll each pay $3,379.50 or 7.51 percent of $45,000. Any salary above the maximum is not taxed by the social security system.

It works out that rich people pay proportionately less in social security taxes than not-so-rich people. A person earning $200,000 pays social security taxes only on the first $45,000 earned—which works out to a tax of only 1.7 percent of his total $200,000 salary. But the person making $20,000 pays social security on every penny of it, which works out to a full 7.51 percent chunk of his annual income.

Everything that you normally think of as "wages"—and then some—counts in figuring the tax. That includes salary, bonuses, commissions, straight time, overtime, vacation pay, etc. It also may include "freebies" such as use of a company car or meal allowances. It doesn't matter when you work, or how often—if you earn it, it's taxed by the social security system.

If you changed jobs or worked more than one job during the year, each of your employers must withhold social security taxes from your salary. If your combined wages exceeded the maximum for which you should be taxed, then the two employers will end up withholding too much—but you'll get it back. When you file your federal income tax return, you can use this overpayment either to reduce the total income tax you owe Uncle Sam, or have it refunded to you. (Incidentally, your employer doesn't get credited for its share of the overpayment.)

What if You're Self-Employed?

Self-employed people must pay social security taxes on all net annual income over $400. This income is more or less the same as the income reported on IRS Tax Schedule SE. If a person has more than one type of self-employment income, then the profit and losses from all are added together.

Self-employed people pay a higher rate of social security taxes than regular employees. For 1988 the rate is 15.02 percent of their earnings, up to the maximum taxable amount. Self-employed people currently do pay less in social security taxes than an employee and employer combined would pay. But that difference will be eliminated in 1990, when the self-employed tax increases to twice the regular employee tax.

If you're employed and self-employed at the same time, you pay the self-employed social security tax rate only if your regular employer-paid earnings are less than the maximum taxable amount.

Example: James, an accountant with a big company, earns a salary of $37,800 in 1988. He also moonlights by preparing tax returns in his spare time, earning $12,000 after expenses. James pays self-employed social security taxes on only $7,200 of his self-employment income, enough to bring the total of his regular salary and outside income to the maximum $45,000 limit.

OBSERVATION: If you have a net loss from your self-employed activities, you cannot use that loss to reduce social security taxes on your wages as an employee.

ARE YOU IN THE RETIREMENT SYSTEM?

Most likely yes! Today nearly all workers, including self-employed persons, are included in the social security system. For decades, employees of Uncle Sam were excluded from the system, but as of 1984 all newly hired federal workers also are covered. The same is true for employees of not-for-profit organizations such as charities, who until 1984 were ineligible for social security benefits. State and local governments have the option to cover their employees or not—but about 70 percent of them do. Among the few people still not covered by social security are members of the clergy and railroad workers.

Basically anyone who works at least ten years is considered "fully insured," which means you'll be able to apply for and receive retirement benefits from the government. It also means your spouse, former spouse (if you're divorced) and any dependents could be entitled to benefits as well. You do not have to actually be retired to receive social security retirement benefits as long as you reach a certain age. Any eligible worker can start receiving social security benefits when he reaches social security's standard retirement age (presently 65, but being gradually raised to 67) or early retirement age (62 and holding steady).

The social security folks rate your eligibility to collect benefits by counting what they call "quarters of coverage." Until 1978, workers earned a quarter of coverage for every three consecutive months in which they earned at least $50. In 1978, the rules were changed so that the amount you must earn to be credited with one quarter of coverage is raised each year based on cost-of-living factors. It also no longer matters when you earn the money during the year. For 1988, the minimum is $470 to earn each quarter of coverage so that a total of $1,880 will give you four quarters for the year.

You need forty "quarters of coverage" to be fully covered. This generally works out to a minimum of ten years full-time employment to be fully insured.

Workers born before 1929 get a special break. They need to accumulate only from twenty-six to thirty-nine quarters of coverage, with one less quarter required for each year before 1929 that the person was born. The chart on page 18 illustrates this.

There also are special exceptions on eligibility for workers who become disabled or die before becoming fully insured. Those are described later on in this chapter.

Being fully insured is only the start. The actual amount of your social security benefits will be based

Year of Birth	*Quarters Needed*
1915	26
1916	27
1917	28
1918	29
1919	30
1920	31
1921	32
1922	33
1923	34
1924	35
1925	36
1926	37
1927	38
1928	39
1929	40

on three factors: how much money you earned while you worked, at what age you retire and how much retirement income you have besides social security.

CHECKING YOUR ACCOUNT

It's critical that the government give you proper credit for all your earnings, since that is what your retirement benefits will be based on. The Social Security Administration keeps a record of all employees' wages, including salary, bonuses and self-employment income. But with 115 million workers to keep track of, mistakes can and do happen. If all of your earnings are not recorded, you ultimately could be denied or receive less social security benefits than you are entitled to. Right now, the Social Security Administration reports that over $75 *billion* in earnings have not been credited to anyone's account because officials have no idea who earned the money. That's enough earnings to enable over 100,000 people to retire on full benefits!

To protect your rights, you should request a copy of your social security earnings record about every three years. Don't wait much longer between checks, because it is more difficult and sometimes impossible to correct older mistakes. Simply call, write or stop in at your nearest social security office and ask for a postcard request form. A completed form is shown on page 20.

Social security will send you your earnings record, broken down by:

your earnings for each year since 1984
your total earnings from 1951–1983
your total earnings from 1937–1950

Since the Social Security Administration is about a year behind in its record keeping, your most recent year's earnings won't be included.

Compare the statement with your old W–2 forms. If there is any discrepancy, contact your local social security office immediately! You will probably be asked to fill out a simple form and send it to them along with a copy of your old W–2, the name of your employer

Social Security Form SSA 7004-PC-OP1
Request for Statement of Earnings

FOLD HERE

FOR SSA USE ONLY

AX

SP

REQUEST FOR STATEMENT OF EARNINGS
(PLEASE PRINT IN INK OR USE TYPEWRITER)

I REQUEST A SUMMARY STATEMENT OF EARNINGS FROM MY SOCIAL SECURITY RECORD

NH — Full name you use in work or business
First: DOLORES
Middle Initial: A.
Last: JONES

SN — Social Security number shown on your card: 111-11-1111

DB — Your date of birth: Month 10 Day 19 Year 51 A

MA — Other Social Security number(s) you have used: None

SX — Your Sex: ☐ Male ☒ Female

AK — Other name(s) you have used (Include your maiden name): DOLORES A. SMITH

FOLD HERE

PRIVACY STATEMENT

The Social Security Administration (SSA) is authorized to collect information asked on this form under section 205 of the Social Security Act. It is needed so SSA can quickly identify your record and prepare the earnings statement you requested. While you are not required to furnish the information, failure to do so may prevent your request from being processed. The information will be used primarily for issuing your earnings statement.

I am the individual to whom the record pertains. I understand that if I knowingly and willingly request or receive a record about an individual under false pretenses I would be guilty of a Federal crime and could be fined up to $5000.

Sign your name here: (Do not print) *Dolores A. Jones*
TELEPHONE NO (Area Code): (212) 715-8052
DATE: 9/1/86

SEND THE STATEMENT TO (to be completed in ALL cases)

PN — Name: DOLORES A. JONES

AD — Address (Number and Street, Apt No, P O Box, or Rural Route): 1 West Street
City and state: New York, New York
ZP — Zip Code: 10001

Form SSA-7004-PC-OP1 (9/85)
Destroy prior editions

(or your old tax returns if you were self-employed) as proof of your earnings, along with some other documentation. If caught soon enough, the mistake can be corrected; but errors which are over 3¼ years old may be impossible to correct.

OBSERVATION: If you had more than one employer during the same year, the social security office will list total earnings, even if it exceeds the maximum for that year. But your earnings only count up to the maximum.

In addition to making the three-year review, be sure to notify your local social security office if you change your name—for instance, if you get married—so that your records are not lost.

Just in case you're not asked to use the form, here is a sample letter to the Social Security Administration asking that a mistake be corrected:

[date]

Local Social Security Administrative Office
[Address]

[Your Name]
[Your Social Security Number]

Dear Sir:
I recently received a Summary Statement of Earnings (copy attached) which shows that my covered earnings for 1984 totaled $18,000.00. This is an error. My actual 1984 earnings were

$30,000.00. The names, addresses and earnings from my two employers in 1984 were:

1. XYZ Co. $18,000
   377 Main Street
   NY, NY
2. Acme, Inc. $12,000
   1 Penn Plaza
   Stamford, CT

I am also enclosing one copy each of my Forms W–2 for 1984. Please correct your records at once and notify me when you have done so. I may be reached at:
[Address]

Sincerely yours,
[Your Name]

HOW SOCIAL SECURITY BENEFITS ARE FIGURED

Calculating your exact social security benefit by yourself is difficult because it requires detailed information about your year-by-year social security earnings record. But you can use the following short-cut income chart to get a rough estimate of your monthly social security income, based on 1988 benefits.

Income	*Age 65 (Regular Retirement)*
$12,000	$462
18,000	604
35,000	810
45,000 and above	838

This chart works best for someone with a relatively stable earnings record. It is less useful for someone who stopped working for a number of years in mid-career (e.g., to raise a family) or whose income fluctuated considerably from year to year.

Another way to look at this information is in terms of what percentage of your salary it will replace. The following chart will allow you to do just that, again assuming your salary remains steady, you retire at about age 65 and—most importantly—the system does not change radically.

Salary	*Salary Replaced (One Worker)*	*Salary Replaced (Worker and Dependent Spouse)*
$ 12,000	46%	69%
18,000	40	60
35,000	28	42
45,000	22	33
55,000	18	27
100,000	10	15

The "Salary Replaced (One Worker)" column shows what you'd receive if you were single. The "Salary Replaced (Worker and Dependent Spouse)" column shows what a worker with a nonworking spouse (also of retirement age) could expect to receive.

OBSERVATION: Once you are nearing retirement, you can write to the social security office to get an accurate estimate of your benefits. (Chapter 11 tells you how.)

Remember that benefits also are paid to a worker's dependent child or to a nonworking spouse who is of retirement age. Their benefit is usually one-half of the working spouse's benefit, but increases to 75 percent if the worker dies. Thus, a worker earning at the maximum rate with a dependent spouse who is also 65-years old would get a total family benefit of about $1,257 a month or $15,084 a year. There also are retirement benefits for dependent parents and children, and disability benefits for you and your dependents. If you think you are eligible now for any of these benefits, check with your local social security office.

OBSERVATION: There's a ceiling on the maximum combined benefit that a worker's family can receive, usually not more than one and a half times the worker's benefit.

OBSERVATION: Many divorced "dependent spouses" also qualify for benefits.

WHAT ABOUT TWO-EARNER COUPLES?

The social security system is geared toward the traditional married couple with one wage earner. When both spouses work, they each are entitled to a separate benefit. But sometimes a two-earner couple will receive a lower benefit on their combined income than a one-earner couple with the same total income.

To estimate their retirement benefit, the two-wage-earner couples should use the one worker column in the previous chart for each salary. If one spouse earned $35,000 and the other $45,000, they could expect a social security benefit of 28 percent of the $35,000 paycheck and 22 percent of the $45,000 check. But that combined benefit could be reduced because of the family limit.

Where Do You Stand?

Depending on your income level, you probably are delighted, horrified or unmoved by your replacement ratio. To the "delighted" crowd, please reread the first section of this chapter, "How Secure is Social Security?" Hopefully, that will knock that smile of contentment off your face and shock you into planning (saving) for your own retirement.

Those "horrified"—probably the above-average earners and two-wage-earner couples—may feel even worse after reading the next chapter about your company's retirement plan. Good! The bottom line is that you've got to be ready to make it on your own when you retire.

Hats off to the unmoved—you have learned to ignore social security. If it pays you a nice benefit—fine. If not—you'll be ready with retirement income of your own.

DISABILITY BENEFITS

A healthy individual should know enough about social security disability and death benefits to decide how much outside insurance protection he needs to buy now. (*See* Chapter 7 – Insurance.) The government considers you "disabled" if you cannot work in any meaningful way because of either mental or physical problems. The government's definition of "work" may be stricter than your own; not only must you be unable to do your job, but you must be incapable of "other substantial gainful activity." The disability must be expected to last at least twelve months—or to kill you before then.

Most workers are entitled to disability benefits about equal to the amount their normal retirement benefit would have been. However, if you didn't start working by age 21 or took some time off after that, your disability benefit could be substantially lower than your eventual retirement benefit. Why? Because your benefit is based, more or less, on the average salary you've earned since the age of 21. So if you didn't start working until age 25, you'll have four "zero" years figured into your average. The zero income years won't matter as much if you retire at age 65, and have lots of higher-income working years built up, but it will hurt you if you become disabled at age 30.

You are eligible for disability benefits if you have enough quarters of coverage and a certain number of quarters were earned in recent years. The following chart will help you figure out how many quarters of coverage you need to be fully insured:

Age When Disabled	*Quarters of Coverage Needed*
Under 24	6 earned in last 3 years
24	7 earned after age 21
25	9 earned after age 21
26	11 earned after age 21
27	13 earned after age 21
28	15 earned after age 21
29	17 earned after age 21
30	19 earned after age 21
31 and older	1 quarter for each year after age 21 (or 1950 if you were born before 1930), including 20 quarters earned over last ten years

You must wait five *full* months after becoming disabled before becoming eligible for benefits. That means if you become disabled on May 2, May doesn't count as a full month and benefits would begin in November. But your "November" check would arrive no earlier than December 3.

You'll also get an additional payment equal to one-half of your own benefit for each child under 18 (19 if they're in high school) and for your spouse (if you have a child under 16 or your spouse is over age 65). Unfortunately there is also a maximum limit on family benefits, usually no more than one and a half times a worker's benefit.

Observation: This is only a brief sketch of a very complicated system. Again, if you think you are eligible for disability benefits, you should apply for them immediately. (*See* Chapter 11 for the best way how.)

DEATH BENEFITS

Your spouse and dependents may be entitled to a special social security benefit upon your death if you are either currently insured or fully insured. Currently insured means you have accumulated six quarters of coverage over the last three and a quarter years. To be fully insured for death benefits in which case your survivors may collect more—you must have accumulated a minimum number of quarters, based on your age at death, while you are working. The following chart will help you estimate how many quarters of coverage you need to be fully insured for death benefits:

Age at Death	*Quarters of Coverage Needed*
28 and under	6
29–65	6 + 1 for each year you're older than 28
66	26
67	27
68	28
69	29
70	30

For example, if you are 30 years old, you need eight quarters (6 + 2) to be fully insured.

Assuming you are fully covered at your death, the list of people eligible to collect the benefit is:

- a spouse caring for your natural or adopted child under age 16 (unless you died in an accident or military duty, your spouse must have been married to you for at least nine months)
- a child (natural or adopted under age 18, but can be 19 if in high school)
- a spouse over age 60

If your spouse or child is disabled, the coverage may be extended. And, if you're fully insured, your dependent parent over age 62 may also qualify for benefits.

The chart on page 30 roughly estimates the monthly benefits that would be payable to your family if you died in 1988, assuming you had worked steadily and had received average pay raises. To figure your exact benefit, you must contact your local social security office.

YOU'RE ON YOUR OWN

You should now have a basic idea of what to expect and not expect from social security. The system works mostly as a safety net for people who have a financial crisis, such as the death or disability of the family

Exhibit 2
Monthly Benefits If You Should Die

Your age in 1988	*Who receives benefits*	*Your Present Annual Earnings*				
		$12,000	*$18,000*	*$26,000*	*$35,000*	*$45,000 & up*
65	Spouse, age 65	$462	$ 604	$ 768	$ 810	$ 838
	Spouse, age 60	329	432	548	579	599
	Child; spouse caring for child	345	453	575	607	628
	Maximum family benefit	817	1,086	1,342	1,417	1,467
60	Spouse, age 65	478	624	786	834	858
	Spouse, age 60	341	446	562	595	613
	Child; spouse caring for child	358	468	590	624	643
	Maximum family benefit	803	1,151	1,377	1,458	1,502
55	Spouse, age 65	478	626	794	842	870
	Spouse, age 60	341	447	567	602	622
	Child; spouse caring for child	358	469	595	631	653
	Maximum family benefit	803	1,152	1,389	1,473	1,524
50	Spouse, age 65	478	626	802	858	892
	Spouse, age 60	341	447	574	613	638
	Child; spouse caring for child	358	469	602	643	669
	Maximum family benefit	803	1,152	1,405	1,501	1,562
45	Spouse, age 65	478	626	808	878	923
	Spouse, age 60	341	447	578	628	660
	Child; spouse caring for child	358	469	606	658	692
	Maximum family benefit	803	1,152	1,415	1,537	1,616
40	Spouse, age 65	478	626	810	901	963
	Spouse, age 60	341	447	579	644	688
	Child; spouse caring for child	358	469	607	675	722
	Maximum family benefit	803	1,152	1,418	1,577	1,686
35	Spouse, age 65	479	626	810	914	1,010
	Spouse, age 60	342	447	579	653	722
	Child; spouse caring for child	359	469	608	685	758
	Maximum family benefit	807	1,152	1,418	1,600	1,769
30	Spouse, age 65	481	630	813	917	1,039
	Spouse, age 60	344	450	581	656	742
	Child; spouse caring for child	361	472	609	688	779
	Maximum family benefit	813	1,159	1,423	1,606	1,818

Source: William M. Mercer-Meidinger-Hansen, Inc.

breadwinner. It's also there to help put food on the table for low-income retirees, and to provide supplemental retirement income for middle-income families.

More importantly, in terms of your financial plan you must realize what not to expect: social security is *not* there to support middle- and upper-income earners in their accustomed style. The younger you are, the less you can expect in benefits as the system struggles to handle America's aging population. If you want any measure of security in your golden years, social security isn't going to give it to you. You've got to do it on your own!

Q. Does Tax Reform affect my social security benefits?

A. No. But neither was anything done to financially shore up the system.

Q. How about any other laws?

A. Yes. The 1987 budget law states that social security benefits will automatically rise each year with inflation. In the past, it took inflation of at least 3% before benefits increased.

CHAPTER 2

WHAT YOUR COMPANY WON'T TELL YOU ABOUT YOUR RETIREMENT PLAN

Today, most larger corporations and many smaller ones offer at least one kind of retirement plan to their employees.

But a company retirement plan may not do you that much good financially, depending on the way it is structured.

For one thing, you must carefully evaluate your company's retirement plan to see what benefit, if any, you'll be entitled to when you retire or leave the company. If you change jobs before retirement, you'll need to understand what rights and what investment options you'll have for your retirement benefits. And of course you'll need to look at the effects of Tax Reform. Only then can you develop an intelligent financial plan and determine how much money you need to save on your own toward retirement.

THE FOUR HORSEMEN OF RETIREMENT PLANS

There are four business trends today that may threaten the value of your company retirement benefits.

The first is an increasingly high employee turnover rate. Today's mobile work force changes jobs and sometimes careers with a frequency that would have been shocking in their parents' generation. Instead of patiently waiting for that promotion or pay raise, more and more people are willing to change jobs to get it. The problem is that the vast majority of big and medium-size companies (85 percent) require that a participant be employed at least ten full years before he can collect a dime from the company's retirement plan. The technical term for being entitled to a benefit is being "vested." An employee loses his entire benefit if he leaves the company before accumulating those minimum years of service and becoming vested. Tax Reform has added some new rules which will make it easier for workers to become vested. But as we'll see, these rules won't take effect until 1989.

Even people who have worked long enough to become vested will discover that most company retirement plans are designed mostly for the benefit of longtime employees. To receive full benefits, you may have to stick it out at your company for twenty-five to thirty years! The U.S. government estimates that on average, even employees who do work those thirty years will receive only a little over one-quarter of their final salary in company retirement benefits. Employees with less than thirty years service receive proportionately smaller pensions. That's bad news for most employees.

What's even worse news is that over half of all plans are designed so that the more highly paid the worker is, the bigger his retirement benefits will be. The cutoff point is usually the social security wage base (about $43,800 in 1987). Workers earning at or below that level get a disproportionately *smaller* benefit than those earning above it. As discussed later in this chapter, the theory behind giving better company benefits to higher-paid workers is that lower-paid workers will receive much more in social security benefits—which, as we've seen, is far from the truth.

The second negative trend in company retirement plans is the instability of corporate America. Corporations are regularly taking each other over and when they're not involved with takeovers, they're swapping subsidiary companies. At the same time, some companies in certain industries—such as steel, heavy equipment, agriculture and banking—are in big financial trouble. The rate of company bankruptcies and near bankruptcies is approaching the levels of the Great Depression.

The result of this corporate instability: you can do a good job and still lose it. After a takeover, many employees are declared "redundant," which is a polite explanation for being unnecessary. For instance, where before each company had its own accounting department, after the merger they're one big company and two full accounting departments are too many. When things settle down after the takeover, the dominant company will decide just how many accountants they really need and fire the redundant ones.

For companies in financial difficulty, a favorite method of cost cutting is firing employees. Even a good worker intending to stay with his employer forever may find himself in trouble through no fault of his own if his once-stable company undergoes radical changes.

The third trend is the growing instability of the pension world. Pensions are a large expense to companies and are all too often eyed greedily by cost-cutting executives who might freeze benefits, reduce them, or eliminate them altogether. This would not affect workers already retired, whose payments by law cannot be reduced; but it can hurt current employees' retirement planning. Sometimes, financially troubled companies reduce their annual contribution to their employees' pension fund. Over time this causes "underfunding"—meaning that the plan does not have enough money to pay everyone's benefits. The federal Pension Benefit Guaranty Corporation (PBGC) provides insurance for a *portion* of any pension lost because of underfunding. But these days, so many plans are underfunded that the PBGC may be broke some day unless Congress keeps a close eye on it. Recently, the LTV Corporation declared bankruptcy and may dump an additional $1.5 billion in liabilities on the PBGC.

The fourth trend is inflation. It may not seem much of a problem now, with prices rising at an annual rate of only 3 percent or 4 percent and many economists saying that the days of double-digit inflation are over. But the amount of most pensions is fixed at retirement and their value can be eroded quickly by even single-digit inflation: a modest clip of 3 percent inflation a year means that after ten years, the value of your pension would be reduced by 25 percent. Even those companies that offer retirees so-called cost-of-living adjustments do so when and how they please, and the increases may not cover the real loss of income.

THE RETIREMENT PLAN PRIMER

Since 1974, all company retirement plans have been regulated by the Employee Retirement Income Security Act, more affectionately known as "ERISA." In a nutshell, ERISA makes it more likely—but by no means guarantees—that you will get whatever retirement benefit your company has promised you. The ERISA rules help ensure that your company pension plan will not run into the same cash crunch that the social security system now faces.

Under ERISA, a retirement benefit must be paid from a specific trust fund set aside exclusively for employees. The company makes contributions to the fund and invests the money. Once the money is put in that trust fund nobody, including your company, can get their hands on it until after everyone gets their retirement benefit in full. But most plans state that if the trust doesn't have enough money the company *won't* make up the difference; that's the rub. And a company is permitted to change the amount of its contributions.

Like a great deal of federal legislation, ERISA was put together in a hurry. When Congress didn't have time to agree on or think through a particular rule, it was simply left vague or ignored altogether. Since 1974, there have been no fewer than seven major revisions of ERISA and a dozen more are in the works. The result is that lawyers, actuaries and accountants are the only ones who can figure out what ERISA really says. Those "experts" often fail miserably when trying to explain to laymen what their ERISA rights are all about.

The best way to understand your company's retirement plan is to read a standardized document that every plan must have. It's called the Summary Plan Description, or "SPD," and explains the basic features of your company's plan. If you are covered by your company's retirement plan, your company under the law must give you a free copy of the SPD upon request.

Before reviewing your SPD, be sure to ask whether the SPD is updated for all recent plan amendments and, if not, ask for a description of the changes. By law your company must update its SPD within 210 days after the end of any year in which there were substantial changes made in the plan. This means your SPD could be almost two full years behind the times.

Observation: If you have lost your SPD, you are entitled to a second free copy from your company's employee benefits or personnel department. If your company refuses to give you a copy of the SPD for your retirement plan, contact the U.S. Department of Labor (they're listed in the back of this book) or your lawyer.

The Plain English Dilemma

SPDs are supposed to be written in "plain English." Unfortunately, that's not usually the case. Some companies do make an effort to make their plans comprehensible. They turn the task of writing the SPD over to highly paid consultants who describe the plan in glowing, glossy, easy-to-read terms with lots of pictures and diagrams. But when the company's lawyers get their hands on the SPD, the first thing they usually do is cross out all the examples and sexy stuff written by the consultants. Instead, they substitute long, drawn-out sentences that make little sense to anyone except other lawyers.

Although the consultants fight with the lawyers over whose language will prevail, the lawyers usually win because an SPD is something akin to a contract. In cases where the pension benefit the SPD describes is made to sound more generous than the actual plan, some courts have made the company pay the employee the extra amount. Many companies prefer to listen to their attorneys rather than risk having an outside consultant overrate their retirement plans.

OBSERVATION: Every SPD contains a standard disclaimer that it's only a summary of the plan and that any discrepancies are resolved based on what the actual plan says. But if your company ever tries to give you less than what you believe the SPD promises, then run, don't walk, to a good ERISA lawyer. You might very well have a strong case for getting the better benefit.

What follows is an explanation—in true plain English—of what you really need to know about your company's retirement plan. It covers the three main features of any plan: the eligibility rules, the vesting schedule and the benefit formula. Or, to put it more simply, the questions "Are you in?," "Do you get to keep it?" and "How much?"

1. *Are You In?*

The first important question to answer is if and when you will be allowed to participate in your company's retirement plan. Most plans require that employees reach a minimum age—usually 21—and work for the company a specified period of time—usually one year—before they are eligible to participate. That doesn't mean you are vested—only that you have the potential to earn benefits toward your retirement.

EXAMPLE: John is 19 years old when he is hired by Company X. Company X's pension plan says that all employees can participate in the plan if they are at least 21 years old and have worked for the company for one year. Because of his age, John will have to work for the company two years before he can participate in the plan. But if John had been 25 years old when he was hired by Company X, he could have started participating in the plan after only one year.

OBSERVATION: Many companies have different retirement plans for different workers. For example, there could be one plan for employees who are paid on an hourly basis and another for those who earn a flat weekly salary. Always check to see which plan covers you.

Determining your eligiblity to be in your company's retirement plan is just the first and simplest hurdle. Next, you must figure out:

2. *What Do You Get To Keep?*

Usually, you must work for the company a minimum number of years before you are allowed to keep all or a part of your benefits if you quit or are fired. When you reach that point, you are considered to be vested.

Once you have fulfilled the vesting requirements of your company's particular plan, you have a right to receive your retirement benefits. That applies whether you quit, retire, are fired or elope with the boss's youngest daughter (or son).

A company has a choice of vesting its employees at once after a certain period, or of phasing in vesting over a period of time. In the first case, an employee who leaves a company any time before the vesting period will receive no retirement benefits. In the second case, an employee who leaves the company with graduated vesting after only, say, three years might be 30 percent vested—meaning that he will be entitled to 30 percent of the retirement benefits he has earned with that company. In any case, by law you are considered completely vested when you reach the plan's "normal retirement age," which is usually age 65.

While you should check your SPD to see what vesting method your company uses, the vast majority of companies do not phase in vesting. They use what is called "ten-year cliff vesting": that means if you leave the company after ten years you are fully vested, but if you leave anytime before ten years you receive nothing.

Here's what it looks like:

10-Year Cliff Vesting

Years of Employment	*Percent Vested*
0–9	nothing
10 or more	100%

But under the Tax Reform Act, all plans will be required to use one of two much faster vesting schedules. Here's what they'll look like:

5-Year Cliff

Years of Employment	*Percent Vested*
0–4	nothing
5	100%

7-Year Graduated Vesting

Years of Employment	*Percent Vested*
0–2	nothing
3	20%
4	40
5	60
6	80
7	100

All plans must use one of these two schedules starting with the 1989 "plan year." A plan year is the twelve-month cycle that the plan uses as its financial year and isn't necessarily the standard January to December calendar year. You only have to be in the plan for one hour in the 1989 plan year to take advantage of the faster vesting. And the new, more generous vesting rules will apply to all retirement plan benefits, not just those earned starting in 1989.

EXAMPLE: Betty is head cashier of Acme Bank with five years of employment in 1988. Because under the old tax law Acme's retirement plan used ten-year cliff vesting, she had no vested benefit. But if Acme chooses the new five-year vesting, starting in 1989 Betty will be instantly 100 percent vested. If they choose seven-year graduated vesting, Betty will automatically be 60 percent vested.

OBSERVATION: If you are thinking about quitting your job in 1988, consider waiting until the 1989 retirement plan year, when you may be entitled to a larger vested benefit.

Sometimes a smaller company's plan is skewed in favor of management, which is called being "top heavy." In that case, ERISA requires that the company use one of two special vesting schedules (which are even faster than the new tax reform methods) to compensate nonmanagement employees. This is how the more popular of the two schedules works:

Top Heavy

Years of Employment	*Percent Vested*
1	nothing
2	20%
3	40
4	60
5	80
6	100

Counting the Years. Figuring out your years of employment in terms of retirement benefits is not as simple as it sounds. Many plans count a year as any plan year in which you've worked at least 1,000 hours.

But some plans don't even bother counting hours because figuring the definition of an "hour of work" (for example, paid vacations and lunch do count) is rather difficult. Instead they count a year of employment as any plan year in which you worked at any time. For example, if you worked the first and the last day of the plan year you'd generally have a year of employment, even if you were absent (e.g., quit and then came back) the rest of the year.

If you quit your job before being vested and then return within a certain period, generally you will be allowed credit for all your years of employment. You usually can return to work within five years or the number of plan years of employment you accumulated before you quit, whichever is more. The first year you are gone from your job due to the birth or adoption of a child does not count as a year off from work. There are also special rules for part-time workers.

OBSERVATION: This discussion of years of employment is only a summary of some very complicated legal rules. Generally, if you are a steady full-time worker you usually do not have to worry about meeting the technical requirements for a year of employment.

OBSERVATION: Before you quit your job, find out exactly where you stand vestingwise by simply asking your company for a special benefit statement discussed at the end of the next section. If you are close to becoming vested, it may be well worth it to stick to your job a little longer so that you will be entitled to keep your retirement benefit when you leave.

3. *How Large a Benefit?*

In most retirement plans, benefits are based on how many years you have worked for the company after becoming eligible to participate in the plan. The amount of the benefit you have earned toward retirement (which in legalese is called "accrued") is usually based on your salary under what is called a "benefit formula."

There are two basic kinds of retirement plans—

pension plans and profit-sharing plans. The difference between them is how the benefit is calculated.

Pension Plans. By far the most popular, a pension plan promises you a guaranteed, fixed payment (or pension) each year after you retire for the rest of your life. Retirement age—the age at which payment is scheduled to start—is usually age 65. Your company invests the money in its pension plan but, unless the plan runs out of money, the earnings or losses do not affect the size of employees' pensions.

A typical benefit formula for a pension plan might work something like this: beginning at age 65, a fully vested retiree is paid a yearly pension equal to 1 percent of his average salary multiplied by the number of years he has participated in the company's pension plan.

EXAMPLE: Using the above pension formula, assume Peter joined the Acme Company at age 34 and became eligible to start earning benefits under its pension plan one year later, at age 35. He eventually becomes fully vested and retires from the Acme Company after thirty years at age 65, having earned an average salary at the company of $24,000. His annual pension will be 30 percent of $24,000, or $7,200 a year for life. The amount of Peter's pension is determined like this:

1. Years worked (after becoming a plan participant)	30
2. 30 years multipled by 1%	30%
3. 30% of his average salary of $24,000	$7,200

How Is Average Salary Figured? How your company figures your average salary can make a tremendous difference in how much money you collect when you retire. The two basic methods are called: (1) career average salary; and (2) final average salary.

Your career average salary is simply the average salary you have been paid by the company for the entire time you have been in its pension plan. If you have been participating in the plan for ten years, add up your total salary for those ten years and divide by ten.

The final average salary method is more complicated but can be more lucrative for the employee. Final average salary is the average salary you earned during your final few years of employment, usually the last five years.

If you have been working for the same company for a long time, your final average salary is going to be a lot higher than your career average salary. For one thing, inflation has been especially high over the last fifteen or so years. If your company has been giving you cost-of-living raises, your salary in recent years probably has skyrocketed (in terms of dollars, not purchasing power). And if you have gotten promotions or merit raises along the way, your current salary is even higher compared to your starting salary way back when. The longer you work for a company, the bigger the difference will be between the two average salary figures.

EXAMPLE: Susan has been working for the Acme Company for fifteen years. When she retires, Susan will be paid a yearly pension equal to 15 percent of her average salary over the entire fifteen years. This is her salary history:

Year	*Salary*
1	$ 7,000
2	7,200
3	7,500
4	8,000
5	8,400
6	9,100
7	12,000
8	13,800
9	15,000
10	17,000
11	20,000
12	23,000
13	25,000
14	31,000
15	36,000
Total	$240,000

If Acme used the career average method, Susan's average salary would be $16,000 ($240,000 divided by 15) and her pension would be $2,400 a year (15 percent of $16,000).

However, if Acme based the pension on her average salary over her last five years, her average salary would be $27,000 ($135,000 divided by 5) and her pension would be almost twice as much—$4,050 a year (15 percent of $27,000).

Under the final average salary method, an employee's pension will end up being closer to what he was earning when he left the company. This means that workers who change jobs often and do not stay with any company for very long will not benefit from a final average salary plan.

OBSERVATION: When a company terminates a pension plan that uses a final average salary formula, it really penalizes those employees intending to stay until retirement. Not only do they stop earning any additional pension benefits, but their final pension generally will not reflect the additional salary increases they will receive until retirement.

OBSERVATION: Most companies count everything they pay you as "salary" when figuring your retirement benefits. But they don't have to: some plans ignore items such as bonuses, overtime and commissions and include only straight salary. Since it's up to the company, you should check your SPD to see what's included and what's not.

Profit-Sharing Plans. In a profit-sharing plan, your retirement benefit is based on how well your company does financially during the years you work there. That can be either very good, or very bad.

It works like this: each year a company decides how much money, if any, it wants to put into a fund for that year. Based on a certain formula, the money is divided into individual accounts for all the employees who are participating in the plan. The money in the profit-sharing plan is then invested, usually by the company. If someone quits before his or her benefit becomes vested, that benefit is forfeited and usually added to the other accounts. When you leave the company, your benefit will be based on your share of the company contributions, the investment income and other people's forfeited benefits.

OBSERVATION: Before you quit your job, find out if you have to be employed on the last day of the plan year in order to earn a benefit for that year. If you are close to that date and at least partially vested, it may be worthwhile to postpone quitting a little longer to earn an extra year's benefit.

The benefit formula in a profit-sharing plan is based on employees' "relative salary"—that is, their salary relative to everyone else in the plan. For example, if your annual salary is equal to 1 percent of the combined salary of everyone in the plan, you get 1 percent of the company's annual contribution to the plan. But, as you will see later in this chapter, a benefit formula can be designed so that higher-paid employees get a disproportionately larger share of the profits.

OBSERVATION: A company can have more than one retirement plan for its employees. So it's possible that you could be a member of *both* a pension and a profit-sharing plan at the same time.

Pension Plan vs. Profit-Sharing Plan

Even though your company doesn't give you a choice of retirement plans, you should know the differences.

	Pension Plan	*Profit-Sharing Plan*
1. Amount	A fixed pension for life figured under a formula usually based on your salary	Your share of the amount paid to the plan by your company plus income earned by plan
2. Risk	The amount of the pension is guaranteed even if the company loses money or makes poor investments with money in the plan. If the plan goes broke, you generally get only what PBGC guarantees	You risk the company having a bad year or making bad investments. If the company makes a lot of money by investing the plan's assets, then you profit
3. Guarantee	Portion of benefit insured by PBGC	Benefit not insured by PBGC
4. Who Benefits Most	Long-term older employees	Short-term younger employees

How to Find Out How Much You've Earned

By law a company must give any plan member who requests it an annual statement which shows the amount of the member's earned retirement benefits, how much is vested and when it will be 100 percent vested. This rule applies to all plans, including pension and profit-sharing plans. Generally, your company must send your statement to you within thirty days after your request. The only exception is for companies that automatically send everyone a statement each year; in that case you must wait for your annual statement.

You should keep these benefit statements along with *every* updated version of your company SPD in your permanent records.

Double Whammy: Integration

Integration is the exception to all the rules just explained about company retirement plans. Basically, it is a highly technical and complicated way for companies to give proportionately higher retirement benefits to their better-paid workers. The concept takes advantage of a seemingly noble idea behind ERISA: that all workers in a company should—when social security is taken into account—earn the same benefit relative to their salary and years in the plan.

As you will remember, social security taxes are currently paid only on salary up to $43,800. This means that someone earning $50,000 or $200,000 pays the same amount in social security taxes as someone earning $43,800. Those higher-paid workers also will receive the same social security pension when they retire, so that the higher-paid worker's social security benefit will be much less, compared with his former salary, than a lower-paid worker's. In fact, they probably don't need social security as much, either. But to make up for this "injustice," the law allows a company to give a higher-paid worker a proportionately larger pension than will be given to lower-paid workers.

401(K) AND SAVINGS PLANS

Sometimes a company will let employees put extra money of their own into their pension or profit-sharing account. That employee-paid part of the plan is like a plan within a plan. There are two ways to do it: 401(k) plans and savings plans.

In a 401(k) plan, which is part of a profit-sharing plan, the company will withhold, at your request, a portion of your salary and invest it in a special account. You do not pay any federal income tax on that money, or on the income you earn, until you withdraw the money. In that aspect, a 401(k) account is like an IRA. And, as with an IRA, there are restrictions on when the money can be withdrawn—usually not until you leave the company and are over age 59½.

A savings plan, on the other hand, can be part of either a pension or profit-sharing plan. If you request it, your company will withhold a portion of your salary and put it into its retirement plan. You pay income tax on the money put into the account, but you do not have to pay any tax on the investment income until the money is withdrawn. Although policies vary from company to company, generally the money cannot be withdrawn until you leave the firm's employment.

(Chapter 5 will explain how 401(k) and savings plans can be a good way to save money toward retirement and will compare them with IRAs.)

Some Other Kinds of Plans

Pension and profit-sharing plans are by far the most common, but not the only kinds of company retirement plans in use today. For example, there is a plan in which your company pays a specified amount of money into separate accounts for each member. That plan, called a money-purchase plan, is like a profit-sharing plan except that your company *must* contribute the same amount annually to the plan.

All kinds of combination plans are also in use. For example, a company could have a combined pension plan and profit-sharing plan. Employees would be members of both plans, but when they retire they might only get a benefit from whichever plan had the larger benefit and nothing from the other plan.

Two other forms of retirement plans, called Employee Stock Ownership Plans and cash-balance pension plans, are both discussed at the end of this chapter.

Women's Equity

A longtime problem with company pension plans was that in some cases, the primary family breadwinner (usually the husband) would spend his entire company pension before he died, leaving his widow without financial means. For example, the husband might have collected his pension in one lump sum or have chosen a pension that was payable only as long as he lived, rather than a smaller pension over the life of both himself and his spouse.

Congress eventually recognized this problem and, in early 1981, former U.S. Representative Geraldine Ferraro proposed legislation to protect pensioners' survivors. Representative Ferraro's bill followed a tortuous path through many highly technical debates and political compromises until, in 1984, election-year politics finally forced unanimous passage. The resulting Retirement Equity Act is a well-intentioned but confusing legal horror.

For purposes of your plans to retire rich, one thing about the law is clear: your employer may be required to ask you to make certain choices now about your future pension that will dramatically affect how much you receive at retirement.

OBSERVATION: Although it was intended as a women's rights bill, these rules apply equally to both men and women.

What You Need to Know

Under the 1984 equity law, all pension plans and some profit-sharing plans must offer a special benefit to the widow or widower of a vested employee. This "spousal death benefit" is generally paid if the employee dies before reaching the minimum plan retirement age. The death benefit must equal at least half of what the employee would have received if the employee had quit on the date of death and lived until retirement. Therefore, for the death benefit to apply, you must be married and at least partially vested in your pension plan.

EXAMPLE: Sarah and Michael are married and are each 35 years old. Michael is vested in his company pension plan. If he quit today, he would be entitled to a monthly pension of $200 starting at age 65. By law, Michael's company must offer him and Sarah the option of spousal death benefit protection. This means that if Michael died, Sarah would get a pension of $100 a month (half of Michael's earned pension) starting on what would have been Michael's 65th birthday.

There's only one catch: your actual pension may be reduced for each year the spousal death benefit protection is in effect. It's similar to life insurance in that you pay for each year your spouse is covered. But instead of annual insurance premiums, you pay for that protection by settling for a lower pension.

EXAMPLE: Steve, who is married to Cindy, is about to retire at age 65. Without spousal death benefit protection, he would be entitled to a $550-a-month lifetime pension. But because they opted for the spousal death benefit starting when Steve was 30, his pension is reduced to $487 a month.

Steve's pension was reduced by a full $33 a month. In terms of present dollars, that's worth a total sum of about $6,100. That's a lot of money to pay for a guarantee that if Steve died before age 65, Cindy would get half of his earned pension, beginning at Steve's 65th birthday.

OBSERVATION: The above examples assume that the plan retirement age is 65, but many plans allow long-standing employees to retire at an earlier age, usually age 55. Once you reach your plan's earliest retirement age, your death benefit protection depends on many factors, including when you choose to retire. (*See* Chapter 11.)

Spousal death benefits are not always a good buy. Married couples should compare the cost of term life insurance (*see* Chapter 7) with what their company pension will charge them for spousal death benefits to see which is cheaper; life insurance can work out better. Those highly technical calculations require the services of an actuary who can compare the cost of insurance premiums with the reduction in your expected pension.

Since you probably don't have an actuary handy, I recommend that you check with your company's benefits department. Sometimes companies reduce your pension by only a fraction of what it really costs the plan to provide spousal death benefits. This is called a "subsidized death benefit." If they subsidize the cost, then it *might* be worth your while to use the plan. But keep in mind that if you do live to retirement age, the protection will have given your spouse nothing other than peace of mind. If they do charge you the full amount, then you probably are better off with life insurance—a good salesman will tell you how much insurance coverage you need to replace the death benefit. And life insurance payments on death are usually tax free. But don't let him try to sell you cash value insurance. (*See* Chapter 7.)

OBSERVATION: A few companies are starting to allow employees to pay a flat monthly amount (usually through payroll withholding) for spousal death benefit protection, rather than having their pension reduced. This makes it easier to compare the cost with insurance and lets you pay for the protection through your salary rather than your retirement chest.

Opting Out

If your pension plan charges for spousal death benefit protection, then you and your spouse must be given the option not to be covered. Your company will give you a special form for this purpose when you are either vested (all or partially) or reach age 35 (or quit before 35), whichever comes later. If you decide not to have protection, both you and your spouse must sign the form. To make sure there is no hanky-panky, the law requires that your spouse either sign in front of a plan representative or have the signature notarized. If you do not fill out the form properly, your spouse will be covered automatically.

OBSERVATION: There are special rules if your spouse cannot be located; if you are in that situation, ask your company.

Your spouse's election not to be covered only applies to him or her. If that spouse dies or you get divorced and remarry, you and your new spouse must sign a new form.

WHAT HAPPENS WHEN YOU QUIT YOUR JOB?

Let's say you leave your job before retirement and have a vested retirement benefit. The main questions to ask are: (1) Can you take it with you? (2) How much is it worth now? (3) What should you do with it? (These subjects are also discussed from a retiree's point of view in Chapter 11.)

CAN YOU TAKE IT WITH YOU?

Some employers will not allow you to collect a pension plan benefit until you reach retirement age, even if you quit when you're only 30. One reason is that the company is afraid you might spend your retirement benefit the moment you got your hands on it. The other is that they want to hold on to the money as long as possible. On the other hand, some companies consider it a bother to have to keep track of former employees until they reach the age of 65. Those companies usually pay or "cash out" someone's entire benefit soon after they quit.

But if the value of your benefits is more than $3,500, the law requires that your company obtain your written permission to cash you out when you quit. If you're married, they also must obtain your spouse's written consent (notarized or signed in the presence of a plan representative). If you don't consent, then your benefit stays in the plan until you reach retirement age. If your benefit is worth $3,500 or less, they don't need your approval to cash you out.

If your vested benefit stays in the plan after you quit, your company must send you an annual statement of your benefits and notify you of any changes in the plan that affect you. If you move, be sure to give your former employer your new address.

When you leave a company with a vested benefit, your company must tell you about your rights to receive payment, what choices you have, and must give you a benefit statement telling you:

How Much It's Worth

If it's a profit-sharing plan, your benefit is worth whatever vested dollar amount is in your account. So if you're 50 percent vested and have $6,000 in your account, you're entitled to $3,000.

In a pension plan, your benefit is stated as the monthly or annual amount that will be paid to you at retirement age. For example, you might have a pension of $300 a month for life, beginning at age 65. In order to cash you out, your company must calculate what that pension is worth today in a single cash sum.

Let's say you're 100 percent vested and will be entitled to a pension of $300 a month for life starting at age 65. The following chart roughly estimates what you'd receive in a single cash sum depending on your age when you leave the company:

Age	*Single Cash Sum*
35	$ 2,200
40	3,400
45	5,200
55	12,300
65	29,000

As you can see, the value of a pension grows dramatically as you near retirement age. Someone who is young and changes jobs often is likely never to build up much of a pension.

Starting in 1987, the IRS will charge a 10 percent penalty on any payments from a retirement plan made before age 59½.

The only exceptions are if:

1. you're disabled
2. it's made to your beneficiary after your death
3. it's paid in equal installments for the rest of your life or that of you and your beneficiary
4. you are at least 55 years old and have elected early retirement from your company plan
5. you use the money for certain permitted medical expenses
6. it's made to your ex-spouse on divorce or separation
7. it's made from an ESOP

8. it's made before March 15, 1987, if you left your job in 1986 and agreed to be taxed on the payment on your 1986 tax return
9. it's rolled over to an IRA.

Surveys show that 70 percent of all early retirement plan payments are spent right away. The 10 percent penalty is intended to discourage you from spending your benefits before you retire.

The penalty is applied to the amount of the early payment and must be paid in addition to the regular income taxes due. However, no taxes or penalty are due on any payment that represents a return of your own contributions to the plan since you've already paid tax on that money.

The new law leaves you one other way to get the payment and still avoid the 10 percent penalty—roll it over tax free to an IRA or your new company's plan. That way you avoid paying any income taxes or penalties while saving for your retirement.

With these rules in mind, the question then becomes:

WHAT SHOULD YOU DO WITH YOUR RIGHT TO A SINGLE-SUM PAYMENT?

Given the choice to receive a payout now or wait until retirement, your decision will be based in part on what kind of plan it is. In a profit-sharing plan, your account will continue to earn income if you leave it with the plan. If you're satisfied with the way your company has been managing the profit-sharing plan, it might be best to leave your money where it is and enjoy the convenience of not having to manage the money yourself. Moreover, you won't pay any taxes on your benefit until you take it out.

On occasion, a company will separate the accounts of people who have quit from everyone else's. This segregated account may be invested differently (usually more conservatively) than the regular accounts.

If you do choose to allow your benefit to remain with the plan after you quit, you probably won't have another opportunity to withdraw your money until you reach the plan's retirement age. This lack of flexibility removes the temptation to spend your retirement benefit before you retire.

OBSERVATION: Before doing anything, you should read your SPD and whatever other material your company gives you to understand what will happen if you leave your benefit in the plan. You should also confirm in *writing* your conclusions about the plan with your company benefits department.

In a pension plan, the decision is more complex. If you leave the company your benefit will not grow with future investment earnings, but your benefit does become more valuable to you as you near retirement age. Your pension will be paid for from the same pension fund "pot" that the rest of the participating employees and former employees are depending on.

Your concerns should be the financial soundness of the plan and of your company (it may be standing behind the plan if it runs out of money). To check on the plan's finances, ask your company if there would be enough money for everybody's benefit if the pension plan was *terminated* today. Even if the answer is yes, that's no guarantee of what things will be like in fifteen or twenty years. You also should have some idea about your company's financial soundness simply from working there. You should evaluate your company as if you were considering investing in its stock (*see* Chapter 9).

Once you're comfortable about your company's finances, you'll want to know if you will be entitled to any "subsidized" benefits if you leave your money in the plan until retirement. As discussed above, some plans provide low-cost or free preretirement spousal death benefit protection. In addition, your plan could also provide subsidized benefits for those who live to retirement age. For example, some companies continue—without any charge—a worker's full pension to his spouse after the worker's death.

To find out if you would be eligible for any of these subsidized benefits, first check your SPD. If you're still uncertain, ask your plan administrator for a *written* explanation of these benefits. Remember that if your plan does give subsidized benefits, you'll lose the subsidy if you withdraw the money when you leave the company.

A final option is to call a few reputable life insurance companies to find out how much they would charge for a retirement annuity in the same form and amount as your pension. (Annuities are discussed in Chapter 11.) If their charge is less than the single-sum payment, it might be a better deal for you to take the cash now and roll it over to an IRA.

EXAMPLE: Pam is a 35-year-old employee who's quitting her job. She has a choice of receiving a yearly pension of $4,000 starting when she's 65 or a $2,576 cash sum today. Pam finds out that a reputable insurance company would charge her a single premium of $2,200 for an annuity that would pay her $4,000 a year starting at age 65. Pam decides that the cash sum is better.

Most workers, given a choice, choose an immediate cash payout when they quit. They then face another important choice:

What To Do with the Benefit Check

Anyone who doesn't desperately need the benefit money but pockets it anyway may be making three mistakes: Shrinking their check by a 10 percent penalty, paying taxes today they could postpone until retirement and spending part of their retirement nest egg.

Rollover to IRA

Part or all of the money you receive when you're cashed out can be transferred (rolled over) tax free into an IRA (Individual Retirement Account) within sixty days of payment. There are two requirements: first, you must have received at least half of your retirement benefit in a single year. (This is rarely a problem when you're cashed out because you usually receive it all in the same year.) The second requirement is that payment must have been made on account of certain events such as your retirement, reaching age 59½ or terminating employment. Because the rules are complicated, you should always check with your company or tax accountant to make sure you're eligible.

But you do not have to meet the usual requirements for contributing to an IRA. For instance, it doesn't matter if you have too much or too little earned income for that year and the usual restrictions for people age 70½ don't apply. Nor is there any penalty for contributing more than $2,000 annually from a distribution to an IRA.

EXAMPLE: Maureen has quit her job with a vested benefit in her company profit-sharing plan of $6,000. She has chosen to receive the entire benefit right away. Maureen can roll over any portion of the $6,000 to an IRA within sixty days of payment.

OBSERVATION: Again, any portion you receive that is only a return of your own after-tax contributions (as shown on the Form 1099) isn't eligible for a rollover.

Of course, you are taxed and possibly penalized on any part of the distribution that is not put into an IRA. If you receive property instead of cash from the retirement plan, you must roll over either the property or the cash proceeds from the sale of the property.

Once the money is in the IRA, it is governed by the regular IRA rules. This means that if you are over age 70½ when you roll over your retirement payment to an IRA, you must start withdrawing money from the IRA each year. Your IRA trustee can tell you the amount that you must withdraw.

To roll over a single-sum distribution to an IRA, you simply fill out a form that is available from your IRA custodian and attach it to your rollover check.

OBSERVATION: Don't take a chance of losing your benefits check or missing the sixty-day rollover deadline. Make your rollover the very day you receive your lump-sum distribution.

(IRAs, including how to start one and how to invest your IRA money, are fully discussed in Chapter 5.)

Rollover to a New Company Plan

You may be able to transfer your cash payment directly to your new company's retirement plan if three rules are met. First, your new company's plan must accept rollovers. Second, you must have received your *entire* benefit in a single cash sum. Third, you must roll over that entire benefit (not including your own contributions) within sixty days after receiving it.

OBSERVATION: Any money you roll over to your new company's plan is immediately 100 percent vested.

There are some good reasons why you might want to roll over your money to your new company's plan. As with IRA rollover, you avoid the 10 percent premature distribution penalty and delay paying any income taxes until you take the money out of the new plan. You get the investment management abilities of your new company rather than having to do it on your own in your IRA. You also avoid some of the restrictions that apply only to IRAs. And the rollover might qualify you for special income averaging when it's paid to you from the new plan. (Income averaging will be discussed in detail in Chapter 11, "When You're Almost Ready to Retire.") This would happen if somewhere down the road—say, when you retire—your entire benefit from the new plan is paid to you in a single sum along with the money you rolled over. This payment from the new plan would also have to qualify as a lump-sum distribution.

EXAMPLE: Julie is quitting her job at Widget, Inc. to join the Acme Company. Julie has $10,000 in her Widget retirement plan. Acme's profit-sharing plan accepts rollovers and Julie has her $10,000 transferred to the Acme plan. Twelve years later Julie leaves Acme and receives her entire account, including the money transferred from Widget, in a lump-sum distribution. Julie can use special income averaging on the *entire* distribution.

To find out if your new company's plan accepts rollovers, just ask. If the answer is yes, ask how the money will be invested and if there are any restrictions on taking it out. You may find that you prefer rolling the money over to your new company's plan rather than to an IRA.

OBSERVATION: If you think you might be interested in a rollover to your new company's plan, you should ask them about it as soon as possible, preferably when you accept the job.

If for any reason you cannot or do not want to directly roll over your benefit to another plan right away, you can use an IRA as a "stopover." Money put into a stopover IRA can eventually be rolled over to a company plan. But the stopover IRA can have no money other than what was paid from your first plan. And you must have received and rolled over your entire benefit from the first plan.

EXAMPLE: Todd has just been paid $16,000 from his company pension plan after quitting his job to become a free-lance writer. He puts the entire $16,000 in a new IRA. Todd never puts any other money in that IRA (he has a second IRA for his own contributions). After a few years Todd stops free-lancing and gets a new job with a company that accepts roll overs. Todd empties his stopover IRA and puts the money in the new plan without paying any taxes on it.

There are special (and complicated) rules on rollovers to a company plan for people who were "key employees" in a "top heavy plan." Most workers don't have to worry about those rules. But if you were an owner, high-paid employee or officer in a small business that had a retirement plan, you should ask your lawyer or accountant before ever rolling over money to a new plan. Rollovers to an IRA are always fine.

A Vacation Saved Is a Villa Earned

But even if you can save some income taxes by using income averaging, or avoid the new 10 percent penalty, you should hesitate before pocketing a plan payment. This money was intended for retirement, not enjoyment today and will be worth much more if you hold onto it.

EXAMPLE: Tom is 35 years old and has just quit his job. He receives a $12,000 check from his company profit-sharing plan and decides to spend $7,000 on a four-week cruise to the Greek Islands. The remaining $5,000 is eaten up by the 10 percent penalty and income taxes on the whole $12,000 payment. But if Tom had rolled the entire $12,000 into an IRA and earned a steady 9 percent interest rate, he'd have accumulated $159,000 before taxes by age 65. That's enough to buy a Greek villa, instead of a four-week vacation to Greece.

WILL YOUR PENSION HAVE THE MONEY TO PAY?

The answer for the vast majority of companies is yes. But for some companies, particularly in the steel, auto and heavy equipment industries, the answer may be no! Companies in financial hard times may help make ends meet by cutting their contributions to their pension funds to the lowest legal limits. Sometimes a company gets government approval to miss a few years' contributions to the pension plan. So as employees continue to earn additional benefits, the size of their pension funds is shrinking. The result is that a number of pension plans have become seriously underfunded.

When a pension plan is underfunded, employees

may have a legal right to expect the company to compensate for any shortfall. But if there's not enough money in the plan because the company is financially troubled, that expectation won't matter much. The employees would have to stand on a long line with the rest of the company's creditors, probably without much satisfaction. That's when the Pension Benefit Guaranty Corporation steps in.

WHAT'S INSURED?

The PBGC is like the FDIC of pensions. It is a federal agency that insures many—but not all—pension plans.

First, the PBGC insures only pension plans which qualify under certain IRS rules (most of them do). Pension plans of governments, churches, foreigners, and small professional service employers (doctors, lawyers, etc.) are not covered.

Second, only pension benefits that were vested before the plan terminated are insured.

Third, the PBGC insures benefits only up to a certain maximum level of roughly $1,800 a month or $21,600 a year. The maximum is raised by PBGC each year based on increases in the social security wage index. However, the maximum is phased in 20 percent a year during the plan's first five years.

Fourth, the PBGC insures only pensions that are scheduled to begin at age 65 and are paid over the life of the employee. Extras, such as an early retirement benefit, are not covered.

Rarely will an underfunded pension plan literally run out of money. What actually happens is that when the company or the PBGC realizes that the situation is hopeless, the plan is terminated. All further benefit increases are stopped and the plan funds are split up among participants according to a legal list of priorities. The batting order for paying out the funds is:

1. Employee contributions
2. Retiree benefits
3. Employee (nonretiree) vested benefits that are insured by the PBGC
4. Other vested benefits
5. Nonvested benefits

Usually the money runs out somewhere between categories 2 and 3. The PBGC guarantees all pensions up to category 3. People with part or all of their pension in categories 4 and 5 are out of luck.

EXAMPLE: The Acme Company is bankrupt and its pension plan has just enough money to pay back employee contributions and pay retirees their pension. Employee Stacy, 45, is 100 percent vested in her Acme pension of $25,000 a year. Keith, 30, is 50 percent vested in a pension of $9,000 a year. When Stacy reaches age 65 the PBGC will pay her a lifetime pension of $21,600, which is the PBGC maximum. When Keith is 65, the PBGC will pay him a pension of $4,500 a year, since he is 50 percent vested. Stacy and Keith also can sue Acme for their lost pension through the company's bankruptcy proceedings but they're unlikely to get much more money, if anything at all.

Is the PBGC Solvent?

Sort of. Although a government agency, the PBGC is not funded by Uncle Sam. Instead, the PBGC's revenues come from premiums that the government requires each employer pay to insure its pension plans. But when Congress set these premiums, it underestimated just how much the PBGC was going to have to pay to bail out problem pension plans.

Over the last few years a number of major plans that were very underfunded have been terminated, dumping their monstrous liabilities on the PBGC. For example, the Wheeling-Pittsburgh Steel Company has dumped $475 million in liability on the PBGC, Allis-Chalmers an additional $165 million and recently LTV another $1.5 billion. There remain many other seriously underfunded company plans that could end up in the PBGC's lap. All in all the PBGC already is in the hole for about $1 billion! The executive director of the PBGC has said that the agency's insurance program is in danger of imminent collapse.

Although the PBGC potentially could exhaust its funds within the decade, it would be political suicide for Congress to let that happen. So Congress has sharply increased premiums and attempted to reform the system to make it harder for companies to dump their plans on the PBGC. For the time being, the PBGC is once again solvent. But further increases will soon be necessary.

WHAT HAPPENS WHEN THERE'S TOO MUCH MONEY IN A PENSION PLAN?

The pension world is really a "tale of two cities." While some plans are seriously underfunded, many other companies have highly profitable pension plans which have earned much more money than is needed to pay every participant's benefits. These plans are said to have "excess" assets—although have you ever known of any plan, person or company who had *too* much money?

It's estimated that about three-quarters of America's biggest companies have excess assets in their pension plans that altogether total about $34 billion! The excess money came largely from excellent plan investments in the booming stock market of the 1980s, but also was helped by a higher-than-expected employee turnover rate that led to more benefit forfeitures.

Until recently, some companies had been using their excess assets to pay for cost-of-living increases for retired workers and to give benefit increases to active employees. Other firms treated their excess as a financial cushion in case the stock market went way down or the company's business went sour.

But as the pile of excess money grew even larger, companies started to eye these funds greedily, looking for a way to tap the excess funds. Under ERISA rules, a company cannot take the extra money out of its pension trust fund while the plan is operating. The legal solution is for a company to terminate its plan, pay participants their entire benefits and then keep whatever money is left over. In other words, the employees do not reap the extra profits.

The PBGC must approve all pension plan terminations. Usually, the company will also ask the IRS to rule that the termination won't cause any bad tax side effects. It takes about six months to a year to get these government approvals and generally all payments (except to retired people) are held off until they are okayed. Many times, however, both agencies virtually rubber-stamp their permission.

Since 1980, over 500 companies have terminated their pension plans, reaping about $5 billion in extra assets. Congress was not happy about the situation and added to the new Tax Reform laws a 10 percent penalty on a company that terminates its pension plan.

WHAT HAPPENS WHEN A PENSION PLAN IS TERMINATED?

When a pension plan is terminated, participants immediately stop earning any further benefits and become completely 100 percent vested in whatever benefit they have accumulated so far.

In order to continue paying retired employees their pensions and to pay other employees when they retire, the company buys annuity contracts from an insurance company. These contracts guarantee to pay everyone their normal pension at the same time at which they would have been paid under the old pension plan. The insurance company is fully responsible for paying out all pensions; the company and the PBGC both are probably off the hook once the annuity contracts are purchased.

Instead of having an insurance company take over the pension plan, some companies give workers the choice of being paid the present worth of their pension in a single cash sum or transferring that same sum to another company retirement plan. In those cases, younger workers won't receive much: for example, a $100-a-month pension would be worth only about $730 in cash to a 35-year-old worker. If the total cash value of your pension is $3,500 or less, your company can force you to take a single-sum payment. They don't need your permission and they don't have to offer you an annuity contract.

Remember, anyone who simply pockets a cash payment (instead of rolling it into an IRA) from a terminated pension plan must pay taxes and perhaps a 10 percent early payment penalty on the money.

Your company also might offer to let you roll over your benefit into another of its plans, usually a profit-sharing plan. You don't pay taxes or a penalty on such a rollover. Given the choice, you should choose the rollover if you like the way your money will be invested in the other plan. Otherwise, put it into an IRA. (IRAs are covered in Chapter 5.)

OBSERVATION: When your company offers a rollover to its own plan, it usually makes all the arrangements for you. All you'll have to do is fill out a form.

EXAMPLE: Jane is 35 years old and has earned a pension of $100 a month from her company starting on her 65th birthday. The benefit isn't vested yet. But one day Jane's company decides to terminate its employee pension plan. As a result, Jane immediately becomes 100 percent vested and will be entitled to receive $100 monthly from an insurance company when she turns 65.

Becoming immediately 100 percent vested is the good side of a pension termination. The bad news is now that your pension plan is gone, the amount of your benefit is frozen at that level. That especially hurts long-term older employees, as well as those younger employees who intended to stick with their company for many years. You'll be especially hard hit if your pension is figured on your highest average salary, because future raises won't be included in your average. And there won't be any cost-of-living increases after you retire.

OBSERVATION: Some companies, by giving regular cost-of-living increases or by mentioning them in an SPD, employee booklet or the plan itself, are considered legally responsible to continue giving them—

after their plan terminates—through the insurance company that takes over the plan. If you think you might be entitled to cost-of-living increases from a terminated plan, ask a good pension lawyer for advice. You may have an excellent case.

What Happens after the Termination?

In about half the cases in which a company terminates its pension plan, it substitutes a new plan, usually a profit-sharing plan. This is usually good for younger workers who plan to leave the company after a few years and, again, not so good for everyone else. Sometimes a company starts a "mirror-image" plan, meaning a pension plan that is identical to the old plan, except that it is without the excess assets.

When a company terminates a pension plan and then sets up a mirror-image plan it can just roll everyone's benefit over to the new plan. This way the new plan just takes over for the old plan.

WHAT CAN HAPPEN TO YOUR PENSION AFTER A TAKEOVER?

If you read newspapers or watch TV, you've heard about the recent wave of company takeovers and mergers. If your company hasn't been involved in one yet, it very well could take place soon. Sometimes the takeovers are friendly: the company being taken over (called the target) and the company doing the taking over (often dubbed Darth Vader, after the space-movie villain) want to join forces. But frequently Darth's companionship isn't welcome and a hostile legal battle develops. (That's why the aggressor company is called Darth Vader.) But no matter how it happens, employees and their pensions are affected by the results. Here's how.

Basically, Darth Vader takes over a target company to make more money. One common way is to terminate the target company's pension plans, and use any excess assets to help pay for buying the target company. For example, when Texaco took over Getty it got $250 million dollars in assets by terminating Getty's overfunded pension plans. Occidental Petroleum did even better; it got $400 million in extra assets from the Cities Service pension. If it happened today, they'd have to cough up the new 10 percent penalty because of changes in the new tax act.

Another way of making money is by making the target a leaner and more efficient business—which often means firing office workers because of overstaffing or because there are people at the takeover company and the target company doing the same job. Usually, the employees at the target companies are the ones who get fired.

Once you are fired, your immediate problem is finding a new job. Retirement is the farthest thing from your mind. But it still is important to find out how your retirement benefits will be affected if you are not vested.

"Free" Vesting

If your company has fired a lot of people, you may not have to forfeit anything. If so many workers are fired over a short period of time that the retirement plan shrinks drastically, it's considered the same as if the company terminated the plan. That situation is called a partial termination and the fired workers immediately become 100 percent vested.

The only trouble is, there is no IRS rule that specifies how many workers have to be fired before a partial termination is in effect. If you're fired, not 100 percent vested and you think enough people have been dismissed so that a partial termination applies, ask a lawyer for advice. You might also contact the IRS (which is in charge of partial terminations) for their view. The phone number for the IRS is at the end of this book.

Pension Parachutes

To prevent their pension from being "raped" in case of a hostile takeover, some companies attempt to safeguard any excess assets. For example, a company could state in its pension plan that if the company is ever taken over, excess assets can be used only to increase benefits to employees or pay for existing or new benefits, such as health and medical benefits. Usually a company does not reveal these special pension rules until a takeover is threatened.

OBSERVATION: If your company is a takeover target and you're thinking of changing jobs, try to find out if you'd be entitled to any extra pension benefits after the takeover. It might be worthwhile to delay changing jobs under such circumstances.

ESOP'S FABLES

Employee Stock Ownership Plans—ESOPs—are another form of company retirement plan. They are based on the noble idea of the worker as company owner. While owning stock in the company where you work is, in theory, a major plus in retirement planning, it also can backfire.

In an ESOP, each employee receives a certain amount of company stock—based on his salary—and the dividends from the stock are added to his account. Often, ESOPs are started by companies worried about the future—either because of hard times or because of a possible takeover. In the first case, an ESOP helps raise cash by having the company sell stock to the plan. In the second case, forming an ESOP puts more of the company's stock in friendly hands.

Usually, you have to leave a company before you can cash in your stock from an ESOP. Depending on the going price of the stock at that point, you might choose to sell it or hold onto it if you think the price might go up. Some ESOPs offer employees the option of taking cash instead of stock, which saves you the bother and expense of selling the stock yourself.

OBSERVATION: There are special and complicated tax rules governing stock payments from an ESOP. If you're in this situation you should seek help from your accountant.

But there are problems with ESOPs. Although ESOPs are managed by trustees, sometimes the trustees are controlled by the company management and simply rubber-stamp whatever is in management's best interests without much say from the workers. One critic dubbed such a plan a "MESOP"—for management enrichment stock ownership plan. There have been lawsuits filed by company employees who were dissatisfied with how the trustees were managing their ESOP. But no real consensus has emerged in the courts on the issue of how an ESOP should be managed in the best interests of the workers.

ESOPs also are risky because an employee has his retirement fortunes tied to how well his company is doing—since that will determine the value of his stock. Sometimes a company will replace its pension plan with an ESOP—substituting a safe, secure, if unspectacular employee retirement plan with a much riskier proposition. A company might do that if the retirement plan has excess assets: terminate the plan, set aside the money needed to cover the actual retirement benefits and either pocket the extra assets or use them to buy company stock for the new ESOP.

THE NEW AND IMPROVED PENSION PLAN

Recently a new type of pension plan has come into being. Some pension people have named it the Cash Account Pension Plan, others the Account Balance Pension Plan, and still others call it a Cash Balance Pension Plan. Because there's a chance that this type of plan will become popular, it's worth knowing about its advantages and its potential problems.

A Cash Balance Pension Plan resembles a profit-sharing plan. Each year a certain percentage of each participant's salary is earmarked in an account and that account grows with interest at a specified rate, either the rate of inflation for the year or the rate Uncle Sam pays on his short-term Treasury Bills, whichever is more. When someone quits or retires, he or she gets whatever amount in the account has become vested.

The difference is that—unlike a profit-sharing plan—the interest actually being earned by a cash-balance plan is not necessarily the fixed rate of interest being earned by the participants. Usually, the interest rate for participants is pegged at a little *less* than what the plan will actually earn on its investments. The company keeps the difference, which can result in significant savings.

Like a profit-sharing plan, this newfangled plan is easier for employees to understand than a traditional pension plan. Your benefit is the amount in your account rather than a pension based on a complicated formula calculated in part on your retirement age.

If your company changes from a pension plan to a Cash Balance Pension Plan, you won't lose your existing benefit but your future benefits usually will be based on the rules of the new plan. However, if you're an older or long-term worker your company may give you "grandfather" protection—that is, allow you to continue earning your retirement benefits under the old rules.

It's also possible that your company will pass on their savings from switching to a Cash Balance Pension Plan in the form of higher or new benefits for employees. (BankAmerica, the first major company to switch to a Cash Balance Pension Plan, says it gave its employees grandfather protection and passed on the cost savings to all employees.) If your company does not do these things, then you will be hurt if you are (or become) an older, long-term employee. If you're young and leave the company after a relatively short period, you're likely to be better off with a Cash Balance Pension Plan than a regular pension plan—although neither plan would be as good for you as a profit-sharing plan.

THE BOTTOM LINE: IT'S UP TO YOU

Now that you've gathered all this information about your company's retirement plan, what next? Think about what your benefit is worth today and what you figure it will be worth when you leave the company (which could be long before you actually retire). If you change jobs frequently you probably have realized that your employer's various retirement plans are worth little to you. On the other hand, if you have been (or plan to be) with the same company for a long time, your benefit could be a big help toward retirement as long as a takeover, cost cuttings, plan termination or bankruptcy don't interfere.

In any case, it should now be clear that a company retirement plan and social security alone won't see you through your golden years in comfort and style. If you want to retire rich, you must take things into your own hands and start saving today!

Q. Will Tax Reform help me keep my retirement benefits?

A. Maybe. Starting in 1989, the new law requires all company retirement plans to use a faster vesting system. For example, under the old rules, a company could forfeit the benefit of any worker who quit before ten years of service. Starting in 1989, all workers must be vested within seven years

Q. Will my taxes on retirement payments go up?

A. For some people, yes. First, there is a new 10 percent penalty (in addition to regular taxes) on many payments made to an employee from a plan before age 59½. There are ways to avoid the penalty, including rolling it over to an IRA. Second, the special income averaging tax breaks on lump sum distributions under the old law have been sharply reduced, so that they will offer less savings to fewer people. These changes are discussed in Chapter 11.

Q. Anything else I should know about?

A. Yes. Tax Reform added about 1,000 highly technical rules for retirement plans. A few, such as those dealing with social security integration, may work out to increase some employee's benefits. But most of the rules are designed to make it harder for you to get your money before retirement and to make it harder for companies to give their highly paid workers larger benefits. That latter change, combined with the hassles of dealing with all the new rules, may prompt some companies to throw in the towel and scratch their retirement plans altogether.

PART II

SELF-RELIANCE

To retire rich you must get into the savings habit. As the first part of this book showed, most likely Uncle Sam and your company will pay you some benefits—but not enough. And the younger you are, the less government and business is likely to help. It's the rare person whose social security and company retirement benefits will support him in comfort and cushion a shrinking check against inflation.

So if you've got to do it on your own, you must start saving now. Most people feel they cannot afford to put aside any money—that's simply a symptom of overconsumption. Our whole culture is built on spending all you can so that even raises and unexpected bonuses get spent before you know it. This is all a result of bad habits and thinking you need more "stuff" than you really do to be happy.

But the truth is you can't afford not to save and it's not as hard as you might think. The next chapter shows you how to organize your finances and *painlessly* save for retirement. And in today's uncertain economy that's more important than ever.

But managing your finances has just gotten far more complicated because Congress has rewritten our tax laws. Tax Reform changes every aspect of America's finances, from the way we save, invest and spend to the decisions to build a factory or apartment buildings or drill for oil. And the new system is anything but simple.

Chapter 4 explains the basics of the new rules, including how to estimate your 1987 and 1988 taxes. You may find that your current financial plan no longer makes good sense under the new system.

For many Americans, only the way they're taxed has changed, but their actual tax bill may remain about the same. That's due to the counteracting forces of lower rates and fewer deductions. Generally, it still makes sense to use the traditional strategy of sheltering your money from taxes in investments that offer a good return and the amount of risk with which you're comfortable.

One of the best places to start may still be the simplest of tax shelters, the IRA. Another device is a company savings plan, especially the saver's delight, the 401 (k) plan. Chapter 5 discusses how to use both IRAs and 401 (k)s under the new rules, including figuring if they're still right for you and selecting, managing, investing and changing your account. Those who don't have the cash to invest in both an IRA and 401(k) can learn how to choose between them.

If you're self-employed, you really have your financial destiny in your hands. You can still set up your own retirement plan—sometimes called a Keogh plan—and save up to 50 times as much as you could with an IRA. You'll need the help of an expert to set up a Keogh plan but Chapter 6 tells you what you need to know *before* you sign on the dotted line. An educated financial consumer gets the best deal.

CHAPTER 3

SAVINGS: THE KEY TO RETIRING RICH

UNLEARNING TO SPEND YOUR MONEY

When I landed my first job after graduating from law school, I thought I was in financial heaven. I was still living with my parents (rent free), my student loan payments had not yet started, and except for carfare and lunch, I had no expenses. My first paycheck seemed enormous and undeserved since at work I was doing the same things—researching and writing papers—that I had been paying law school tuition to do. Two weeks later, I was handed a second equally "enormous" paycheck, before I had even put a dent in my first check.

As the months went by my paycheck didn't seem quite so large as before; somehow I "learned" to spend more and more of my paycheck each week. Although my living expenses had not changed, that once-enormous paycheck slowly shrunk to just enough to get by on. Saving money for the future seemed out of the question.

The moral of the story is that it's very easy to spend all the money you earn, no matter how much or how little. And once you do that, it seems very hard to put away savings and get by on less. There's the same tendency with raises: you gradually get accustomed to spending the increased salary and before too long you're convinced you cannot get by on less. But you can!

Whether you make a million dollars a year or seem to be just above the poverty line, you must train yourself to spend less than you earn. Just as you can easily get used to spending your raises, you'll find you can also get used to doing with a little less and putting the difference toward retirement.

SETTING A GOAL

Many people think of saving as a "money-diet" because you have to avoid most of the things you like to do best. You may feel deprived, frustrated and depressed. But saving can be a lot easier and more enjoyable than a diet. After all, when you are saving money:

1. you can still eat almost anything you want, if not at the fanciest restaurant;
2. you don't have to exercise;
3. you can get a great tax break from the government; and

4. you enjoy the satisfaction of watching your money grow.

But even on a full stomach, saving can seem difficult. Always keep in mind what you are saving for: financial freedom. Think about retiring with the security and luxury of owning your own home, having a good sum socked away in an IRA and other investments and maybe even receiving a monthly pension. Then consider the alternative: being dependent on social security benefits and a pension without any significant cushion to give you real comfort. That's the hard fact of life being faced by many retirees today—people who have found that their retirement income is simply not enough.

Faced with the choice, you can find the incentive to resist spending your entire paycheck—no matter what you earn. The trick is to plan for retirement while you're still working and can do something about it—it's too late to maneuver at age 65.

The only sensible way to save is to set certain short-term and long-term goals. The first step is getting a handle on your current finances, and the easiest way to do that is by writing out a personal balance sheet. The two hours a year you spend figuring out just what you own will be well worth it.

How to Prepare Your Balance Sheet

First, list the value of all your investments and all the cash (e.g., money in a checking account) you have on hand. Next, put down all of your debts, including mortgages, other loans and credit card balances. Ignore assets such as clothes, cars and jewelry, because even if you wanted to sell them, they would not be worth much cash. Finally, write down your annual income—check your tax return for the exact figure—as well as any tax-free income such as interest on an IRA.

With the exception of your house, you should use the current value of each of your assets on the balance sheet. I prefer to list a home at its purchase price because a house is difficult to value and chances are you would use all the proceeds from the sale to buy your new home anyway. People also tend to overestimate how much their home is really worth. ("The Petersons next door sold their home for $128,000 and ours has an even nicer play room.") If you feel compelled to list what you think is your home's "true" worth, then list it separately. When you're through listing everything, subtract your debt from your assets—that's your equity.

Your balance sheet must be prepared "as of" a certain date—for instance, as of December 31. Although the date itself doesn't matter, you must use the same date each year, otherwise it will be difficult to compare one year's finances to the next.

A sample balance sheet is shown on page 96.

OBSERVATION: Use rough figures in your balance sheet—you need only a good estimate of what you own and owe.

Once you've prepared your balance sheet, you should consider whether your finances could use the extra help of a budget.

Greg and Gail Greenshade
Balance Sheet As of December 31, 1988

Assets		*Amount*
Checking account		$ 300
Savings account		2,200
IRA: X bank C.D. (pays 11%, due 1991)		5,000
Money market		2,200
Acme Company stock		5,800
Acme Company bond		2,010
Tax refund due from IRS		350
House at 111 Tree Lane Blvd. ($120,000 real value)		58,000
	Total	$75,860
Debt		
Pledge to charity		$ 1,600
30-year 7% mortgage– 20 years to go		45,000
3-year car loan–1 year to go		2,000
	Total	$48,600
Equity		$27,260
Income for 1988		
Salary		$35,000
Interest		1,200
Dividends		600
	Total	$36,800

Do You Need a Budget?

A budget shows you where your money's going and how to split your earnings between your present and future needs.

It's a fact that budgets can be a bother: they're cumbersome to put together and, if overdone, can have you searching through every nook and cranny of your house trying to find receipts for the shoelaces you bought last year. But a budget does point out in black and white some financial facts of life you may have been hiding from yourself: for example, that you spend too much on things like new cars, vacations and clothes. Your budget may make you realize that you shouldn't spend $4,200 on a family vacation this year or that you'd be better off keeping the old car another year.

Budgets are especially helpful for impulsive spenders or people who are about to embark on a large financial commitment, such as buying a new house or starting a business. Those people need to maintain a tight rein on their finances.

It's actually quite easy to prepare a budget—it just takes patience. You can prepare a budget for a single month or for the whole year, whatever suits you best. When possible, you should use up-to-date figures, such as your current mortgage payments. With other less predictable items, such as income taxes, use last year's numbers. For income tax rates, last year's numbers won't do; the rules have changed so dramatically that you'll have to figure it out yourself. Chapter 4 will show you how to estimate your 1987 and 1988 taxes under the new system. There are two basic methods of preparing a budget: the "standard" way and the "shortcut" way.

Standard Budget

Start by listing your expected income (both taxable and not taxable), including salary, interest, dividends and major gifts. Now list your expenses. The most common are:

1. Federal income taxes
2. State and local income taxes
3. Social security taxes
4. Mortgage or rent payments
5. Property taxes
6. Auto loan payments
7. Other loan payments (including student, credit card and personal loans)
8. Life insurance premium payments
9. Other insurance (health, disability, homeowners, car) premium payments
10. Utilities
11. Education
12. Food
13. Car: gas, oil and repairs
14. Medical, dental and drugs
15. Clothing and cleaning
16. Home repair
17. Child care
18. IRA and company savings plan contributions
19. Vacation

20. Entertainment
21. Charity
22. Children's allowances
23. Special purchases: furniture, TV, VCR, stereo
24. Gifts
25. Miscellaneous

Now subtract your income from your expenses—that's your savings. If you're satisfied with what you have left, then fine. (But don't use your budget to decide you can afford to spend more!) If you're not satisfied, go through your expenses and cut back until you're where you want to be. But you'll usually find that most items are untouchable. You have to pay taxes (although you might be able to reduce them with an IRA or Keogh plan), you have to eat and if the car breaks down it has to be fixed. That's when it's helpful to use the Shortcut Budget.

Shortcut Budget

With this method, you ignore your income and all expenses that are out of your control and concentrate instead on those few items that you *can* do something about. Namely:

1. Loan payments–can you pay off a loan early and save on the interest?
2. Clothing–is that new coat, pair of shoes, etc., really necessary?
3. Vacation–why not borrow an uncle's vacation house rather than going to Europe?

4. Entertainment–do you really need to eat out so often or as expensively?
5. Major replacement items–what's really wrong with the old TV?
6. Gifts–does your family really need to exchange such expensive presents each holiday?
7. Miscellaneous–the nickel and dime expenses that really add up

SHORT-TERM GOALS

Once your finances are in order, the next step is setting short-term savings goals. If you invest your money right, the small amount you save each week will snowball into a large fortune by the time you retire.

"Small" can mean saving only 4 percent or 5 percent of your before-tax salary from each paycheck—not enough to cramp your life-style. If your annual salary is $20,000, try saving between $800 and $1,000 the first year. If your annual salary is $60,000, then your first year's savings goal should be between $2,400 and $3,000.

If 4 percent or 5 percent seems like an awful lot to save in one year, think of it on a weekly or even a daily basis: $1,000 a year works out to only $19.23 a week or a very manageable $2.74 a day. Once you get into the savings habit, you can start increasing the amount. It is relatively easy to start saving 8 percent a year if you're already saving 5 percent a year.

Getting a handle on the spending money that disappears from your pocket can also help you save. Coffee and doughnuts from the snack wagon, drinks after work, expensive lunches, new gizmos that you don't need and books (Why didn't you just borrow this one from the library?)—all these small expenses help make life comfortable, but you have to get them under control. Perhaps the easiest way is to simply limit how much cash you carry around—it's hard to spend what's not in your hand.

The results will surprise you. If you save (don't spend) just $5 each workday, you'll end up with nearly $1,200 at the end of the year. At 9 percent interest, that adds up to $265,000 after 35 years—more than most people save in a lifetime, just from holding onto some pocket money.

PAINLESS WAYS TO SAVE

The basic rule of painless saving is that you are unlikely to spend money that never reaches your pocket. Here are eight ways to do it:

1. *Pay Yourself First*

This method is so easy and obvious that most people never think of it. All you do is: first thing each payday deposit a set sum of the money in the bank. Then forget it. By paying yourself first, you remove temptation and take advantage of the "you can't spend what you don't have" psychology.

OBSERVATION: This tactic is meaningless if you simply use your credit cards when you run out of cash.

2. Tax Refund Saving

As you are doubtless very aware, your company withholds money from your paycheck and passes it along to the government as an "advance payment" on your annual income tax. Come April 15, you file a tax return and if your company has deducted too much, you get a tax refund. In effect, you've been forced into painlessly saving money each week. It was easy, because you never got a chance to spend it.

When that tax refund check arrives, be strong. Resist temptation, ignore all TV and magazine ads—and as fast as you can—put that government check somewhere where you won't even think about spending it.

One place is an IRA. As you will see in the next chapter, even with the new rules many people will still be able to deduct their IRA contributions right off the top of their income. For other people, even the new nondeductible IRA may make sense because it lets your investment earnings grow tax free. Either way, having an IRA can help you get another income tax refund the following year. You will then be on the right side of the spending/saving cycle because each year you will be saving more without having to give it much thought.

Of course, tax refund saving is not an efficient way to save, since the government does not pay you any interest while it holds onto your money (although you'll be charged interest and penalties if you withhold too little). However, it does offer the distinct advantage of requiring no willpower—and for some people it's the only method that works.

OBSERVATION: If you're expecting a tax refund, file

your return as early as possible. By avoiding the annual April 15 crunch, you will get your refund check quicker and start earning interest on it sooner.

3. *Holiday Clubs*

Offered by many banks, holiday clubs operate on the same principle as tax refund saving: you won't spend what you don't see. But instead of using the money in your club account for a vacation or gifts, when it comes due put the money in your account directly into an IRA or other safe investment.

OBSERVATION: Some banks are starting to pay interest on their holiday club accounts—make sure yours does, too. Otherwise, you're making an interest-free loan to the bank.

4. *IRA Clubs*

A few banks are now offering IRA "plans" in which a few dollars a month is automatically taken from your checking or savings account and deposited in an IRA for you. If you can't find a bank that offers this service, then start your own IRA club. Put a certain amount each week into a savings account, even if it's only $5. At the end of the year, you'll have accumulated enough to put away in an IRA. Either way, you won't miss that small amount, but your savings will mushroom with interest.

5. *Payroll Deductions*

Many companies offer a payroll savings plan for their employees, in which money is automatically withheld from an employee's check and then invested in a credit union or used to purchase the company's own stock. Sometimes the savings plan is part of a company retirement plan, in which case there is a tax break in addition to saving money. Your company may even match your contribution. This will all be discussed later in this section.

Start by asking your employer to withhold a small amount from your check, then gradually increase the amount. You'll find that you hardly notice the dent in your paycheck.

EXAMPLE: Susan makes $25,000 a year and spends it just as fast as it comes in. Feeling a little guilty, she agrees to have her employer withhold 2 percent of her pay—about $9.60 a week—and put it in the company's savings plan. After a while, she gets used to living with her slightly smaller paycheck. So she increases the withholding to 3 percent or an extra $4.80 a week. Finally, Susan takes the big plunge and agrees to save 4 percent of her salary each week. It still amounts to only about $19 withheld from each paycheck, but over the year it adds up to $1,000, plus interest. If Susan invests that $1,000 in an IRA at the end of the year, she'll have saved a bundle and given herself a good tax break with minimal effort.

6. *Hide Your Raise*

Next time you get a raise, don't tell yourself. What I mean is, start saving the extra money before you get used to spending it.

EXAMPLE: Sam is making $25,000 a year and just got a $50 a week raise. After taxes, his paycheck will be about $32.50 fatter. Sam decides to have his cake—a little less—and eat it, too. He starts to put $25 each week into a bank account. This will amount to $1,300 at the end of the year, which he will invest in an IRA (thereby increasing his tax refund saving). The other $12.50 a week of his raise is all his to spend. He enjoys a little more spending money while still building a fat IRA.

7. *Equity Saving*

Owning your own home is not only another painless way to save, but an essential step toward being able to retire rich. That's because part of every mortgage payment goes to pay off the principal of the loan. This not only forces you to save, but allows you to deduct the interest costs and real estate taxes from your income taxes. A home can also be a great investment, because its value tends to keep up with inflation. (Chapter 8 illustrates the ins and outs of homeownership in greater detail, including a discussion of the new tax rules.)

8. *Mug Yourself*

That's right. The evening before every payday, empty your wallet of all the bills and loose change left over from your last paycheck—if there's any left—and put it aside. Add the money you "steal" to whatever money you have automatically saved as part of your short-term savings plan. This way, if you have had a relatively inexpensive week you can save a little more without depriving yourself.

EXAMPLE: It is Thursday evening and Max will be paid tomorrow. As he is walking past his closet he suddenly tells himself, "Your money or your life." His alter ego says, "Don't hurt me—here's the $28 I have left over from last week's paycheck." But, Max pleads with himself, "I need $2 carfare to get to work tomorrow." So he leaves himself $2, packs a paper bag lunch and adds the $26 to the 5 percent of his salary he already puts aside each week. Sometimes crime does pay!

The Saver's Number One Enemy

Seven out of ten people use it. Those who do have an average of 5.2 of them in their wallets at any one time. It's small, plastic and very easy to get. And, more than anything else in this world, it makes saving very difficult. It's a credit card.

Not that there is anything wrong with credit cards themselves. They're a convenient way to purchase items on your budget. They give you a one-month interest-free loan—you buy in one month, but don't have to repay until you're billed the next month.

But the little plastic demons are easy to abuse. First, credit cards make impulse buying a cinch. See something in the store window that you like, don't have the cash, not enough in your checking account, that's OK—you can CHARGE IT! You'll get a hefty bill for the item next month—long after the excitement has worn off.

The second problem with credit cards is that many people don't pay the entire balance when it's due. Instead they pay only the minimum amount required each month and are charged as much as 24 percent interest on the remaining balance. That's a rip-off—and it's foolish—considering that even banks charge only about 12 percent to 16 percent interest on personal loans. And, with the new tax rules, credit card interest is no longer deductible. More on that later.

Yet it's estimated that Americans owe about $75 billion in credit card debt. One in every three credit card holders borrowed at least $1,500 with their plastic. For holders of premium cards, the *average* debt was $2,000. At 24 percent interest, a $1,500 balance translates to $360 a year in interest. If you had invested that interest every year, at 9 percent you'd have $77,656 after 35 years.

Credit card debt is a sure sign of personal financial mismanagement. So what should you do? If you've got the cash, pay off all your credit card loans immediately. If you don't have the cash—and that means you're using plastic to buy more than you can afford—leave your cards at home. If your willpower is weak, cancel them altogether and save the annual fees. If you find this difficult to do, it may be because you're living beyond your means. And if you're having trouble making ends meet now, what will you do if things get rough? If nothing else ever has, the crash should inspire you to have control over your money.

Finally, let's talk about premium "gold" cards. Those are credit cards that charge extra fees for the privileges of a higher credit limit (and getting their subscribers to pay 24 percent interest on even more money). These cards sometimes give you preferential treatment on limousines, luxury hotels and other daily "necessities" of life. But those status symbols don't offer anything useful for nine out of ten people. Premium cards are basically a waste of money and, if you're weak-willed, they're dangerous too. Stay away from them.

Do You Need a Financial Adviser?

Most people get some financial advice from their accountant, lawyer, insurance salesman or stockbroker. A finncial adviser is a specialist who offers guidance about your overall budget, taxes, investments, life insurance, home purchase and most other areas of personal finance.

Generally, you should not consider paying for financial advice unless your income is more than $70,000 if you're single or $90,000 if you're married. However, some people with smaller incomes do need professional help in deciding whether to purchase a home or if their personal finances are in a real mess.

If you decide to seek professional help, be careful. The field has no standards or requirements—anyone can hang out a shingle, call himself a financial adviser, and start handing out advice. Some of them are fools or charlatans. While several institutions offer "certified" financial planner programs, the academic requirements are not standardized and not always rigorous. For example, the *Wall Street Journal* recently reported that one organization had awarded a certificate to a pet poodle whose owner had submitted a bogus application in the animal's name. Nor is Uncle Sam that strict: someone can generally become a registered financial adviser with the federal Securities and Exchange Commission simply by filling out a short form and paying a $150 fee.

The best way to select a financial adviser is to first ask for recommendations from friends, business associates, your accountant or your lawyer. Also check out any free lectures or seminars that are offered by financial advisers. The International Association for Financial Planning, the Institute of Certified Financial Planners or the National Association of Personal Financial Advisors can give you names of some certified planners in your area, although you should regard their recommendations with many grains of salt. Those agencies' addresses are listed in the back of this book.

Interview at least three candidates. Look for someone with a similar approach to investments to your own–how much risk to take, how much you need to save, etc. Don't be impressed by someone who just tells you what you want to hear: "Sure you can take that expensive vacation, even though you and I both know you can't really afford it."

Ask about credentials: education, experience, previous occupations and whether the person is part of a firm that has other resources and talent available to draw upon. How many clients does he handle and, on average, how much money do they have? You don't want to be a big fish in a small pond or a small fish in a big pond.

Ask to see a sample financial plan he drew up for

someone else (with the client's name deleted, of course).

Ask what he thinks he can do for you (be wary of someone who promises the moon and stars).

Ask if he is knowledgeable about all areas of financial planning or specializes in one or two areas, such as life insurance.

Ask whether the advice you'll receive will be custom-tailored to fit your needs or just a standardized plan.

Most important of all, ask about fees. Most advisers will promise to save you enough money to pay for their services, but don't believe it unless they can prove it on paper. Ask if they charge by time (fees can range from $40 to $120 an hour), a flat rate, a percentage of your net worth or commissions. If you pay commissions, the adviser makes money every time you buy something such as insurance, stocks or tax shelters. The more you buy, the more they make—and that makes it unlikely, if not impossible, that your financial adviser will be anything close to objective.

Some financial advisers get kickbacks. For example, the adviser could suggest that you use a particular stockbroker and that stockbroker could reward your adviser by paying him a portion of his own fees. This is worse than being charged a direct commission for advice because you don't know about it. Avoid any adviser who takes kickbacks and don't be afraid to ask if they do.

What to Do When Your Debt Gets Out of Control

In a recent national survey, one out of ten Americans said they felt trapped by their debt. Interestingly, the figures were even higher for people with household incomes of over $50,000. In that same survey, a significant number of people also said that their level of debt was hurting their marriage, family and friendships.

The purpose of this book is not to counsel individuals who need help beyond basic financial planning—it's doubtful any one book can solve serious money problems. But there are other places to turn. If your problems are due to gross mismanagement or an unexpected financial crisis, consider getting the help of a financial planner. There may also be social service agencies in your area that can offer free help. Call the National Foundation for Consumer Credit for advice on where to go in your area. Their address and phone number are listed at the back of this book.

If you think you might be a compulsive spender, consider an organization called Debtors Anonymous. DA is modeled after Alcoholics Anonymous and offers a similar mix of group support and self-help. They also have a list of 15 questions to help you decide if you're a compulsive debtor. DA's address and telephone number are listed at the back of this book.

Finally, you may need legal advice about your rights as a debtor, including the option of declaring bankruptcy. (Interestingly, Debtors Anonymous does not recommend bankruptcy to compulsive debtors.) If you don't have a lawyer, ask your local bar association or legal aid office for help.

Whatever you do, don't let things get (or continue) out of control; there are plenty of qualified people around to help you help yourself.

INFLATION AND TAXES: A DOUBLE WHAMMY

Once you've gotten into the savings habit, you'll find your two greatest obstacles to retiring rich are inflation and income taxes. Inflation alone can cut deeply into the purchasing power of the money you save. When inflation is combined with income taxes, even after Tax Reform, the result can be devastating: you can actually lose money by saving!

Inflation—What Will Your Money Be Worth Tomorrow?

At the end of the Little League baseball season, star shortstop Sally decided she wanted a new glove for next year. Sally figured out that if she saved $1 a week from her allowance, she could afford to buy a $35 glove by next spring. She managed to save the money over the winter and, one week before spring practice began, proudly marched into the store, $35 in hand. But she discovered that the price of the glove had gone up to $39 since last year—so she had to wait four weeks more, until she was able to save the extra $4. Sally had discovered inflation.

Inflation is an enemy of your savings and it has plagued man since he began using money: the Roman Emperor Diocletian mandated wage and price controls to fight raging inflation almost 2,000 years ago! The last time prices actually went down in this country over a significant period was during the Depression of the 1930s; otherwise the value of your money has steadily eroded.

What exactly is inflation? Inflation means that prices are going up and thus the value of your dollars is going down. An inflation rate of 5 percent, for instance, means it will take $105 at the end of the year to buy what $100 would have bought at the start of the year.

Inflation gets worse even when it seems to be getting better. This is why: let's say the rate of inflation is 5 percent for two years in a row. At the end of the first year it will take $105, $5 more, to buy what $100 used to buy. But at the end of the second year it will take $5.25 more—not just $5 more—to buy the same goods; even though the inflation rate did not increase. The reason is that each year's inflation builds on the previous year's, in the same way that your savings account compounds with interest.

If the rate of inflation is more than a few percent, the value of your money goes down drastically within only a few years. For example, at an annual 8 percent inflation rate, the value of a dollar will be 68 cents after five years, 46 cents after ten years, 32 cents after fifteen years and five cents after forty years! Even at a more modest clip of 4 percent a year, your dollar will be worth only 56 cents after fifteen years.

EXAMPLE: Ida Swan invested $1,000 in a money market account paying 8 percent interest. After one year she has $1,080 in her account—the $1,000 she saved plus $80 in interest. During the same year the rate of inflation was 4 percent. So Ida's $1,080 is really only worth about $1,038. But she still seems to be ahead: the purchasing power of her money has gone down 4 percent while she earned 8 percent interest.

But Ida forgot to figure for another very important thing—income taxes on the $80 of interest income. Ida is in a 28 percent tax bracket, meaning that she must pay about $22 in taxes on her $80 interest. Figuring for the effects of both inflation and taxes, she really ends up with $1,017—an increase of only $17 for the entire year.

The solution is to invest your money wisely enough to keep ahead of inflation and taxes. We'll see how later on.

CHAPTER 4

THE TAX REFORM STORM

The Tax Reform Act of 1986 will dramatically change the financial life of every taxpayer in this country. The complicated new law affects how you save, invest, spend and earn your money—so much so that Congress has actually renamed our tax laws the Internal Revenue Code of 1986.

Chances are that taxes will still be one of your largest expenses, even after the new law takes effect. But now that the rules of the game are changed, all taxpayers need to review their savings and investment strategy to figure how to save for retirement and make the new system work for them.

Before going into specifics, let's take an overall look at Tax Reform to see what the new law does and does not do.

WHO PAYS WHAT?

Over the next five years, individuals should save a total of about $121 billion in federal taxes, which in theory should save the average taxpayer a nice piece of change. But there is no such thing as an "average taxpayer" and, in reality, about one of every four taxpayers will see a rate *increase*.

The biggest winners are our nation's very poorest and very richest. Approximately six million poor families have been taken off the tax rolls entirely, while the very rich enjoy a sizeable tax cut as their bracket drops from 50 percent to 28 percent. The biggest losers are taxpayers in the vast middle range ($25,000–$200,000) who until now had been taking advantage of common deductions like the two-earner deduction, sales tax, consumer interest, IRA contributions and the like (all of which have been eliminated or limited under the new law), and people who previously avoided paying taxes through tax shelters, most of which won't work anymore. The rest of us will probably end up saving some money, but not a whole lot. A method of estimating your new tax bill will be explained later on.

On the business side, it's estimated that over the next five years corporate taxes will go up about $120 billion. "Good," you say, "it's about time they paid their fair share of taxes." But it's not so simple. Corporations don't pay taxes; people do. When Congress raises corporate taxes, and thereby cuts into corporate profits, the general public loses out in one of two ways. First, a company's shareholders—that's individual people owning stock in the company—earn less on their investment. Second, corporations faced with higher taxes can pay for the extra expense by simply charging more for the cars, toothpaste, or whatever else they sell. Either way, higher corporate taxes end up being paid by all of us. Congress giveth and it taketh away.

Simplicity?

Albert Einstein once said that the hardest thing in the world to understand is the income tax. He would be appalled by the new reform law which—despite rhetoric about "tax simplification"—is almost 2,000 pages long. One of the most confusing aspects of the new system is that it will be phased in gradually, so that over the next few years some people will be taxed under both the old and new rules at the same time. It should take about four or five years before the dust settles and taxpayers can figure out what's going on.

Tax Rates Won't Stay Down

Representative Dan Rostenkowski (one of the principal authors of the Tax Reform Act) said it publicly and most lawmakers and experts say it privately: taxes eventually will have to be raised. One reason is that there is no way anyone or his computer can figure out what the real bottom line effect of the new tax rates will be on government revenue. According to some of its supporters, the new law is "revenue neutral," which means that for every dollar somebody saves in taxes, someone else's taxes go up a dollar and the government does not lose any money. However, more likely than not the new law is a money loser. Government statisticians were pressured to inflate revenue estimates from the new tax rules so the law would pass and legislators would have something to brag about for the 1986 election year. Well the elections are over and this could come back to haunt us in a few years when the money lost by Tax Reform swells an already awesome federal deficit.

That's reason number two. Even if the new law *is* revenue neutral, in a few years our nation's growing deficit is likely to reach a point when something unpopular will have to be done. That "something" will almost surely include a tax increase—possibly through higher rates, fewer tax deductions, a new national sales tax, or all three. But before worrying about the future, let's see how the Tax Reform Act will affect you now.

The New Tax Rates

The old tax system had 15 different tax brackets and a maximum rate of 50 percent that applied to taxable income over $175,250. Under the new system, there are a handful of lower tax rates just for 1987 and a second set of even lower, "permanent" rates starting in 1988. Here are the 1987 rates:

1987 Tax Rates

Tax Rate	Taxable Income Married	Single
11%	0–$3,000	0-$1,800
15	3,000–28,000	1,800–16,800
28	28,000–45,000	16,800–27,000
35	45,000–90,000	27,000–54,000
38.5	Above 90,000	Above 54,000

Starting in 1988, there are fewer tax brackets, but they're more complicated:

1988 Tax Rates

Tax Rate	Taxable Income Married	Single
15%	0–$29,750	0–$17,850
28	29,750–71,890	17,850–43,150
33	71,890–171,090	43,150–100,480
28	Above 171,090	Above 100,480

You're probably wondering why the highest earners will be paying 28 percent while people earning less money are in the 33 percent tax bracket. Aren't tax rates supposed to be progressive, meaning that as your income increases your rate goes up? Not anymore. Under the new system, you pay 15 percent on the first dollars you earn (up to $29,750 if you're married and $17,850 if you're single) and 28 percent on income in the next level. For example, a married couple with a taxable income of $35,000 in 1988 would pay $5,932 in taxes as follows:

15% × $29,750	=	$4,462
28% × $5,250 [35,000-29,750]	=	1,470
		$5,932

So far, this is similar to how the old system worked, only with fewer brackets. But it gets tricky in the next level ($71,890 to $171,090 for marrieds and $43,150 to $100,480 for singles). They pay 33 percent on that income, even though the politicians, the press and the experts claim that the top rate is only 28 percent. The 33 percent rate compensates for the advantage of the 15 percent bracket for people in this third level of income. In other words, the rate is raised for taxpayers in this level so that they will end up paying a flat 28 percent rate on *all* their income, even the part that belongs in the lower 15 percent level. But it's even worse for some people in the 33 percent bracket, because they also lose the benefit of their personal exemptions. More on that in a moment.

Taxable Income

Under the new system, your taxable income equals your gross income minus certain special deductions that come "off the top" (such as the IRA) to get your Adjusted Gross Income. That figure then is reduced by your "itemized deductions" or your "standard deduction," whichever is larger, minus your personal exemptions. That figure is your taxable income.

With one big and one little exception, figuring out your gross income under the new law is no different: it's your salary, interest (not including tax-free municipal bond interest), long-term capital gains, etc. The big difference applies to long-term capital gains. (A long-term capital gain is profit on the sale of stocks, bonds, real estate and other "capital" items that you owned for more than six months.)

Under the old system, you were taxed on 40 percent of your long-term capital gains while the other 60 percent was tax-free. That meant that the highest rate on capital gains was a mere 20 percent. Starting in 1987, capital gains will be taxed fully, just like your regular income, except that in 1987 the tax rate cannot exceed 28 percent even if you're in a higher bracket. This of course means it will no longer make sense to delay selling a profitable investment just to get a long-term gain.

The other change is that your first $200 in dividends ($100 if you're single), which under the old system was tax-free, is now taxable.

Under the old tax law, you could immediately deduct certain items in calculating your Adjusted Gross Income before computing any itemized deductions. The most common of these off-the-top deductions were employee business expenses (job-related costs that your boss didn't reimburse); up to $3,000 of your two-earner deduction if your spouse worked; some moving expenses; and your IRA contribution. Out of those four deductions, only IRA's are left in the Tax Reform Act as an off-the-top deduction and even those are no longer tax deductible for everyone. (IRA's are discussed in detail in the next chapter.)

From your Adjusted Gross Income, deduct either all your itemized deductions or the standard deduction, whichever is larger. In 1987 the standard deduction is $3,800 for married couples and $2,750 for singles. In 1988, it's $5,000 for marrieds and $3,000 for singles. So a married couple in 1988 with more than $5,000 in itemized deductions would be better off not using the standard deduction and itemizing instead.

What Is an Itemized Deduction?

Under the old system, you were permitted to count many of the costs of living and earning money as an itemized deduction. Under the new system, that list of eligible deductions has shrunk. For the "average" taxpayer, here's a list of the most common items and whether or not they are still deductible under the new law.

Itemized Deductions That Are Still O.K.

1. Most interest on your home and a second home (See Chapter 8 for details)
2. State, city and local *income* taxes
3. Real estate and property taxes

4. Medical expenses *above* 7.5% of your Adjusted Gross Income
5. Charitable deductions
6. Employee business expenses and certain investment expenses *above* 2% of your Adjusted Gross Income
7. Certain moving expenses, if you moved to take a new job that was at least 35 miles from both your old job and your old home

Itemized Deductions
That Are No Longer O.K

1. State, city and local *sales* taxes.
2. Consumer interest, e.g., interest on credit cards, student loans, auto loans, etc. However, this new rule is being gradually phased in. In 1987 you can take up to 65 percent of consumer interest as an itemized deduction; in 1988, 40 percent; in 1989, 20 percent; in 1990, 10 percent; and nothing after that
3. Investment interest (e.g., interest on a loan to buy stocks) is only deductible against any investment income (e.g., dividends) you have.
4. Employee business expenses and investment expenses below the 2% floor
5. 20 percent of otherwise deductible meal and entertainment expenses. (The five-martini lunch is now the four-martini lunch.)

People who use tax shelters have more problems. Tax shelters are "investments" in housing projects, oil and gas ventures, race horses, etc. which gave the "investor" paper or fake losses that they could deduct. Generally, those paper losses are no longer deductible and tax shelter investors need the help of a tax advisor, fast.

Personal Exemptions

You now have figured out your gross income, minus certain deductions to get Adjusted Gross Income, minus your itemized deductions or standard deductions. Now you subtract your personal exemptions to get your taxable income (finally!).

In 1987 you are allowed a $1,900 deduction for yourself (married couples get two deductions) and for each dependent. In 1988 the deduction per person is $1,950 and in 1989 it's $2,000. The other change is that starting in 1988, only a smaller and sometimes zero personal exemption will be allowed for married couples with taxable income over $149,250 or for singles with taxable income over $89,560. (The rules are tricky, so if you're not earning these bucks skip the rest of the paragraph.) As with the 15 percent rate, the takeaway comes in the form of being stuck in the 33 percent tax bracket for a longer period. Basically, you'll be in the 33 percent bracket for $10,920 of your taxable income above the $149,250/$89,560 cut-off point for each personal exemption you take. (The chart for 1988 tax rates assumes the married couple and single person did not have any personal exemptions other than themselves.)

Estimating Your New Taxes

To estimate how much more or less you'll owe in taxes under the new rules, start with your 1986 tax return. Go through it line by line, crossing out the deductions that are no longer available. Taking into account the new standard deduction and personal deduction, figure out your taxable income. Then, use the tables with the new rates to figure out what your tax bill would be under the new system. In using the new tax tables, don't forget to use the different rates for each level of income. Now compare your estimated tax bill with your 1986 taxes. That, in the short run, is what the 1986 Tax Reform Act means to you.

OBSERVATION: Also changed is the way you figure your taxes. Five-year averaging, which allowed people whose income jumped up a lot in one year to reduce their tax bite, has been eliminated.

EXAMPLE: Lou and Denise, a married couple with one child, want to estimate their 1988 taxes. Here's a summary of their 1986 return:

Gross Income	$45,000
Less two-earner deduction	(2,500)
Less 60% capital gain deduction	(800)
Adjusted Gross Income	41,700
Less itemized deductions (including $700 sales tax, $250 interest on a student loan, and $400 in employee business expenses)	(6,000)
	35,700
Less personal exemptions (3)	3,120

Taxable income	32,580
Tax liability	$ 6,248

Here's how they would figure their 1988 taxes:

Gross Income	$45,000
Two-earner deduction	–0–
60% capital gain deduction	–0–
Adjusted Gross Income	$45,000
Less standard deduction which is more than their $4,750 in itemized deductions (see below)	(5,000)
	40,000
Less personal exemptions	(5,850)
Taxable income	$34,150
Tax liability	$ 6,184

For 1988, Lou and Denise estimate their taxes should go down by about $64.00.

How Lou and Denise figured their 1988 itemized deductions:

1986 itemized deductions	$6,000
Less sales tax not deductible	(700)
Less 60% of interest not deductible	(150)

Less employee business expenses not deductible because they were under 2% of their Adjusted Gross Income | (400)

Less employee business expenses not deductible because they were under 2% of their Adjusted Gross Income	(400)
1988 Itemized Deductions	$4,750

OBSERVATION: If your taxes will be significantly less under the new law, put aside the savings for retirement!

MARGINAL TAX BRACKET

Your marginal tax bracket is a key number in retirement planning, because it is the rate you are likely to pay on your investment income. If your marginal tax bracket is 15 percent, it means you end up earning only 8.5 percent on a money market account that pays 10 percent interest. If you're in the 28 percent bracket, then the same 10 percent interest rate puts only 7.20 percent in your pocket after taxes; and if you're in the 33 percent bracket, the after-tax return on that 10 percent investment is a measly 6.7 percent.

To figure out your marginal tax bracket, figure your taxable income using the methods just explained. Then use the charts with the new 1987 and 1988 rates and look to see what your tax bracket will be. Of course, if you know your income has gone up or down a lot, make the necessary adjustment.

Don't forget about state and local income taxes. Most states and some cities tax investment income and, sometimes, all income including salary. Unless you itemize your deductions, this number should be added to your federal marginal tax bracket. If you itemize, you'll be able to deduct the state and local taxes you paid during the year on your federal return; this means that Uncle Sam picks up part of your state and local tax bill. The higher your federal tax bracket, the more Uncle Sam pays for.

New York State is among the worst culprits: income over $26,000 is taxed at the rate of 13 percent. If you live in New York City, add on another 4.3 percent. This means that if you're in the 35 percent federal tax bracket and live in New York City, you'd end up in the 52.3 percent marginal tax bracket if you don't itemize and in about a 46 percent bracket if you do itemize.

To figure your combined marginal tax bracket, check last year's state tax return to determine your state and local tax bracket.

EXAMPLE: John is in the 33 percent federal tax bracket and the 10 percent state bracket. If he doesn't itemize, then his combined marginal tax bracket is 43 percent (33 percent federal plus 10 percent state). But if he itemizes, his combined marginal tax bracket is about 40 percent. To get this number John calculates as follows:

(a) 100−33% (federal tax bracket) = 67% (John's share of state taxes)

(b) 67% × 10% = 6.7% (out-of-pocket cost of 10% state taxes)

(c) 33% + 6.7% = 39.7% (combined marginal bracket)

OBSERVATION: Don't worry if you don't understand the calculations—most people don't. Just follow the steps and you'll get the correct answers.

For the record, a list of each state's highest marginal income tax rates is shown on pages 130–133:

BEAT THE SYSTEM

In the "old days" before Tax Reform the trick to saving on taxes was to earn the income now but postpone paying the taxes until you retire, when chances were you'd be in a much lower tax bracket than when you first earned the money. Investing your savings to postpone taxes was the basic idea of a tax shelter.

But now the rules of the game have changed. For some people it may be a good idea to pay taxes now because they might be in a *higher* bracket when they retire. For many others it will still be a good idea to postpone taxes in order to save more money for retirement. For these people the best-known tax shelter is still the IRA. With the new rules everyone will still be allowed to put money in an IRA, but for some it will no longer be *deductible*. But there are also the Keogh or self-employed retirement plan, the SEP or company-paid IRA, the company retirement plan and special types of investments—like buying your own home and life insurance—that help you dodge the tax bullet. These shelters are available to rich and poor alike and

HIGHEST MARGINAL INCOME TAX RATES BY STATE

State	*Maximum Rate of Tax*		
Alabama	5%	on income over	$ 6,000
Arizona	8	on income over	6,738
Arkansas	7	on income over	25,000
California	11	on income over	27,820
Colorado	8	on income over	14,151
Connecticut	13	on dividend and interest income over $100,000 and 7% on all net capital gains	
Delaware	8.8	on income over	40,000
District of Columbia	11	on income over	25,000
Georgia	6	on income over	10,000
Hawaii	11	on income over	61,000
Idaho	7.5	on income over	5,000

State		*Maximum Rate of Tax*	
Illinois	2.5%	on all taxable income	
Indiana	3	on adjusted gross income	
Iowa	13	on income over	$76,725
Kansas	9	on income over	25,000
Kentucky	6	on income over	8,000
Louisiana	6	on income over	50,000
Maine	10	on income over	25,000
Maryland	5	on income over	3,000
Massachusetts	5	on earned income and 10% on interest, capital gains and dividends	
Michigan	4.6	on all income	
Minnesota	14	on income over	31,750
Mississippi	5	on income over	10,000
Missouri	6	on income over	9,000
Montana	11	on income over	45,600

State	*Maximum Rate of Tax*		
Nebraska	19%	of adjusted federal income tax liability	
New Hampshire	5	of interest and income dividends	
New Jersey	3.5	on income over	$50,000
New Mexico	7.8	on income over	100,000
New York	13	on income over	26,000
North Carolina	7	on income over	10,000
North Dakota	9	on income over	50,000
Ohio	8.075	on income over	100,000
Oklahoma	6	on income over	15,000
Oregon	10	on income over	5,000
Pennsylvania	2.2	on some income	
Rhode Island	22.21	of adjusted federal income tax liability	
South Carolina	7	on income over	13,840
Tennessee	6	on interest and dividends	

State		*Maximum Rate of Tax*	
Utah	7.75%	on income over	$7,500
Vermont	26.5	on federal income tax	
Virginia	5.75	on income over	12,000
West Virginia	13	on income over	120,000
Wisconsin	7.9	on income over	51,600

and Some Selected Cities

Birmingham	1%
Detroit	3
Kansas City, Missouri	1
Newark, New Jersey	0.75
New York	4.3
Philadelphia	4.3%
Pittsburgh	2.1
Portland, Oregon	0.6
St. Louis	1
San Francisco	1.5

don't require you to take any risks or lose sleep worrying about an IRS audit. For these other shelters, the rules are basically the same. But the new tax rates and the possibility of a tax increase make using (or not using) them to your best advantage a difficult choice. The next chapters discuss how to make the right choice.

CHAPTER 5

IRAs AND 401(k)s: STILL AMERICA'S TAX SHELTERS

TOO GOOD TO STAY TRUE

Before the Tax Reform Act of 1986, Individual Retirement Accounts were clearly the easiest, safest and all-around best tax shelter for virtually all taxpayers. The new laws don't change who can have an IRA, how much you can put in or what happens to any money you've already put in an IRA. The income earned on all IRA money is still tax-free until withdrawn and most people will get an income tax deduction for at least some of the money they put in an IRA.

But Tax Reform *will* mean that from now on, IRAs will be a bigger tax boon for some people than others—which means taxpayers now should think twice about whether an IRA is really their best bet in retirement planning. One of the biggest changes resulting from Tax

Reform is that not everyone will be able to automatically get a full dollar for dollar deduction on their income taxes for money put in an IRA. Starting in 1987, anyone who is in a company retirement plan *and* earns above a certain level ($40,000 for married couples and $25,000 for singles) won't be able to deduct all, or perhaps any, of their IRA contributions. More on that later.

There is another aspect of tax reform to keep in mind. Now that the new lower tax rates have fully kicked in, the value of an IRA's tax savings is reduced. For a few people that might make IRA's (deductible or nondeductible) not the best choice for retirement planning. Much more on that later. In general, you should always plan on leaving money in an IRA for at least ten years to make it worthwhile.

But IRAs are still incredibly flexible. Most working people can invest any amount up to $2,000 each year. You can invest the full $2,000 one year, $600 the next and nothing in the third year. You also can make multiple contributions during the year, as long as the total amount you deposit is within the annual limit. That means you could deposit $400 at the start of the year, $600 in June and another $1,000 in November. Your IRA funds can be invested in almost anything you want: money market funds, certificates of deposit, mutual funds, stocks, bonds, etc. And you can change investments as often as you like.

The paperwork involved in opening an IRA is minimal. They are available at almost any commercial bank, savings and loan association, mutual fund, stock brokerage firm or insurance company. You can maintain more than one IRA at a time—you can put money in a bank IRA in one year and open a second IRA with a brokerage firm the next year.

The biggest catch is that the government wants you to keep your money in the IRA until you are at least 59½ years old. For that reason, there is a 10 percent penalty tax on any money withdrawn before then, in addition to the regular income tax you would pay on the money. But the penalty does help you resist the temptation to dip into your retirement savings prematurely. After age 59½, you can withdraw money from your IRA whenever and in whatever amounts you want, even if you're still working.

OBSERVATION: Most people have until April 15, 1987 to put money in an IRA for the 1986 year and take a tax deduction on their 1986 return, before the lower rates and new rules take effect.

The great features of an IRA—and then some—may also be available to you if your company has a retirement option called a 401(k) plan. If you're lucky enough to work for a company that offers a 401(k) plan, you can take advantage of it and an IRA at the same time. The 401(k) plans are discussed and compared to IRAs in the last part of this chapter.

WHO CAN SET UP AN IRA?

Anyone who works and is under age 70½!

With Tax Reform, the requirements for setting up

an IRA are still the same—only now not everyone will be allowed to deduct their contributions. Before getting into the new deduction rules, let's take a quick look at what the law means when it says you have to work to have an IRA.

Working means you have "earned income." The amount reported on your annual W-2 income tax form is earned income. Basically earned income includes:

1. wages and salary
2. company bonuses
3. sales commissions
4. tips
5. vacation pay
6. overtime pay
7. self-employment income.

Self-employment income —money you earn "on your own" without working for a company or boss—also is considered earned income. If you own your own business, your business revenues minus your business expenses is your self-employment income. If you do handiwork, repairs, wash cars, mow lawns, clean houses or paint apartments, all your fees are counted as self-employment income. So are professional fees earned by a doctor, lawyer or dentist, royalties collected by a writer, actor or actress and sales made by an artist or inventor. It doesn't matter if you work sixty hours a week or once a month—any money you make on your own counts in terms of an IRA.

OBSERVATION: If your self-employed business loses money but you also have a salaried job, the only income that counts for IRA purposes is your salary.

"Passive" income such as interest, dividends and profit from the sale of a house doesn't count as earned income. You can argue in vain that you worked for the money that you invested and "worked" very hard making the right investments, but the IRS says no. Once you retire, your company pension and social security checks also are treated as passive income. Again, it does not matter that you had to work to receive that money. The only exception to the earned-income rule is alimony payments. A divorcee (or legally separated spouse) can count all alimony or separate maintenance checks as income.

If your earned income for the year is at least $2,000, you can put the maximum $2,000 allowed by law into an IRA that year. That $ 2,000 cap applies to deductible and nondeductible contributions together. If your earned income for the year is less than $2,000, the most you can contribute to an IRA is the amount of the income.

Until 1987, anyone can take a dollar-for-dollar deduction on their income taxes for any money put into an IRA. But after 1987, the new tax rules eliminate that automatic deduction for anyone who is covered by a company retirement plan *and* whose income is above a certain amount.

Being covered by a company retirement plan (the tax law calls it being "an active participant in an employer-maintained retirement plan") means you are a member of a:

1. company pension plan
2. company profit-sharing plan
3. 401(k) plan (discussed later in this chapter)
4. ESOP
5. Keogh plan
6. retirement plan for federal, state, city or other government employees, or
7. SEP (discussed later in this chapter).

You're considered covered by such a plan if you were eligible to earn any benefits or to contribute your own money for at least one day during the year. It doesn't matter if you're not vested in that benefit, or if you were not covered by the plan at the time you contributed to the IRA.

But even if you're covered by a company plan, you still get the full IRA deduction if your Adjusted Gross Income (see Chapter 4) before deducting the IRA contribution is less than a certain amount. The limit is $25,000 if you're single or $40,000 if you're married and file a joint tax return with your spouse (as most couples do). If your income is above that amount and you're in a company plan, your IRA deduction is gradually phased out depending on your income, as shown in the chart on page 141. But just to make your financial life more complicated, the new rules also allow everyone earning at or below the $50,000/$35,000 cutoff to deduct the first $200 they put into an IRA.

If either spouse participates in a company retirement plan, both are treated taxwise as if both are cov-

Adjusted Gross Income		
Married	*Single*	*Amount of IRA Contribution Deductible*
$40,000	$25,000	Fully deductible
41,000	26,000	$1,800
42,000	27,000	1,600
43,000	28,000	1,400
44,000	29,000	1,200
45,000	30,000	1,000
46,000	31,000	800
47,000	32,000	600
48,000	33,000	400
49,000	34,000	200
50,000	35,000	200

ered by the plan. But if the couple files separate tax returns, the spouse who isn't covered by the company plan can deduct his or her IRA contributions without worrying about the income limit.

EXAMPLE: Rochelle put $2,000 in an IRA during 1988. When she sits down to fill out her tax return for that year, she calculates that her Adjusted Gross Income is $30,000 for the year, before deducting the IRA contribution. Rochelle was a member of her company's pension plan in 1987. According to the chart, Rochelle will be able to deduct $1,000 (50 percent of the $2,000 contribution) on their tax return.

What about the remaining $1,000? It counts as a nondeductible contribution. It may be worth putting that money in an IRA even without getting a tax deduction, because the earnings on all IRA contributions—deductible and nondeductible alike—are tax-free until withdrawn. As we'll see later in this chapter, that can be a boost in your plans to retire rich.

How IRA Tax Deductions Work

Your IRA tax deduction is listed "above the line" on your tax return, so it doesn't matter whether you itemize your deductions. Simply state what part of the money you're putting into the IRA is deductible. If you put $2,000 in an IRA and can deduct all of it (say because you're not in a company plan), put down the entire $2,000 deduction. If you can only deduct half that amount (like Rochelle in the above example), only list a $1,000 deduction. If you go over the legal deduction limit, you may be penalized.

Observation: You're not allowed to exceed the $2,000 annual contribution limit in any case. For instance, a single person in the 50 percent deductible range can't put $4,000 in an IRA in order to get the full $2,000 deduction.

WHEN CAN YOU SET UP AN IRA?

You have until the day your income tax return is normally due (April 15 for almost everybody) to set up and put money into an IRA for that tax year, even if you get an extension of time to actually file your return.

EXAMPLE: Larry, who was not in his company pension plan and earned $35,000 in 1988, did not put any money into an IRA. It's now April 14, 1988, and Larry has just realized how much he owes the government in taxes. So Larry quickly puts $2,000 into his IRA that day, and deducts it from his 1988 return—immediately reducing his taxable income for that year to $33,000.

You also can set up and contribute to your IRA after filing your income tax return, so long as you make the contribution by April 15. That means you could file your income tax return early and claim an IRA deduction but wait until April 15 to actually deposit the money. This is a terrific deal if you are expecting a tax refund—file early, claim an IRA deduction and use your tax refund to pay for it by April 15.

OBSERVATION: If you claim an IRA deduction but don't put the money in by April 15, you must amend your return and pay the extra taxes, with interest. You may also be penalized 5 percent for being negligent or in some cases even 50 percent for filing a fraudulent return.

WHICH YEAR?

Because the government gives you until April 15 to make your IRA payment for the previous tax year, it's actually possible to put $4,000 into your IRA in the same calendar year. In other words, any time before

April 15 you can make a $2,000 contribution for the previous year and another $2,000 contribution for the current year—assuming you hadn't yet put any money into an IRA for last year.

If you have the choice of designating an IRA payment for the previous tax year or the current year, it's better to count it toward the previous tax year if you can take the tax deduction.

However, that advantage is lost if you won't be allowed much of a tax deduction for last year, but expect to be able to deduct it this year *and* you don't expect to be able to save more money. In that case, use the money you've saved for this year's IRA. That way, you'll get the most out of your IRA tax deduction.

Special Rules for Working Couples

A husband and wife who both work can maintain entirely separate IRAs, each with the usual $2,000 annual contribution limit based on their individual incomes. If each working spouse invests up to the $2,000 annual limit, they can put a total of $4,000 a year into IRAs. Over time, this can translate into big money. If a 35-year-old working couple starts putting aside $4,000 a year in IRAs at 9 percent interest, they'd have a total of $545,230 when they reached the age of 65. If one or both spouses are covered by a company retirement plan and their Adjusted Gross Income is above the

$40,000 cut-off, then the new deduction limit applies to each spouse. For example, if a couple's Adjusted Gross Income is $45,000, thus limiting their IRA deduction to $1,000, then each spouse can deduct $1,000 of his or her IRA contribution. So if they each put $1,000 into an IRA, they would get a total $2,000 tax deduction on their joint return. A married couple cannot maintain a joint IRA.

IRA Contributions for a Nonworking Spouse

One-earner families should not despair. Under a special rule, if the couple files a joint tax return the working spouse can use part of his or her earned income to put money into a separate IRA for the nonworking spouse.

The working and nonworking spouses can put a maximum of $2,250 into the two IRAs each year, as long as no more than $2,000 is put into either person's IRA. For example, the working spouse can put $1,000 into his or her IRA and $1,250 in the nonworking spouse's. It's their decision.

Example: Dick and Jane are married. Dick earned $25,000 during the year and Jane, who is a full-time law student, did not earn anything. They decide they want to make the most of the IRA tax shelter, so Dick invests $2,000 in his IRA. Jane also opens a separate IRA to which Dick contributes $250. Or they might decide to have smaller but equal IRAs—say $1,125 in each.

Each spouse can have a completely different type of IRA. Dick's IRA could be invested in General Motors stock while Jane could buy a CD (certificate of deposit) for her IRA.

Even if a "nonworking" spouse earns some compensation during the year—say $10—he or she can still contribute money to a spousal IRA that year.

EXAMPLE: Back to Dick and Jane: If Jane worked after school for a few weeks one year and earned $100, Dick could still put $250 in a spousal IRA.

USE IT OR LOSE IT

If you don't put money into an IRA for one tax year, you can't double up your payment the following year. If it's April 16, 1989, and you haven't invested in an IRA, you still can put money in for 1989, but the 1988 tax benefit is lost to you forever.

Throughout this book I have been urging you to start saving *now*. The obvious reason is that the sooner you start, the more money you'll have. The first dollars you save in an IRA—the dollars you save today—are the most important in your plan to retire rich, because they will earn interest for the longest period. But more importantly, if the interest is reinvested, it too earns income. Over time the income earned on the income—called compounding—grows into a truly hefty sum.

For example, if you start putting $2,000 a year into an IRA when you are 40 and earn 9 percent interest every year, you'll have $169,402 in your IRA at age 65. Not bad, but if you had started saving *just five years earlier*, when you were 35, you'd end up with $272,615. Through the magic of compounding, the extra $10,000—put into the IRA by starting to save just five years earlier—grew to $103,213!

What about inflation? Let's assume that the average rate of inflation is 5 percent—four percentage points less than your 9 percent rate of interest. Even with inflation, the $272,615 in your IRA still will be worth about $112,170 in terms of today's purchasing power.

Should You Put Money in an IRA?

The answer depends on whether you can make deductible or nondeductible contributions, how long you plan on leaving your money in the IRA and what your tax bracket is.

If you are able to deduct your entire IRA contribution, then in effect Uncle Sam is sharing the cost of your IRA. If you put $2,000 into an IRA, you'll get an automatic $2,000 income tax deduction. That means the $2,000 you put into an IRA actually saves you $660 in taxes if you're in the 33 percent bracket, $560 if you're in the 28 percent bracket, and $300 if you're in the 15 percent bracket. Think about that: the government lets you pay less taxes if you save for your own retirement. That's not a free lunch, it's a free dinner!

You can use the IRA tax deduction to save even more. For example, if you have saved up $1,440 to put into an IRA and you're in the 28 percent bracket, you really can afford to put $2,000 into an IRA because, after your tax savings, a $2,000 IRA investment cost you only $1,440.

Let's compare how much money would be left after taxes if you put a fully deductible $1,000 annually into an IRA, compared to the earnings you'd get from a taxable savings account that pays the same interest, after 5, 10, 15 and 30 years, assuming you're in either the 15, 28 or 33 percent tax bracket.

15 Percent Bracket

Time Invested	*IRA*	*No IRA*	*Savings*
5 years	$ 5,087	$ 4,952	$ 135
10 years	12,914	12,111	803
15 years	24,957	22,460	2,497
30 years	115,861	90,321	25,540

28 Percent Bracket

Time Invested	*IRA*	*No IRA*	*Savings*
5 years	$ 4,309	$ 4,098	$ 211
10 years	10,939	9,707	1,232
15 years	21,140	17,385	3,755
30 years	98,141	61,969	36,172

33 Percent Bracket

Time Invested	*IRA*	*No IRA*	*Savings*
5 years	$ 4,010	$ 3,777	$ 233
10 years	10,179	8,831	1,348
15 years	19,672	15,595	4,077
30 years	91,326	52,969	38,357

These charts illustrate two important points. First, the higher your tax bracket, the more those deductible IRA contributions swell your next egg. Second, for your IRA to mean much of a savings difference, you must leave the money untouched for a fairly long period. No matter what your tax bracket, after only five years an IRA won't give you much more in savings. But after ten years, an IRA will save you about 7 percent more, even if you're only in the 15 percent bracket. If you're in the 33 percent bracket, then an IRA would increase your savings by a full 15 percent.

But there's another advantage to IRAs that even people who can't deduct their contributions enjoy: postponing paying tax on all their earnings from the IRA investments.

The reason an IRA still can work out to your advantage is when you reinvest your income, you earn income on your income. By letting your income compound over time, you can greatly increase your nest egg. On the other hand, if you have to use part of your earnings to pay taxes, the magic of compounding vanishes. The higher your tax bracket, the more your advantage from making even nondeductible IRA contributions, because you save even more.

Let's compare how much money would be left after taxes if you put $1,000 annually, nondeductible, into an IRA versus a taxable savings account–both paying the same interest–after five, 10, 15 and 30 years, assuming you're in either the 29 percent or 33 percent tax bracket. (There's no point in doing the analysis for the 15 percent bracket, because those people should be able to automatically deduct their entire IRA contributions.)

28 Percent Bracket

Time Invested	*IRA*	*No IRA*	*Savings*
5 years	$ 4,110	$ 4,098	$ 12
10 years	9,892	9,707	185
15 years	18,245	17,385	860
30 years	76,710	61,969	14,741

33 Percent Bracket

Time Invested	*IRA*	*No IRA*	*Savings*
5 years	$ 3,792	$ 3,777	$ 15
10 years	9,031	8,831	200
15 years	16,497	15,595	902
30 years	67,821	52,969	14,852

As is the case with deductible contributions, with nondeductible contributions the higher your tax bracket and the longer you leave money in, the more financial sense it makes to invest in an IRA. In fact, federal regulations on IRAs encourage you to leave your money in for a long time and penalize you if you don't. As discussed in more detail later, there's a 10 percent penalty (in addition to your regular income taxes) on money taken out of an IRA before age 59½ (except for money you take out that came directly from your nondeductible contributions).

Also consider the fact that many states let you deduct your IRA contributions from your state income tax return. If you live in one of these states, saving money on state taxes will increase the power of your IRA even if you can't save on your federal taxes. Ask your tax advisor or the financial institution where you have your IRA about the laws in your state.

The possibility of a federal income tax hike is a final consideration. As we saw in Chapter 4, our enormous federal deficit may force higher taxes eventually. If your taxes go up, the advantage of putting money in an IRA today goes down. For example, if you're in the 28 percent tax bracket now but Congress raises your bracket to 35 percent by the time you withdraw your IRA at retirement, your strategy of saving taxes would backfire. However, chances are that because there are so few tax deductions left, Congress probably could raise taxes by only a percentage point or two to raise lots of revenue. Meanwhile, you'll probably have less income by the time you retire. That combination of less income and higher tax rates just might keep you in the same tax bracket.

OBSERVATION: Tax Reform added a new 15 percent excise tax on all payments from IRAs, Keoghs and other retirement plans that total above $112,500 in any year. The new rule is discussed in Chapter 11.

Considering all that, after Tax Reform is it still worthwhile to invest in an IRA? It should be worth it for everyone to make deductible contributions to an IRA in 1987, when tax rates will still be relatively high. After that, the answer is an easy "yes," regardless of your tax bracket, if you can leave the money in until you're at least age 59½. The exception would be if you're in the 15 percent bracket now but expect an increase in income over the years that would put you in a higher tax bracket by the time you retire. In that case, you may be better off skipping an IRA and investing in regular taxable accounts, unless the 10 percent withdrawal penalty will give you the willpower to leave your retirement savings untouched until retirement.

Should You Borrow Money to Put in Your Ira?

Probably not. If the tax return deadline is fast approaching and you don't have the money to invest in an IRA, a loan will allow you to make an IRA payment for that tax year. Because interest rates on short-term consumer loans are very high and, after Tax Reform, no longer deductible, you should repay the loan as soon as possible to make it profitable. Perhaps the taxes you'll save by deducting the IRA payment can be used to help repay the loan.

But be careful. If you get caught on a treadmill of borrowing money for each year's IRA investment, it's time to reexamine your finances. You should not need more than twelve months to save for your IRA payment. If you're repaying the loan each year, then you're obviously capable of saving the necessary money and borrowing is just a way of making up for poor financial planning.

IRA MANAGEMENT

Where Should You Open an IRA?

Today, virtually every financial institution offers IRAs. Among your choices are banks (including commercial banks, savings and loan associations and credit unions), mutual funds, brokerage firms and life insurance companies. Although they all claim to have the best IRAs around, the biggest difference between the various institutions is the investments they permit, the services they offer and the fees they charge. Before going into any further detail, let's take a quick look at what these four institutions have to offer.

1. *Commercial Banks and Savings and Loan Associations*

Most banks or savings and loans do not charge any fees for IRAs, which is helpful if you're just starting out. Most banks limit your IRA investment options to the bank's own investments, usually just CDs and some form of bank money market account. In most cases, your investment is insured by the Federal Deposit Insurance Corporation (FDIC) for up to $100,000.

Some banks also now offer brokerage services, so that in addition to the traditional bank investments you also can buy stocks and bonds. Of course, the bank charges a commission every time you buy or sell a stock or bond and, generally, banks providing brokerage services are more likely to charge a trustee's fee as well.

2. *Mutual Funds*

A mutual fund is a pool of money collected from thousands—and sometimes millions—of individual investors that is jointly invested by professional money managers. Most mutual funds specialize in a specific type of investment, such as relatively risk-free, short-term investments (called money market), relatively low-risk stocks, speculative stocks or coporate bonds.

The advantage of mutual funds is that they make it possible for a small investor to spread his financial risk over a great many stocks and to rely on the expertise of the fund's advisers. They also allow small investors to put their money into stocks or bonds without paying high brokerage commissions.

Often a mutual fund company will combine several of its funds into a "family of funds" that includes a money market fund, a fund that invests only in blue-chip stocks and bonds and various other funds that invest in aggressive growth stocks. Investors can split their money between the funds as they see fit or transfer money between funds, usually without an additional charge.

Some mutual funds are specially designed for IRAs and usually charge an annual fee. Some of those mutual funds are sponsored by stock brokerage firms, so that in addition to investing in the funds you can pick individual stocks and bonds for your IRA.

3. *Brokerage Firms*

A stock brokerage firm usually offers the most investment options for your IRA. You can instruct the broker as to exactly what stocks or bonds to buy and change your investments as often as you like. Most brokerage firms also allow you to invest in one or more mutual funds, including a money market fund.

The brokerage firm will charge a commission each time you buy or sell stocks or bonds. Most brokerage firms also charge an annual flat trustee fee, and sometimes an additional fee based on a percentage of the value of your IRA. Avoid any firm that charges a fee based on a percentage of the amount in your IRA.

To compete for your IRA dollars, some firms (including banks that provide stock brokerage services) are offering reduced brokerage commissions to their customers. These "discount brokers" may charge as much as 80 percent less than regular full-service brokers for buying or selling a stock. Discount brokers usually make up for reduced commissions by providing fewer services (such as investment advice) than full-service brokers. This can mean big savings because commissions are stiffest for sales or purchases of relatively small amounts of stock. Some discount brokers don't charge an annual trustee fee at all. As competition heats up you should be able to find several firms, including full-service brokerage firms, that have eliminated all IRA fees.

4. *Insurance Companies*

Although insurance companies were among the first institutions to offer IRAs, they generally haven't stayed competitive.

Most insurance companies today offer investors only two or three investment options such as an equity fund, a fixed-rate annuity fund (which is somewhat akin to investing in the insurance company itself) and a money market fund. In general, those funds have not done well. Insurance companies also are notorious for charging high fees, being inflexible, and making things so complicated that it's difficult to understand or evaluate your investments. Generally, a mutual fund IRA is preferable to one offered by an insurance company.

Because insurance company IRAs are unique, they will be discussed further in a separate section at the end of this chapter.

Choosing Your IRA Investment

Don't make the mistake of selecting an IRA custodian and then picking your investments—that's like the tail wagging the dog. Choose first what investments you'd like to be able to make, *then* find an IRA custodian who offers those investments.

Choosing IRA investments used to be simple. You had two choices–a bank CD (certificate of deposit) or an insurance company IRA. But in 1981, the federal tax laws were changed, making IRAs available to just about all workers. The number of possible investment alternatives skyrocketed to just about everything, including stocks, bonds, mutual funds, mortgage-backed securities and annuities. Although some advertisements still imply that you must put your IRA money in either a CD or money market account, investing your IRA today is not much different than handling your other investments.

Since there are so many choices available for your IRA, it's best to first discuss:

What You Can't Invest In

Only a few investments are off-limits for an IRA. They include "collectibles"—jewelry, art, gold and silver (except certain gold and silver coins sold by Uncle Sam), stamps and commodities—from copper to pork bellies.

You cannot borrow money from your IRA, use your IRA as collateral for a loan or invest your IRA in your own business. Nor can your IRA borrow money.

If you break any of these rules, you'll have to pay income tax on the IRA money you invested improperly and, if you're under age 59½, the 10 percent early withdrawal penalty on the amount involved.

What You Can Invest In

Everything else from bank money market accounts and CDs to stocks and bonds. Your choices, though, boil down to debt or equity.

Debt means your investment is really a loan for

which you'll collect interest and eventually get repaid. Bank money market accounts, CDs and bonds are all debt investments. They're generally safe because defaults are rare and there are regular interest payments. For this reason debt is sometimes called an "income investment," meaning it's chosen by people who want to collect interest. Certain investments, including most bank CDs, are insured by Uncle Sam.

Equity, on the other hand, is called a growth investment because you are buying a piece of the action, hoping that it will increase in value. Stocks are the most popular equity investments. Although some stocks also pay cash dividends to their shareholders, there is no requirement that they do so.

Since the late 1940s, equity has been a better investment, or average, than debt. To illustrate, let's compare the performance of U.S. Treasury bills (a debt investment loaning money to Uncle Sam) and the average return on stock investments from the years 1947–1981. If you had invested $2,000 in Treasury bills in 1947, you'd have accumulated about $8,441 in 1981. In the same period your $2,000 in stocks would have earned, through dividends and increases in value, about $72,431!

Of course, between 1947 and 1981, there were times when you would have been much better off with debt investments. And just because stocks have in the past outperformed debt is no guarantee for the future. Finally, even if stocks in general go up, it won't matter if the stocks you choose go down in value.

As you can see, choosing which investments are right for your IRA is no easy matter. It helps to keep in mind four "how much" factors: how much risk you're willing to take, how much money you have to invest, how much time you're willing to spend handling your investments and how much financial expertise you have.

How Much Risk Do You Want to Take?

Another way to ask that question is "How much money do you want to make?" You may reply, "Millions." But that means you'll also have to risk losing everything, because investment risk (the odds that something will go wrong and you'll lose your money) and investment return (how much you can earn from an investment) go hand in hand. Risky investments generally offer the lure of the highest possible returns, but you also run the greatest chance of losing your shirt altogether. "Sure" investments pay you less income, but won't keep you awake at night.

There actually are two kinds of risks involved with investments: one is that your investment will go sour and you won't be able to get some or all of your money back; the second risk is that you'll simply get stuck with a low rate of return.

With rare exceptions, the longer a period of time you're willing to commit your money, the higher the return. The reason is that the longer you have to wait to get repaid, the more risk you take that things will go wrong, and so the greater the reward if things go right.

For example, the interest rate for bank money market accounts, where your money is readily available, will be somewhat lower than for a twelve-month bank CD. The difference is even greater between a bank money market account and a bond that matures after thirty years.

How Much Can You Afford to Lose?

The most important question to ask yourself is "What will I be using my IRA for?" The more you'll need your IRA for retirement security, the more cautious you should be. Figure out an estimate of your basic retirement needs and if you cannot risk having your nest egg shrink from poor investments, don't take chances. Stick with sure things like CDs and bank money market accounts.

At the same time, be sure there will be enough money in your IRA at retirement if you invest conservatively now. If the answer is no, you might want to risk dabbling in the stock market for the chance of increasing your gains. Age is another consideration. Someone in their twenties or thirties probably can afford to take more investment risks than someone nearing retirement age, because there's more time to make up for a losing investment.

Yet another factor in choosing your IRA investments is what financiers call "liquidity." Liquidity means how fast you can turn your investments into cold hard cash without loss. You should plan your investments so that they can be easily tapped when the time and price are right. If you're going to need your money soon—say, to buy a retirement home—your IRA should be in liquid investments such as a money market account, where you can quickly withdraw your money without risking a loss or a withdrawal penalty. If you buy stocks and bonds, you might end up having to sell them to raise cash when prices are low. And taking your money out of a CD before it's due could cost you a hefty penalty.

Your Personality

The investments you select should be based as much on your personality as your pocketbook. Some people love gambling with the possibility of scoring big, while others are just the opposite—they agonize about the possibility of losing their money. Financially conservative types are more comfortable with lower-earning—but safe and steady—bank or money market accounts. Gamblers are often more enticed by the stock market. Pick investments that suit your personality.

Mow Much Time Do You Want to Spend?

If you look upon investing as a chore, leave most of the work and worry for someone else and choose investments that require minimum time and effort. As it happens, some of the least risky investments are also the easiest to manage.

But many people enjoy the challenge of managing their money themselves. Through close attention to the stock market and prudent risk taking, they aim to achieve a higher rate of return than the average person. They generally choose directed investment plans at a stock brokerage firm or certain banks, into which they can put their IRA funds in any legal investment from stocks and bonds to bank money market accounts and mutual funds and can change them as often as they like.

A compromise between spending almost no time and a lot of time handling your money is investing in a family of mutual funds. With mutual funds you need to choose only an overall financial strategy, such as investing in stocks; you then pick a fund which fits that strategy and let the professional money managers worry about selecting which stocks are right.

How Much Expertise Do You Have?

The less you know about investments, the simpler you should keep things. If you can't tell the difference between common stock and livestock, then you need a simple, relatively foolproof IRA investment like a bank money market account or a CD. You won't hit it big, but you won't make any major mistakes, either. If you have some knowledge about investments, yet don't feel quite comfortable choosing stocks and bonds, a family of mutual funds would let you pick a type of investment (e.g., safe stock, solid bonds) but leave the details of buying and selling to the professionals.

How Much Do You Have to Invest?

If you are just starting your IRA, play it safe and get a bank money market account or a CD which matures in less than three years. Banks tend not to charge fees and are usually happy to accept smaller deposits. In general, it doesn't make financial sense to invest less than $5,000 (some say $10,000) in stocks and bonds because you won't be able to diversify your investments and the cost of commissions will be high. When you have saved more money, you can decide whether you want to switch to other, riskier investments.

Putting it all together, the chart on page 165 shows the principal features of the three major IRA investment plans.

Now that you know what's available and what you should consider before investing, let's look in more detail at the kinds of investments suitable for IRAs, ranging from the safest to the riskiest.

INVESTMENT SAMPLER

Money Market Accounts

Basically, they're the safest investment for your IRA because there is little risk of losing your money. Because the interest rate fluctuates with the market, you aren't stuck if interest rates go up. But you do sacrifice the chance to lock in a high interest rate if market rates fall. Money market accounts offer the added advantage of flexibility, allowing you to withdraw your money and put it in another investment at any time without any penalty.

Besides being ideal for people just starting an IRA, money market accounts also are a good choice for those who want a place to temporarily "park" their money while they mull over their next investment move.

You can open a money market IRA at a bank, mutual fund or stock brokerage firm. The most conservative and safest money market mutual funds invest only in U.S. Treasury bills and usually have names like "Government Fund" or "Government Reserve Fund." They pay the lowest interest rate of any money market mutual fund. But because money market mutual funds are relatively safe to begin with, you probably are better off investing in one that isn't limited to Treasury bills.

What to Look For in Choosing a Money Market Mutual Fund

You should choose your money market mutual fund based on what the fund has to offer in terms of fees, services and other investment options.

Interest rates aren't a big factor. Although interest rates do vary slightly from fund to fund and from week to week, generally these differences even out. If one fund pays ¼ percent more in a particular week,

	Bank	*Mutual Fund*	*Directed Investment*
1. Risk	minimal	varies greatly	usually higher than others
2. Return	steady and unspectacular	can be high, low or a 100 percent loser	same as mutual fund, but the highs can be higher and the lows even lower
3. Flexibility	almost none	some	the most
4. Fees	none or minimal	minimal	the highest of the three
5. Expertise needed	little	some	a lot
6. Minimum sensible investment	whatever you can afford	$2,000	$5,000–$10,000

the next week another fund is likely to surpass it. Even if it doesn't, a difference of ¼ percent interest on $2,000 for a year comes to only $5. The *Wall Street Journal* and many business sections of Sunday papers list the rates paid by the major money market mutual funds.

Bank Money Market Mutual Funds

As a result of recent changes in federal banking laws, banks now can offer their own money market mutual funds. Like regular bank money market accounts, they are very safe, relatively low-return investments. The only difference is that with a bank money market mutual fund, all your money is being loaned to the bank, rather than being invested in a variety of different government, corporation and bank IOUs.

All federally chartered banks are insured for $100,000 per account by Uncle Sam. Be sure to ask if your bank actually is *federally* insured. If the bank is backed only by a state or regional group, look elsewhere.

CDs

A CD is a loan to a bank for which you are paid a fixed rate of interest for a fixed period of time, at the end of which the bank pays you back the principal plus the earned interest. Since the recent deregulation of the banking industry, a bewildering variety of CDs have come on the market, with terms ranging from six months to as long as ten years.

One or two banks are starting to offer floating CDs where the interest rate varies with market conditions. To take advantage of the float, you have to settle for an initially lower interest rate than a regular CD. But that rate could float up above the fixed rate, or down.

Some stock brokerage firms also are now offering CDs, through an arrangement they make with a bank. However, CDs that are not bought directly from a bank are not insured by the federal government and are not a good idea.

Risk and Return

Because the interest rate is usually fixed—and to compensate for tying up your money for a longer period—CDs usually offer higher interest rates than bank money market accounts. The longer the term of the CD, the higher the rate. If you decide to take your money out of a CD before it comes due, you will be faced with the infamous "substantial penalty for early withdrawal"—usually a loss of three months' interest.

CDs are a relatively safe investment and if the bank is insured by Uncle Sam, there's no risk of losing any money. But a CD does lock your money into a fixed interest rate, leaving you unable to switch into higher-yielding investments without being penalized. If you guess right and interest rates decline after you've invested in your CD, you'll reap the benefits.

If you think interest rates are about to go up, choose a relatively short-term CD, perhaps six months to one year. If you expect rates to go down, invest in a longer-term CD at currently high yields. But if you're like most people, you probably will have a little idea of the direction in which interest rates are heading. In that case, your best bet is to invest in CDs with a maturity of one to one and a half years. That way, whichever way interest rates go, you won't lose big or win big.

What to Look for in Choosing a CD

Before choosing a CD, do some comparison shopping. Compare the rates and penalties for early withdrawal imposed by different banks offering IRAs. Compare interest rates—how often interest is compounded (daily, weekly or monthly) will make a big difference in how much income you actually earn. Look for a figure called the "effective annual yield," which reflects the effects of interest compounding and will tell you which bank really pays the highest interest.

Some banks let you "create" your own CD by choosing the amount you want to invest and for how long. For example, you could decide to put $1,000 in a CD maturing in one and a half years. This is a handy way to custom fit a CD to your needs.

Unless you specifically notify them otherwise, your bank may reinvest your CD automatically. This means that when your CD matures, they will take your principal and interest and use it to buy a new CD of the same maturity–without notifying you in advance. That bank policy has caused headaches for many an investor. Just think of your chagrin if you decide to buy stocks with the money in your expired CD, only to find out that the bank has just bought you a new

CD that won't mature for two more years. You either have to pay the penalty for early withdrawal or wait another two years until the new CD matures. To avoid that predicament, keep track of your CD and instruct the bank in writing, well in advance of the maturity date, what you want done with your CD when it matures.

Stocks and Bonds

Investing in stocks and bonds, whether through a directed investment plan or a mutual fund, is much more involved than other money market instruments or CDs. For that reason the ins and outs of choosing stocks and bonds for investment are discussed separately in Chapter 9.

One Special IRA Consideration

Before Tax Reform there was an important difference between choosing IRA investments versus your "regular" investments: because you don't pay any taxes on IRA investment income until you withdraw the money, it had been preferable to use your IRA for "income" investment, leaving capital gains for your outside investments. As we've seen, with Tax Reform all income is now taxed the same. So pick your IRA and outside investments based on how much total profit (interest, dividends and appreciation) you expect.

SIX THINGS TO CONSIDER BEFORE CHOOSING A CUSTODIAN

Once you've selected the type of IRA custodian you want—bank, mutual fund, etc.—do some comparison shopping among specific institutions. Check the ads in your newspaper's Sunday business section to find out what's currently available. Call up and request each institution's free brochure. Don't be afraid to ask a lot of questions and keep these things in mind:

1. *Fees*

Look for the custodian with the lowest fees. The same is true for stock brokerage commissions. Be sure to check if there are any special fees for closing the account or transferring money to a different IRA. Avoid any IRA that charges an additional fee based on how much money is in your account.

2. *Helpfulness*

Some institutions are better than others about helping you fill out forms, explaining the investments offered and the like. If you need investment advice, pick a place where you think you'll feel comfortable asking questions.

3. *Small Amounts*

Some custodians require a minimum contribution that might be more than you are ready to invest.

4. *Relationship*

There are sometimes financial advantages to doing all your investment business at one place. For example, many banks give cheaper loans and mortgages to "preferred customers," and it's often easy to become one by opening an IRA before you borrow money. When I applied for my home mortgage, I opened up a checking account and an IRA with that bank at the same time. This made me a "preferred customer" and entitled me to a 1 percent reduction in the interest rate on my new mortgage.

5. *Fexibility*

Some IRAs restrict how and when you can take money out of your IRA. Others leave the decision entirely up to you. For instance, some don't allow withdrawals until you're at least 59½ years old. Since you don't know what payout options you'll want, the more flexibility you have, the better.

6. *Free Gifts*

The IRS limits the value of free gifts—for opening an IRA—to $10 in most cases. Everything else being equal, by all means pick the custodian offering the free toaster. But examine the total package closely–things are rarely, if ever, really equal.

OBSERVATION: You can open an IRA by mail, make payments by mail and change your investments by a phone call. So location is not an important consideration, unless you want to be able to drop by and say hello to your custodian.

The Paperwork

To set up an IRA, you can call, write or visit any bank, mutual fund or brokerage firm offering IRAs. The necessary forms are short and easy to fill out. Give the custodian the signed forms and a check or money order and you've opened an IRA.

To make additional contributions to your IRA, you need only send in a check or money order. However, you should include a short letter with your check or money order giving your name, address, social security number and IRA account number. Some institutions provide their customers with special IRA deposit slips that they can be use instead of a covering letter.

In addition, you should always specify for which tax year you're making your payment. For example, if you're contributing $2,000 to an IRA on April 1, 1987, for the 1986 tax year, you must specify that in the covering letter to eliminate any confusion over whether the money is intended for a 1986 or 1987 IRA contribution.

When you open an IRA, you also should fill out a designation of beneficiary form stating whom you want to receive the assets in your IRA if you die. Generally beneficiary can be a living person, a trust or a charity. You can change your beneficiaries as often as you like by filling out a new form each time. Usually you can choose more than one beneficiary (for example, half to a son and half to a daughter) and list contingent beneficiaries in case your first-choice beneficiaries die before you do.

If you die without having named a beneficiary, the assets in your IRA will be handled according to local inheritance law. Generally, this means the money goes to your spouse and children or, if you don't have either, to your parents or estate.

OBSERVATION: Never leave things to chance; fill out your designation of beneficiary form when you open your IRA.

WHAT IF YOU PUT TOO MUCH MONEY IN AN IRA?

There is a special 6 percent penalty for exceeding the annual contribution limits for an IRA. For example, if you've put $3,500 in an IRA in a single year instead of $2,000, you will have to pay the government a 6 percent penalty on the extra $1,500 payment. Even worse, the 6 percent penalty will be charged for each year that the $1,500 overpayment remains in the IRA. Of course, you cannot deduct either the extra $1,500 payment or the overpayment penalty in figuring your income taxes. To avoid paying any penalties, you can simply withdraw the excess money plus the interest that you've earned on the overpayment before it's time to file your income tax return for that year. But you still must pay the regular income tax on that interest by reporting it on your next tax return.

EXAMPLE: If Jonathan puts $3,000 in his IRA on

January 10, 1989, for the 1988 tax year, he has until April 15, 1989, to take out the extra $1,000 plus the interest on the $1,000. If he makes the deadline, he won't have to pay the extra 6 percent penalty. But the income on the extra $1,000 is added to his other earnings on the tax return he files for 1988. If Jonathan misses the deadline, then he'll have to pay the 6 percent penalty.

If Jonathan doesn't take the extra money out by April 15, he can avoid paying a *second* penalty next year on the excess if he counts the $1,000 overpayment toward his IRA contribution for 1989, as long as he doesn't exceed his maximum allowable contribution again. He can even take a $1,000 deduction for 1989.

A third option is to simply withdraw the excess money after April 15, and pay the 6 percent excess contribution penalty for that year. But as you'll see, there is a 10 percent penalty on a withdrawal from an IRA for persons who are under 59½ years old. The penalty would apply in Jonathan's case (unless he was disabled) even though he's taking money out that should never have been put in.

Changing IRAs

You can move money from one IRA to another by means of a "rollover," which is simply a transfer of your money. You don't pay any taxes or penalties on the transfer. Let's say you opened your first IRA at Bank A and over the years save $10,000. Then you decide that it's time to invest in stocks, but Bank A doesn't have brokerage services. So you roll over your money to Brokerage Firm B.

When you roll over from one IRA to another, you generally must put in the new IRA precisely what you took out of the old. For instance, if you withdraw 100 shares of General Motors stock from one IRA, you must either roll over those shares or sell the stock and roll over the cash proceeds.

There are two ways to roll over money from one IRA to another: the slow way and the fast way.

Slow Way

The slow way is to set up the new IRA yourself and tell the custodian of your current IRA to transfer all or some of it to your new IRA.

The problem is that this direct transfer can be painfully slow—delays of six months and more are not uncommon. Why? Because IRA trustees are swamped with just opening new accounts and keeping their records straight. For them, transferring accounts is a computer and bureaucratic headache.

But the headache may be yours if you don't keep track of things. I once lost four months' interest transferring money from a bank IRA to a stock brokerage IRA simply because the bank got my name wrong. I had filled out all the right forms and done everything else I was asked, yet after two months I discovered my stockbroker had never received the rollover check. The bank insisted that my account had been closed two months ago and the money transferred. Finally, we figured out that the bank had put the wrong name on the check and that someone at the brokerage firm had sent it back to the bank—which then couldn't figure out whose money it was. Finally, after four months of telephone calls and aggravation, they completed the transfer.

I learned a few lessons. First, be sure to use the printed form your new IRA custodian provides. Second, have the new custodian send that form to the proper office at your old custodian–get the name of the specific department, correct address, and, if possible, the name of a person in the department. Third, *follow up.* Call your new custodian to be sure the form was sent and call up the old custodian to make sure the money has been transferred. Keep riding both sides until the job is done.

Always give yourself at least four weeks for an IRA transfer and try to avoid doing it at the end of the year. If your change drags over to the new year, you could end up paying annual custodian fees twice–to your old and new custodians.

If you experience delays of more than one month, Uncle Sam may be willing to step into the fray. Write the Securities and Exchange Commission and the New York Stock Exchange about your problem. The addresses are listed at the end of this book.

Observation: The IRS has ruled that if the custodian accidentally puts the rollover money in a regular, non-IRA account and the mistake isn't caught before the sixty-day deadline, the money is treated as a taxable IRA withdrawal.

Fast Way

The quicker way of doing things is to take the money out of the first IRA yourself and walk it over to your new IRA. You have sixty days after you take the money out of the first IRA to put it into the second IRA. But try to do it all on the same day. If you exceed the sixty-day period, you will be taxed on the money and, if you're under age 59½, you will also have to pay a 10 percent penalty. This type of rollover is allowed only once every twelve months for each IRA account you have.

It is possible to make a "partial rollover," in which you transfer only part of the money out of the first IRA into a second IRA. You must pay tax on any money that you keep for yourself and, if you're under 59½, the 10 percent penalty. Otherwise, the same rules apply to partial and full rollovers.

Rollovers from Company Retirement Plans

Money in a company retirement plan may also be rolled over tax free to an IRA. There are two requirements: first, you must have received at least half of the retirement benefit in a single year. The second is that the payment must be made because of certain events such as your leaving your job, retiring or reaching age 59½. Because the rules are complicated you should check to make sure you're eligible.

But you do not have to meet the other usual requirements for contributing to an IRA. For instance, you don't have to have any earned income for that year and the usual restrictions for people age 70½ don't apply. Nor does the usual $2,000 annual contribution limit apply. Of course, you don't get an income tax deduction for the roll over. And any portion of your company fund that is only a return of your own after-tax contributions (as shown on the Form 1099) isn't eligible for a rollover.

EXAMPLE: Maureen has quit her job with a benefit in her company profit-sharing plan of $6,000. If she wants to, Maureen can roll over any portion of the $6,000 to an IRA within sixty days of receiving the payment.

OBSERVATION: In some cases you may be able to roll over your IRA back into a company retirement plan. See Chapter 2 for more information.

To roll over a single-sum distribution to an IRA, you simply fill out a form that is available from your IRA custodian and bring it to them with your rollover check. But certain single-sum payments from a company retirement plan qualify for special income tax treatment. If you roll over all or part of a single-sum payment to an IRA you won't be allowed to use this favorable method of figuring your taxes. (See Chapter 2 for more details.)

You are taxed on any part of a retirement plan distribution that is not put in an IRA. (If you're under age 59½, you may also owe a 10 percent penalty. See Chapter 2 for details.) If you receive property instead of cash from the retirement plan, you must roll over either the property or the cash proceeds from the sale of the property.

Once the money is placed in the IRA, it is governed by regular IRA rules. This means that if you are over age 70½ when you roll over your retirement payment to an IRA, you must start withdrawing money from the IRA each year. Your IRA trustee can tell you the amount that you must withdraw.

OBSERVATION: Don't take a chance of losing your benefits check or missing the sixty-day rollover deadline. Make your rollover the very day you receive your distribution.

TAKING YOUR MONEY OUT

Basically, the rule of thumb is to wait as long as possible to take money out of your IRA. Most of the money you take out of your IRA is taxed as regular income, except that you don't pay any social security tax on it.

However, you do not pay any income taxes on the part of the money that came from your nondeductible contributions since that money was already taxed once. Your IRA custodian should be able to tell you which part of any payment is a return of your nondeductible contribution and which part is taxable as investment income or deductible contributions. But you should keep records in case they don't.

Generally, you should try to take money out of

your IRA only in lower-income years–usually after retirement—since your tax rates go up as your income increases. And, again, income compounding is a good reason in itself to delay taking money out of your IRA.

There are strict rules for when you can withdraw money from your IRA without incurring a penalty. Between the ages of 59½ and 70½, you can take as much money as you choose from your IRA every year. If you're 60 years old and need an extra few thousand dollars—even if you're not yet retired—you can simply tap your IRA. And if you have earned income that same year, you can pay back up to $2,000 to the IRA. Once you reach age 70½, the law says that you *must* begin withdrawing money from your IRA.

EXAMPLE: Peter is 62 years old and is planning a three-month vacation from work. To help pay for it, he takes $12,000 out of his IRA, which is taxed as regular income. When he returns to work, he can put up to $2,000 back into his IRA that same year and take a tax deduction, too.

Early Withdrawal Penalties

You will be penalized 10 percent of any money (except the portion coming from nondeductible contributions) that is taken out of your IRA before you are 59½. The 10 percent penalty applies only to the money taken out, not to the total amount in your IRA. You must also pay income tax on the full amount you take out (again, except the portion coming from nondeductible contributions), and you may not deduct the 10 percent penalty in figuring your taxes.

The penalty doesn't apply if you are disabled when you take the money out or if it's withdrawn by your beneficiary after you die. You are considered disabled if you cannot work because of a physical or mental impairment that is expected to continue indefinitely. The penalty also won't apply if you take the money out in installments over the rest of your life or the life of you and your beneficiary, in much the same way a pension is paid.

EXAMPLE: Brenda is 40 years old and has $30,000 in her IRA, all of which came from deductible contributions. If she decides to withdraw $10,000 now, she would have to pay the government a $1,000 penalty (10 percent of $10,000). She also would owe federal income tax on the $10,000 she withdrew.

If you do make an early withdrawal, you must pay the 10 percent penalty with your next year's income tax return and fill out Form 5329 along with your regular income tax return.

If you know for sure that you will need the money within the next ten years or so, don't put it into an IRA. But don't let the penalties themselves scare you too much. A 10 percent penalty is not that severe and the extra income you earned in the IRA—because you haven't been paying any taxes on it—could pay for that 10 percent penalty. When and if the day comes that you absolutely need to withdraw money from your IRA, chances are that at that point your financial problems will have put you in a lower tax bracket anyhow.

What Happens to Your IRA When You Die?

The tax law sets the limit on when your beneficiary must start taking money out. Otherwise, it's up to your beneficiary and the rules of your IRA custodian. Here's what the law requires:

If an IRA owner has begun taking money out—say in monthly installments—then after he dies the beneficiary can continue on the same installment program or choose a faster payment schedule. If payments hadn't started before death, then the beneficiary must take all the money out within five years.

But there are several exceptions. First, if the IRA is payable to a named beneficiary and payments begin within one year after death, they can be stretched out over the beneficiary's life or life expectancy. The 10 percent penalty doesn't apply to these payments even if the beneficiary is under age 59½. A non-spouse beneficiary may not invest his or her own money in the inherited IRA.

There is another exception if your spouse is the named beneficiary. The spouse can leave the money in the IRA and postpone taking it out until the deceased spouse would have reached age 70½. Another option is for the spouse to treat the inherited IRA as his or her own IRA for deduction and rollover purposes, so that money can be taken out by the spouse at any time between the ages of 59½ and 70½. Before age 59½, withdrawals are subject to the usual 10 percent penalty, and withdrawals must begin by age 70½. All payouts from the IRA are taxable to the spouse.

EXAMPLE: When Jason died, he had $30,000 in an IRA for which his 36-year-old wife Pam was the beneficiary. Pam decides she needs $10,000 to meet her immediate living expenses, but will save the rest for her retirement. So Pam withdraws $10,000 from the IRA. She pays income tax on the $10,000, but not the 10 percent early withdrawal penalty. The other $20,000 remains tax free in the IRA.

Whether a surviving spouse should convert an inherited IRA into cash depends on the person's age and finances. Generally, it's best to keep the entire IRA intact so the money continues to grow tax free. In that case, the inherited IRA money wouldn't be available again until the spouse turns 59½. But if the living spouse is over age 70½, then it's better to leave the money in the IRA for the next five years.

LATE WITHDRAWALS

While you cannot touch your IRA without penalty before age 59½, you *must* begin taking a minimum amount of money out of your IRA annually starting April 1 of the year after you turn age 70½. The minimum is figured so that you can withdraw equal amounts each year of your *expected* life or the expected life of you and your beneficiary. If you take out less than the minimum, you'll face a very stiff penalty: a 50 percent tax on the amount you should have taken out, less the amount you actually took out. The IRS can waive the 50 percent tax if the delay was due to a "reasonable error" and it's corrected when caught.

You can meet the withdrawal requirement by using the money in your IRA to buy an annuity—from an insurance company—that will provide payments to you (or you and your spouse or other beneficiary) for the rest of your life (or lives). A bank or other IRA custodian can calculate how much you are required to withdraw when you are ready to retire. Of course, you can always take out more than the minimum.

Income Tax Withholding on IRA Payments

All payments over $200 from an IRA are subject to income tax withholding, including certain tax-free rollovers from a company pension plan or another IRA, unless you specifically ask not to have any amounts withheld.

Before you receive a distribution from an IRA, the custodian will give you an IRS Form W-4P. That form has a box which you can check in order not to have any amounts withheld. If you do want income taxes taken out, you can specify the number of exemptions you want to claim.

If you're simply rolling over your distribution to an IRA tax free, you should elect no withholding. If you don't, you may be taxed or penalized for violating the rule that requires complete rollovers between IRAs. Before you decide whether you want to elect no withholding, speak to your tax adviser.

OTHER TYPES OF IRAs

Although most people associate IRAs with "individual retirement accounts," there are other types of investments within the IRA family: there are insurance company individual retirement annuities and employer-paid IRAs. Here's how they work:

Individual Retirement Annuity

Individual retirement annuities are offered only by insurance companies. Like regular IRAs, they allow you to invest up to $2,000 annually and deduct the contribution from your taxable income at the end of the year. There usually are three investment choices offered.

One is a "fixed-rate annuity," which pays interest based on how much the insurance company earns on its general bond, real estate and mortgage portfolio. It's something like investing in the company itself: if it does well, you do well and vice versa. Each year's interest rate in a fixed-rate annuity is usually announced at the start of the year. Usually the insurance company also guarantees you a minimum rate for as long as you stick with the investment—but only 3 percent or 4 percent, which is no big deal.

The second investment is usually a variable annuity. This is simply a common stock fund similar to a mutual fund. The earnings depend on how well the fund does each year, with no guarantees.

The third choice is usually some form of money market mutual fund. Most insurance companies allow you to switch from one type of annuity to another or to split your investment among all three.

When you retire, you have the option of taking out the money in the IRA in cash. Or, the insurance company can take the money in the IRA—your payments plus the accumulated interest—and pay you a fixed monthly payment, called an annuity, for the rest of your life. The amount of the annuity depends on how much money is in your account when you retire, your age at retirement and the interest rates at the time the annuity starts.

You can also get a "joint-and-survivor" annuity, which entitles your beneficiary to receive a lifetime annuity if he or she survives you. Because your beneficiary continues to receive payments after you die, the monthly amount paid under a joint-and-survivor annuity will be less than what you would receive if the annuity was paid only during your own lifetime.

Many insurance companies will not accept annual IRA contributions of less than $50. Most also reserve the right to close out your account if you haven't been investing in it regularly or if you haven't been investing enough. In either case, the insurance company would refund all the money in the account, which you can then transfer to a regular IRA to avoid paying taxes and penalties.

Generally speaking, an insurance company annuity is a poor choice for an IRA because of the ridiculously high fees. Fees as high as 8.75 percent of *each* contribution are not uncommon. You also could be charged a fee, sometimes as high as 10 percent, for taking money out in any form other than an annuity. All this could come on top of an annual maintenance fee to boot. Meanwhile, you can get everything an insurance company offers and more by way of investment in a mutual fund—generally at a fraction of the cost.

And if you want a fixed-rate annuity from your IRA when you retire, there are better ways. You can simply transfer the money in your regular IRA to an insurance company when you retire and have them provide the annuity. That way, during your working years you can invest your IRA money however you like.

Another option is to invest your money in conservative, low-risk investments when you retire. You will receive a fixed, guaranteed monthly income but still have the principal to use during your lifetime or to pass on to your beneficiaries. But with an annuity, once you and your beneficiary both have died, the insurance company will be entitled to keep whatever money is left.

Employer-sponsored IRAs

Some companies make arrangements for their employees to make regular payments to an IRA. These IRAs are identical to the ones you can set up yourself—the advantage is that most of the paperwork is done for you and the company usually pays any trustee's fees and handles the investments for you. And, if the company offers a payroll withholding system, the money goes straight from your paycheck to your IRA before you're tempted to spend it.

Some company IRA programs go one step better: the company will put its own money into an IRA for you and you don't have to pay income tax on the contribution. But you cannot take an extra deduction on your taxes. And the money counts toward the $2,000 annual limit and is taxed by the social security system.

You can put money in both a regular IRA and an employer-sponsored IRA as long as you don't exceed the annual contribution limit.

Example: Debbie earns $25,000 working for the Acme Company and the firm also contributes $1,200 into an IRA account for her every year. Debbie can put up to $800 more into a regular IRA each year and take an $800 income tax deduction.

Simplified Employee Pension

A simplified employee pension, or SEP, is a blend of an IRA and a company pension plan. Under the SEP rules, a company can put up to 15 percent of an employee's salary or $30,000, whichever is less, into an IRA annually. The usual $2,000 maximum yearly contribution limit doesn't apply and the employee can still put up to $2,000 of his own earned income into a separate IRA or a special SEP–IRA. But being a member of a SEP, like any other company retirement plan, means that you won't be able to deduct your IRA contributions if your Adjusted Gross Income is too high.

THE 401 (k) MIRACLE

There's a new breed of plan being offered by companies that, for many workers, offers even more tax advantages than an IRA.

These new plans are called by several different names: "salary deferral plans," "cash or deferred plans," or "401 (k) plans"—the last name taken from its place in the Internal Revenue Code.

The basic idea behind a 401 (k) plan is similar to an IRA: you can reduce your taxable income while saving for your retirement. But instead of opening an account yourself, the money in a 401 (k) plan goes into a regular company profit-sharing plan. The difference is important because most of the rules and regulations governing company 401 (k) plans are more generous—meaning better for the employee—than with an IRA.

Here's how these special 401 (k) plans work. At your request, your employer withholds a specific amount from your paycheck and invests it in a special account under your name in the plan's trust fund. How the money is invested usually is up to your company, but sometimes the company will give you some choices. For example, you may be able to divide your account between a money market mutual fund, a blue-chip stock fund or your company's own common stock.

You can contribute much more to a 401(k) plan than the $2,000 annual limit allowed with an IRA. Each company plan sets its own limit, usually between 10 and 15 percent of your total salary, but by law your maximum contribution each year cannot exceed $7,000 (the limit was $30,000 before Tax Reform). In some plans the employer may also match a portion of your own contribution to the plan. That means that if you put 4 percent of your pay into the plan, your company might add another 2 percent. Your own 401(k) contributions will always be 100 percent vested. But watch out: you may not be able to keep the company matching contribution if you don't stay with the company long enough to become vested.

Like an IRA, your 401(k) account will be invested and you will not be taxed on the investment earnings until the money is paid out to you. However, you do pay social security taxes on whatever your employer withholds from your salary to put into the plan. A few states still tax your 401(k) contributions, so you'll have to check with your company or tax adviser to find out for sure.

Your company probably will allow you to change the amount of your salary contribution once or twice a year. Many companies also let you temporarily suspend contributions if you happen to have a cash crunch and need your full paycheck.

Unlike an IRA, with a 401(k) plan you may be able to withdraw your money before age 59½ without incurring the usual 10 percent penalty. For instance, many company plans allow an employee to tap his salary contributions for a severe financial hardship. Unfortunately, the IRS has not yet set any fixed standards for what a "severe hardship" is, but some experts say that buying a house or paying medical bills can count. (Check with your company to be sure.) And, of course, usually all your money can be withdrawn when you reach age 59½, retire, die or become disabled. In those cases you either pay the income tax on the money or perhaps transfer it, tax free, into your new employer's pension plan or an IRA of your own.

If you do decide to keep the money, you might want to reduce your tax burden by figuring your income tax on the basis of "income averaging." The idea is to spread out over several years a sudden increase in income and, of course, spread out the tax bite at the same time. (Chapter 11 will discuss the rules for income averaging in more detail.)

Some 401(k) plans let employees borrow money from their accounts. The loan doesn't count as a taxable distribution as long as you meet the loan terms. This is a good tax-saving way to use your 401(k) money for a while, but should not be used frequently. After Tax Reform, though, you generally won't be able to deduct the interest on the loan. You should plan on repaying the loan as soon as possible.

You are allowed to contribute to both a 401 (k) plan and an IRA in the same year. But if you're not able to deduct your IRA contributions or you can afford only one of the two, the 401 (k) is your best bet. This is especially true if there is a matching company contribution. The major disadvantage to a 401 (k) versus an IRA is that the 401 (k) gives you less flexibility about choosing investments and varying the amount of contributions. You should also find out whether your company uses 401 (k) contributions to reduce other company benefits that are based on your salary (such as your pension or life insurance). Your SPD should have that information.

The chart on page 193 summarizes some of the differences between an IRA and a salary deferral plan.

Q. Did Tax Reform change the rules regarding who can have an IRA?

A. No. Anyone who works and is under age 70½ still can put money in an IRA.

Q. Does Tax Reform affect my existing IRA?

A. No.

Q. Can I deduct future IRA contributions?

A. Maybe. If you're in a company retirement plan *and* have Adjusted Gross Income over $40,000 if you're married and $25,000 if you're single, you'll lose at least part of your IRA deduction. The deduction is phased out over the next $10,000 of income

	IRA	*Salary Deferral Plan*
Where	Almost any financial institution	Only special company plans
How	Must open own IRA	Company withholds salary, may match contributions
Ease	You do all the work	Company does most of work
How much	$2,000 annually or earned income if less than $2,000	Percentage of pay up to $7,000
Taxes	Contributions may be federal-tax deductible; earnings grow tax free; must pay tax on distributions unless rolled over to IRA; not eligible for income averaging	Contributions are federal-tax deductible, but distributions may be eligible for IRA rollover or income averaging
Distribution	Whenever you want, but 10% penalty on distributions before 59½; loans not allowed	Usually at retirement, reaching age 59½ or financial hardship; no 10% penalty if hardship; loans sometimes allowed
Investment choices	Depends on IRA custodian; you pick investment strategy	Depends on plan rules; company usually picks investments or limits your choice

CHAPTER 6

KEOGHS: SELF-HELP FOR THE SELF-EMPLOYED

There is a terrific, no-risk tax shelter that your doctor has known about for years. It offers an easy way for the self-employed person or the owner of a small business to save on taxes now and a painless way to plan for retirement. It's officially known as a qualified retirement plan—but many people call it a Keogh.

Until 1984, only corporations were allowed to enjoy the full financial benefits of qualified retirement plans—that's why so many doctors incorporated themselves as a "P.C." or "P.A.," for professional corporation or association. Unincorporated business had been limited to much more restricted plans.

Since then, qualified retirement plans are equally available to self-employed individuals, partnerships and corporations alike. And unlike IRAs, Tax Reform has not done much to dampen Keoghs for most self-employed people. These retirement plans give you a three-way tax break. First, your business can make tax-deductible contributions of $30,000 or more annually toward your own retirement. Second, the income earned by that money is tax free until withdrawn. Third, you and your employees may pay reduced taxes on the money when you retire.

As we saw in Chapter 1, social security benefits are a relative drop in the bucket toward retirement security. And the $2,000 annual lid on contributions to an IRA, which might not even be deductible, allows you to build only a partial nest egg toward retirement. But with a qualified retirement plan, you can put aside enough money to satisfy most, if not all, of your financial needs through your golden years.

Depending on how your retirement plan is set up, you can vary the amount of your annual contributions and even skip a year or two if business is bad. Or, under certain circumstances, you can terminate your retirement plan well before you're ready to retire and stop contributing altogether.

The biggest down side is that qualified retirement plans are governed by more tax and other governmental regulations—called ERISA—than an IRA.

ERISA IN 150 WORDS OR LESS

The purpose behind the maze of ERISA rules is to prevent a retirement plan from becoming simply a windfall for the owners and the highest-paid employees of a business. To prevent such abuses, ERISA requires that all retirement plans meet certain minimum standards. Generally, all full-time employees who meet certain basic eligibility tests must be members. All members must share the money in the plan, although not necessarily equally. And, members' retirement benefits must become vested, or nonforfeitable, in a relatively short period of time.

There also are rules that prohibit an employer from deliberately firing someone to prevent him from collecting benefits. An employer must file annual reports on the plan with the federal government to show that these rules are being met.

To set up a qualified retirement plan, you need a basic understanding of your financial needs and the help of at least one qualified expert—your lawyer or accountant and maybe an actuary or financial planner as well. But before you talk to any experts, you should understand your basic alternatives so that you aren't talked into making a hasty decision. This chapter will explain in plain, simple English what you should know *before* you set up your plan.

Here's how it all works.

WHO CAN HAVE A QUALIFIED RETIREMENT PLAN?

A qualified retirement plan can be set up by any owner of a small business, including a self-employed person, a partnership or a corporation.

"Self-employed" means you earn at least some

money on your own, without working for a company or a boss. Even if you work only part time at your own business and also work for a company, you are considered self-employed. For example, if you work full time for a big company but run your own shop on weekends, you can set up your own retirement plan, deduct your contributions from your shop income and still remain part of your company's retirement plan.

By law, all your full-time employees must be allowed to participate in the plan, except for employees under age 21 who have been employed less than one year and union members. More on that later.

HOW MUCH CAN YOU SOCK AWAY?

You can choose from four basic types of retirement plans: profit-sharing plans, money-purchase plans, pension plans and target plans. The basic difference between them is how the employer's annual contributions to the plan are figured.

1. *Profit-Sharing Plan*

It's flexible and simple: you decide every year how much money, if any, you want to contribute to the plan that year. Before Tax Reform, contributions had to come from your business profits, but not anymore.

If you have employees, the contributions are split into individual accounts, usually in proportion to each person's salary (or self-employment earnings). The money in that account is invested and, upon retirement, each plan member receives the total contributions in his account along with the income earned. The maximum that can be put in any one person's account each year is usually $30,000, or 15 percent of their compensation for the year, whichever is less.

EXAMPLE: Sam owns a repair shop and employs John to make deliveries. Sam's income from the business in 1986 (after subtracting the $5,000 he intends to put in the plan that year) is $40,000 and John's salary is $10,000, for a total of $50,000. Sam receives 80 percent of the contributions to the profit-sharing plan because his salary is 80 percent of their combined salaries. John gets the other 20 percent. So of the total $5,000 contribution to the profit-sharing plan, $4,000 would be put in Sam's account (80 percent of $5,000) and $1,000 would be put in John's account (20 percent of $5,000).

2. *Money-Purchase Plan*

Instead of the flexibility of a profit-sharing plan, you contribute a fixed percentage of each plan member's salary into an individual account every year. That percentage is decided upon when the plan is set up, but can be amended if you want. Upon retirement, each employee gets the money in his or her account, plus the income.

The maximum amount that can be added to an employee's account in a money-purchase plan each year is $30,000 or a percentage of the person's compensation, whichever is less. For a self-employed person or partnership, the limit is 20 percent of compensation and for an incorporated business, the limit is 25 percent—both more generous limits than profit-sharing plans allow.

You cannot skip or vary the amount of contributions, unless you can prove that making the full contribution would be what the IRS would consider a "substantial business hardship." So, don't even consider starting a money-purchase plan unless you are fairly confident you will be able to make those fixed annual contributions.

EXAMPLE: Ralph is self-employed, with no employees, and has set up a money-purchase plan to which he has decided to contribute 15 percent of his annual compensation each year. If Ralph's self-employment income in 1986 is $50,000, he would put $7,500 into his plan for that tax year.

3. *Pension Plans*

With this setup, you maintain one large retirement account for all plan members. The business' annual contributions to the plan are calculated by an actuary so that there will be enough money in the plan to pay for each employee's pension. Usually, the contribution works out to be about the same every year.

The amount of the pension is based on a plan member's salary and years of employment. For example, the pension could equal 1 percent of a person's annual compensation for every year he has been employed. An employee of twenty years' standing would be entitled to an annual, lifetime pension of 20 percent of his average compensation, starting at retirement age, which is generally 65. The maximum pension allowed is $90,000 a year, or the amount of the member's average salary over his three highest-paid consecutive years, whichever is less.

A pension plan allows contributions well in excess of $30,000 annually to be made for older employees. How? Because the employee has fewer years remaining until retirement, and so more money must be contributed each year to pay for his guaranteed pension. For example, if a 55-year-old business owner starts a plan that guarantees him a lifetime pension of $90,000 a year at age 65, he could put over $100,000 into his plan in each of the ten years remaining until his retirement.

Like a money-purchase plan, the employer cannot change or skip an annual contribution to the plan, unless he obtains an IRS waiver on the ground that he has a substantial business hardship.

4. *Target Plan*

This is a combination pension plan and money-purchase plan, where the employer makes a fixed contribution each year into a separate account for each plan member. The contribution is based on an assumed (or target) pension for each plan member. Again, this means that proportionately more money can be tucked away for relatively older plan members.

But a target pension is not guaranteed. The retiree receives whatever money is in the individual account at retirement—which could be more or less than the target pension, depending on how well the funds were invested. In all other respects a target plan is identical to a money-purchase plan, including the limits on contributions.

WHICH PLAN IS BEST FOR YOU?

Choosing the proper type of plan is the most important decision you'll make; it's something to discuss very carefully with your expert adviser. Generally, you should choose a retirement plan based on the amount of money you can afford to put away and whether you may need to occasionally skip an annual contribution. If your business is new, or if your profits fluctuate a lot from year to year, you might be best off with the flexibility of a profit-sharing plan.

On the other hand, a pension plan is a good choice for the business owner who is over 40 years old and wants to put away as much money toward retirement as quickly as possible. For the same reason, a pension plan allows you to reduce the amount to be contributed every year for younger employees.

An employer may be able to maintain more than one retirement plan at the same time. For example, a store owner could set up a money-purchase plan to which he contributes 10 percent of his compensation, and put another 5 percent of his compensation into a profit-sharing plan. That way, he is committed only to making the 10 percent annual contribution to the money-purchase plan, but has the option of making additional contributions to the profit-sharing plan if he so desires.

HOW ARE PLAN CONTRIBUTIONS INVESTED?

You decide who invests the money in your retirement plan: you can do it yourself, an "investment manager" can or each plan member can invest for his own account. For profit-sharing, money-purchase and target plans the income (or loss) is shared among all members based on the relative amount in each person's account in the plan, unless members invest for their own accounts, in which case each person's account is based on his own investment selections.

Members of a pension plan are not directly affected by how well the investments do, unless the plan doesn't earn enough money to pay for everyone's pension. If the pension plan's investments do especially well, though, the extra profits may be used to increase pension benefits, reduce the company's contributions or, in certain cases, be returned to the company.

The person who manages a retirement plan's assets has what ERISA calls "fiduciary" responsibility. That's rather vaguely defined as requiring that the investments be "prudent" and, in most cases, that they be diversified, meaning split up among different investments. Unfortunately, the law does not offer any more specific guidelines as to how retirement plan money should be invested. But the general aim is that employers choose relatively conservative, low-risk investments such as CDs, U.S. Treasury bills, bank money market accounts, money market mutual funds, stocks and bonds in sound companies and solid mutual funds.

At the same time, not every employer is expected to be an investment genius and not all misjudgments are penalized. However, if you put all your retirement plan's money in an obviously risky venture that doesn't do well, you could be in big trouble. You might be sued and have to repay the losses to the plan.

As a general rule of thumb, don't invest in any of the following without first speaking to a lawyer:

1. your own business or that of a friend or relative
2. a personal loan
3. real estate
4. gold, silver, coins, art, cars, etc.
5. any risky company or venture.

A retirement plan also cannot borrow money, such as buying stock on margin.

By appointing a professional investment manager, you can avoid most of the legal responsibilities and risks. An investment manager can be a bank, brokerage firm or anyone else approved by the U.S. Department of Labor to handle retirement plan investments. You and the manager should sign an investment management agreement prepared or reviewed by a lawyer.

Observation: Most investment managers are expensive and are willing to manage only large sums of money. Many banks and stock brokerage firms offer investment advice and suggestions to small companies, but won't become their investment manager.

A third option that spares you some of the hassles and responsibility is to allow each member to invest his own retirement account funds. This option is open only to members of profit-sharing, money-purchase and target plans. Pension plans must generally be managed by either the employer or a professional investment manager.

The advantage to employees is that they control their future retirement money by choosing their own investments. Employees who manage their own accounts are not covered by the ERISA requirements to be prudent and diversify their investments. But they do face the same prohibitions against investing in gold, silver, other collectibles, their own real estate, etc.

If you want your employees to manage their own funds, make arrangements with a stock brokerage firm or a mutual fund company to provide the necessary services. Separate accounts and regular statements must be provided by the institution for each member. Employees can invest in virtually anything that the institution offers their regular customers and is allowed by ERISA: stocks, bonds, bank money market accounts, money market mutual funds and regular mutual funds.

However, the employer can arrange to limit employees to certain investments. A family of mutual funds is often a good choice: it gives the plan members a wide range of investment choices, but does not require a lot of time or expertise in choosing particular stocks and bonds. It also avoids the need to pay costly stock brokerage commissions. Many mutual funds usually are willing, for a fee, to handle the record-keeping chores. The fees are usually reasonable (e.g., an annual fee of about $50 per account) and can either be deducted from each plan member's account or paid by the employer.

HOW THE TAX SYSTEM WORKS FOR YOU

Remember the three big reasons why a retirement plan is a great way to save for your retirement: an immediate tax deduction for the money you contribute to the plan, the ability to postpone paying taxes on the income earned and being able, in most cases, to pay less tax on the money when you withdraw it at retirement. For example, if you're self-employed and put $10,000 of your income in a retirement plan, you automatically save $2,800 in income taxes if you're in the 28 percent tax bracket and $3,300 in taxes if you're in the 33 percent bracket.

A corporation takes its tax deduction on the corporate tax return, while self-employed persons or partnerships can take the deduction on their personal tax return as a business expense. You do not pay social security taxes on contributions to a retirement plan.

Let's take a look at how much you could save if you put $5,000, $10,000 or $25,000 annually in a retirement plan and earned 9 percent interest over 5, 10, 15, 20 or 30 years:

Time Invested	*$5,000 per year*	*$10,000 per year*	*$25,000 per year*
5 years	$ 29,924	$ 59,847	$ 149,618
10 years	75,965	151,929	379,823
15 years	146,805	293,609	734,023
20 years	255,800	511,601	1,279,003
30 years	681,538	1,363,075	3,407,688

These numbers speak for themselves. Even with inflation, the value of your retirement plan savings can be phenomenal!

OBSERVATION: Tax Reform added a new 15 percent excise tax on all payments from IRAs, Keoghs and other retirement plans which total above $112,500 in any year. This new rule is discussed in Chapter 11.

WHEN DO YOU HAVE TO SET UP A PLAN?

You must set up your qualified retirement plan by the end of the tax year to get a tax deduction for that year. Unlike an IRA, you cannot delay setting up a retirement plan until just before your taxes are due.

But you can delay actually contributing money to the plan up to the normal deadline (*including* extensions) for filing the federal income tax return for that year. For example, if a corporation's income tax return is due March 15, it must contribute to its retirement plan by that date. A self-employed person generally has until April 15, or until August 15 if he files for an automatic extension.

OBSERVATION: A self-employed person who does not have the cash to make a contribution by April 15 should consider filing for an extension until August 15.

Contributions to a pension plan, money-purchase plan or target plan generally must be made within eight and a half months after the close of the plan year, even if that date falls before the employer's income tax return deadline. If you miss that payment date, the IRS will fine you 5 percent of the amount you should have contributed. And, after giving you notice, the IRS can fine you an extra 100 percent if you don't make the contribution or get a waiver.

WHO'S IN THE PLAN?

You don't have much choice. Under ERISA rules most, and usually all, of your "full-time" employees must be included in your retirement plan, except those under age 21 or those who have worked for you less than one year. Of course, you can choose to allow even those employees to participate—a good idea if you are just starting out in business, so you'll be included in your own plan. You usually can exclude from your plan any employees who belong to a union or who work outside the United States.

In addition, the law requires that a minimum of 70 percent of all "full-time" employees who are not "highly compensated" (generally the nonowners) participate in your retirement plan, except for those employees under age 21, union members, etc. For example, if you have ten employees and nine of them are over age 21 and have worked for you for one year, under the 70 percent test you need to include at least seven of them in the plan.

If you have twenty employees or less, it's a wise idea to voluntarily include all of them in the retirement plan. Otherwise, if even one or two employees quit, the plan might no longer meet the 70 percent minimum participation rule. In that case, you would have to quickly amend the plan—which can be difficult—to cover more employees or risk having the plan "disqualified." When a plan is disqualified, the tax benefits of a retirement plan evaporate and each member is taxed immediately on the value of his or her vested benefit.

OBSERVATION: There are exceptions to the 70 percent test for plans that cover a "fair and broad" cross section of employees and a certain percentage of nonhighly compensated employees, but this is rarely available to small plans.

Just What Is a "Full-Time" Employee?

ERISA measures full-time employment in terms of "Years of Service." An employee earns a Year of Service when he or she works 1,000 "Hours of Service" within a twelve-month period, which averages out to about nineteen hours a week. An Hour of Service, in turn, is each hour for which an employee is paid or entitled to be paid, including up to 501 hours a year for vacation time, holidays, illness, disability, layoff, jury duty, military duty or authorized leaves of absence.

Hours of Service are reckoned anew every twelve months. If an employee does not complete 1,000 Hours of Service in his first twelve months on the job, then a whole new twelve-month period begins. The twelve-month period usually starts on the first day of the plan year, but can also begin on the anniversary of the employee's hiring.

Some small businesses keep track of each employee's hours through an easier method called the "elapsed time method." Basically this means that an employee earns a full Year of Service if he works at least one hour during a twelve-month period.

Once an employee becomes eligible, he must join his company's retirement plan within six months or by the beginning of the next plan year, whichever comes first. The specific date on which an eligible employee can become a plan member is called the "entry date." A plan must have at least one entry date a year, but many retirement plans have two or more entry dates, usually on the first day of the plan year and in the middle of the year. For example, if a plan operates on the calendar year the entry dates could be January 1 and June 1. That would mean an employee who met the plan's age and service requirements on May 1 would become a member of the plan on June 1. Ask your adviser for help on what to do.

ARE YOU TOP HEAVY?

The government wants all members of a small business' retirement plan to have a fair share of the benefits. For that reason, there are special regulations, called "top-heavy rules," that apply to certain retirement plans which otherwise might benefit certain "key" employees over lower-paid employees. The main purpose of these rules is to prevent the owners from shortchanging their employees.

What is a key employee? Basically he is any person who is (or was during the last four years):

1. An officer of a business who earns over $90,000 a year;
2. One of the ten employees owning the largest share of the business and earning over $30,000 a year;
3. An owner of more than 5 percent of the business; or
4. An owner of more than 1 percent of the business who earns more than $150,000 annually.

By definition, a plan is considered top heavy if more than 60 percent of the funds in the retirement plan are slated to go to key employees. For instance, an owner would tend to get much more out of a retirement plan than his employees simply because his salary is proportionately greater. But under the tax rules, only the first $200,000 of salary can be counted in figuring benefits.

OBSERVATION: As a practical matter, retirement plans for self-employed people, partnerships and small companies are unavoidably top heavy because there are so few employees involved.

But balanced against the top-heavy rules are two factors that do let an owner benefit more than his employees from a retirement plan: vesting and social security.

How Vesting Can Help an Employer

If an employee is vested, it means his contributions to a retirement plan cannot be taken away from him, even if he leaves the company before retirement. If an employee is partially vested, he gets to keep part of his plan contributions when he leaves and the rest goes back to the plan.

Almost all retirement plans vest an employee's entire benefit if he dies or becomes disabled while still working for the company. Also, an employee is automatically vested when he reaches the plan's retirement age, which is usually 65, even if he has not met the vesting requirements.

Otherwise, you can make it as easy as you want for your employees to become vested. For example, the most generous method would be to vest all employees fully—from the day they start work.

For top-heavy plans, only two relatively generous vesting timetables are allowed: all employees must be either 100 percent vested after their third Year of Service, or 20 percent vested each year after their first Year of Service, which would make them 100 percent vested after six years. You can see the difference between the two vesting schedules on the following charts:

Method 1

Years of Service	*Percent Vested*
1	none
2	none
3 or more	100%

Method 2

Years of Service	*Percent Vested*
1	none
2	20%
3	40
4	60
5	80
6	100

If you vest employees 100 percent after two years of service and use Method 1 you get an additional break: instead of employees automatically joining the plan after they have one Year of Service or reach age 21, you can require them to earn two Years of Service before they can become members.

Most employers use Method 1 for profit-sharing, money-purchase and target plans and Method 2 for pension plans.

In contrast, a small company that is not top heavy may use the following vesting schedule, which makes it more difficult for employees to become 100 percent vested:

Years of Service	*Percent Vested*
1	none
2	none
3	20%
4	40
5	60
6	80
7	100

In profit-sharing plans, a benefit forfeited by a non-vested employee is usually redivided among the remaining employees, using the same formula used to share employer contributions.

EXAMPLE: You have a profit-sharing plan which uses the second vesting table, with employer contributions based on each member's compensation. There are three members of your plan: A, who earns $60,000, and B and C, who each make $15,000 a year. B quits after three years, at which point he is 40 percent vested and has $5,000 in his profit-sharing plan account. B forfeits 60 percent of his benefit, which comes to $3,000. The forfeited $3,000 will be split between A and C, whose combined salary is $75,000, as follows:

$$\$3{,}000 \times \frac{60{,}000}{75{,}000} = \$2{,}400 = \text{A's share}$$

$$\$3{,}000 \times \frac{15{,}000}{75{,}000} = \$600 = \text{C's share}$$

For all other types of retirement plans, the forfeitures are generally used to reduce the employer's contributions to the plan. For instance, if the employees in the previous example were members of a pension plan, their employer's contribution for the year would be reduced by $3,000, the amount of B's forfeiture.

OBSERVATION: There are special rules for figuring Years of Service for vesting purposes and exactly when an employee forfeits a benefit. You should ask a qualified expert before you forfeit all or a part of an employee's benefit.

How Social Security Can Help an Employer

A legal loophole called "integration" also allows an owner to favor himself and higher-paid employees in a retirement plan. Integration simply means that the social security tax paid by an employer is counted as part of the employer's annual contribution to the plan.

It works because an employer pays only social security OASDI (Old Age, Survivors and Disability Insurance) tax on salaries up to a certain maximum income, which for 1987 is 5.7 percent of the first $43,800 earned. As a result, the employer's retirement plan contribution for lower-paid workers is reduced, while the contribution for higher-paid workers and the owners is protected. But the percentage put in below the social security wage base (e.g., $43,800) cannot be more than twice that for salary above the wage base. There is also a restriction on this tactic for top-heavy plans, where an employer must first provide at least the top-heavy minimum benefit before using integration. For profit-sharing and money-purchase plans, that minimum is 3 percent of compensation.

In a top-heavy pension plan, all non-key employees must receive a pension of at least 2 percent of their salary for each Year of Service when the plan was top heavy, up to a total of 20 percent of pay. If the pension plan's regular formula already will provide more to the employee than that minimum pension, then he gets the bigger amount.

EXAMPLE: Drs. Smith and Jones are partners and employ nurses A, B, and C. The doctors earn $200,000 each and nurses A, B, and C each earn $15,000 a year. All five of them participate in a top-heavy, integrated profit-sharing plan to which the doctors annually contribute about 10.7 percent of each member's compensation. But the doctors actually put in only 5 percent of the nurses' salaries, because part of the nurses' 5.7 percent social security tax is counted as part of the plan's contribution. Here's the difference integration could make in how much money is contributed to the plan for each person:

Plan Member	*Amount*
Dr. Smith	$17,900
Dr. Jones	17,900
Nurse A	750
Nurse B	750
Nurse C	750
Total	$38,050

As can be seen, out of a total of $38,050 in contributions to the plan, $35,800—about 94 percent—went to the two doctors.

The chart on page 218 shows how contributions to the four types of plans compare.

HOW TO SET UP A RETIREMENT PLAN

THE PAPERWORK

There's lots of it and it's unavoidable. Foremost is the plan document, which is required by ERISA and describes the terms of your retirement plan, the quali-

	Profit-sharing	*Money-purchase*	*Pension*	*Target*
1. Must you contribute every year?	no	yes	yes	yes
2. Are contributions put into individual accounts for employees?	yes	yes	no	yes
3. Is there a maximum contribution or benefit?	$30,000 or 15%	$30,000 or 20% or 25%	$90,000 pension or 100%	$30,000 or 20% or 25%
4. Is integration allowed?	yes	yes	yes	yes

fications for plan members, how contributions are made, when contributions vest and how the money can be withdrawn.

There are two ways to set up a plan document. The more expensive route is to hire a qualified expert (usually an attorney) to write the plan for you. The charge could be from $500 to $5,000. The cheaper route is to buy a do-it-yourself "prototype plan," which is a standardized form with blank spaces and boxes to check so that you can customize the plan. They are available from banks, brokerage firms or mutual funds.

The organization that furnishes your prototype is called the "sponsor" and usually charges a relatively modest fee of about $50–$60 per employee. In addition to the fees, the broker, banker or mutual fund involved will require you to use their financial services to invest the plan's funds. In other words, if you use a prototype from Merrill Lynch, then Merrill Lynch will be the custodian and all investments will have to be made through Merrill Lynch.

Insurance companies also offer prototype plans, which are geared toward investments in life insurance products. The rules on purchasing life insurance in a retirement plan are complicated and won't be discussed here. Suffice it to say that the insurance company will charge very high fees and that life insurance and retirement plans mix like oil and water. Generally, it's best to keep your life insurance outside of your plan.

If you want to use a prototype, ask these five questions:

1. Does the plan give me what I want from a retirement plan?
2. Does the financial institution have the specific investment services I want?
3. Are the fees, brokerage commissions and other charges reasonable?
4. Do they provide administrative, recordkeeping and other services that I need?
5. Has their prototype plan been approved by the IRS?

The answer to each should be "yes:"

OBSERVATION: Have your attorney or accountant take a look at any prototype plan before you sign on the dotted line.

GETTING THE IRS OK

As a precaution, the IRS should formally review any new retirement plan. If the application was on time, and there is a problem with the plan, the IRS will explain how to correct it. If the IRS decides that the plan conforms with its regulations, you will receive a "determination letter" stating their approval.

Determination letters are not required by law, but they do safeguard you against any errors or omissions in your plan that might come back to haunt you later. Keep in mind that the determination letter applies only to the way the plan is set up—it does not protect you if the plan or its funds are misused.

Observation: Although most prototype plans come with determination letters, that approval might not be adequate if the IRS ever questions your particular plan. Ask your adviser to be sure.

Because the IRS can take as long as one year to review a retirement plan, you might want to implement your plan in the interim. If the IRS does find something wrong with the plan, it usually can be amended easily. If you can't or don't want to correct the problem, then the plan must be closed down or, in legalese, "terminated." New retirement plans should always be written with a clause stating that if the IRS does not approve the plan, then all contributions and the income earned will be returned. Of course, the employer loses the income tax advantages for any contributions that are returned from the plan.

Holding Your Money

The money you put into your retirement plan must be put in either a custodial account or a trust.

A custodial account is nothing more than a special account, opened up at a bank, brokerage firm or insurance company, which then becomes the custodian. The custodian invests the money as directed by you and pays it out to retirees according to your direction and the terms of the plan.

A trust is a more complicated bit of legal hocus-pocus in which one or more persons—who become the trustees—sign a document in which they agree to hold the plan's money and other assets. The "trust" isn't a place or thing, but only a shorthand way of saying that the people signing the document are holding the assets for the benefit of other people. The business owner, including a self-employed person, can be the trustee for his own retirement plan.

Trust accounts must be prepared by an attorney and can be opened by the trustees with a bank, brokerage firm, mutual fund or insurance company. If you adopt a prototype plan, the sponsor may be willing to serve as trustee for little or no extra charge.

OBSERVATION: A corporation's retirement plan can be held only by a trust.

WHAT ABOUT AN EMPLOYEE WHO LEAVES AND THEN COMES BACK TO WORK?

An employer can be less generous about giving retirement benefits to someone who has not been a steady employee. If an employee works less than 501 Hours of Service in one year—or, if the plan uses the elapsed-time method, no hours at all—then the employee has what is called one "Break In Service." Every year in which an employee does not meet the minimum hourly requirements counts as one Break in Service. If the number of Breaks in Service exceeds his Years of Service or five years, whichever is more, the employee loses all his previously earned years and must qualify again from scratch.

OBSERVATION: The first year off due to childbirth, child care, or adoption sometimes is not counted as a Break in Service.

EXAMPLE: Sam has accumulated three Years of Service in his employer's plan when he quits to take a better-paying job. The new job doesn't work out and, after six years, he returns to his first company. Sam now has six Breaks in Service, which is more than the three Years of Service he had earned before he quit his first job. Sam is therefore treated as a completely new employee in terms of the retirement plan, with zero Years of Service.

This is just a summary of the service rules. You should always consult your adviser to be sure everything's proper.

Should You Allow Employees to Make Contributions to the Plan?

There are two major types of employee contributions to a retirement plan, both of which are immediately 100 percent vested:

1. voluntary nondeductible contributions
2. rollover contributions

Voluntary Nondeductible Contributions

Any retirement plan can allow employees to contribute up to 10 percent of their compensation annually to the plan. The 10 percent annual contribution limit is cumulative. If an employee does not make any contributions for several years, he can "catch up" by contributing the total amount from the previous skipped years. Voluntary nondeductible contributions can be made directly by employees or through a payroll deduction system.

These contributions are not tax deductible, but the income earned is tax free until the money is withdrawn from the plan. Generally, employees are allowed to withdraw their voluntary contributions from time to time, but will have to pay tax on any income. Because money grows much faster when it compounds tax free in a retirement plan, though, this feature can be a financial boon for retirement planning.

EXAMPLE: John has belonged to his company's retirement plan for three years, during which time he earned $25,000, $35,000 and $40,000 annually. He has never made a voluntary contribution to the plan. If he wants, he now can contribute up to $10,000 to the plan—which is 10 percent of his combined income over those three years.

The entire amount a worker puts into a plan counts in figuring how much the employer can put into the plan on the worker's behalf.

Rollover Contributions

A vested employee who changes jobs usually can transfer the money from his former employer's plan into his new firm's retirement plan without paying any tax on the rollover.

To qualify for such a rollover, an employee must deposit all the money from his old retirement account into the new retirement account within sixty days. If a retirement plan mistakenly accepts a rollover contribution that does not meet those requirements, the new plan may be disqualified. For that reason, your adviser should approve any rollover in advance.

How Are Benefits Paid Out?

The Tax Reform Act puts an additional 10 percent tax on *all* payments from all retirement plans, including Keoghs, before age 59½ unless they are:

1. paid because of the employee's death or disability,
2. paid in the form of a lifetime pension,
3. paid on account of early retirement on or after age 55 under the plan's rules (not available for all plans),
4. used to pay certain medical expenses, or
5. rolled over to an IRA.

These new rules encourage employees who change jobs to save their retirement benefits for retirement. That's good in terms of retiring rich, but keeping track of former employees' benefits can be a hassle for a small business. To avoid the problem and the 10 percent tax, you should consider offering to pay out an employee's benefits in a lump sum to be rolled over to an IRA.

Retirement plan members can collect their benefit in a single sum, in installments, or in the form of a lifetime annuity, depending on the plan rules. Since it's hard to predict what form of payment you'll want when you retire, try to make sure your plan offers as many choices as possible. Also, if you've got a pension plan, it must offer payment in the form of a lifetime pension with a survivor pension for the worker's spouse. Your plan must also pay half of the benefit of a vested employee who died before payments had started to his surviving spouse. Your adviser should explain these rules to you.

Distributions upon Death

A retirement plan member can name a beneficiary—a person, trust or charity—to inherit his benefits upon his death. As a general rule, a married member must name his or her spouse as a beneficiary, unless the spouse consents in writing to another beneficiary. Your retirement plan might give your beneficiary a choice of how the death benefits will be paid—for example, in one sum or in installments over a fixed period of years. Your adviser or plan sponsor should give you designation of beneficiary forms which each plan member should fill out.

ADMINISTERING YOUR RETIREMENT PLAN

Every retirement plan must have a plan administrator—which is usually the employer—who is responsible for managing the plan. Among the administrator's duties are:

1. keeping track of which employees are eligible for membership in the plan

2. making sure the trustee or custodian has enough information to allocate contributions to each member

3. notifying employees of important information about the plan and their benefits

4. completing and filing the required forms and reports to the IRS, the Department of Labor and to all employees.

Here is a brief summary of the "reporting and disclosure" requirements:

Summary Plan Description

An SPD explains the important terms of the plan in simple English. A copy must be given to all eligible employees within 120 days after the plan is set up and a copy must be sent to the U.S. Department of Labor. An SPD also must be given to new employees and to the beneficiaries of deceased members within ninety days. However, if you request a determination letter, you may wait to file the SPD until 120 days after you get a response from the IRS.

OBSERVATION: If the only members of a plan are the owners of a business and their spouses, an SPD is not required.

Annual Report

Each year an annual report on the plan must be filed with the IRS and the Department of Labor, using Form 5500. This form basically lists the plan's total assets, the contributions made during the year and other basic information. It must be filed annually, even if the employer did not make any contributions to the plan for that year.

Summary Annual Report

This is a short version of Form 5500 that must be sent to all plan members within nine months after the end of the employer's tax year, or two months after filing Form 5500, whichever is later.

Benefit Statement

Members who quit, are fired or retire must be told the exact amount of their vested benefit when they leave the company. In addition, each member must be given a benefit statement at least once a year upon request.

Your accountant, lawyer or other expert who helped you set up your plan can help with the reporting and disclosure requirements. For an additional fee, they will prepare all the necessary forms and documents. If you used a prototype plan, the sponsor may be willing to help you out too.

Fidelity Bond

Generally, retirement plans must have a "fidelity bond" coverage for at least 10 percent of its assets. The bond, which is purchased from a bonding or insurance company, protects plan members from theft or embezzlement. Your qualified expert or plan sponsor should help you get the fidelity bond you need. A bond is not needed for plans if the only plan member is the owner.

PBGC Insurance

The Pension Benefit Guarantee Corporation, or PBGC, is a government agency that insures some pension benefits if there is not enough money in the plan. The employer must pay an annual premium to the PBGC, currently $8.50 per member. The PBGC does not apply to plans in which only the owners are members.

Workers' Rights Under ERISA

As a member of a retirement plan, your employees are entitled under federal law:

1. to examine without charge all plan and other documents including documents filed with the U.S. Department of Labor, such as annual reports and plan descriptions
2. to get copies of all plan documents and other information for a reasonable charge, upon written request.
3. to receive a summary of the plan's annual financial report.
4. to receive a free, annual statement of their status in the plan, including whether they are vested and how much money, if any, they will receive if they leave the company before retirement.

You cannot discharge or otherwise discriminate against an employee in any way to prevent him from obtaining a retirement benefit or exercising his rights under ERISA. If an employee makes a claim for a benefit and the claim is denied, he is entitled to a written explanation of the reason for the denial.

Can You Amend a Retirement Plan?

A retirement plan can be changed or amended by the employer at any time during the year, as long as the changes are made in writing and the employees are notified. However, the employer generally cannot make any change that reduces an employee's earned or vested benefits. An amendment also cannot be made retroactive, except to correct a violation of the law.

Your plan will also be amended from time to time to meet any new legal requirements. Usually when Congress changes the law, you'll have at least a year or more to amend your plan. Your adviser or plan sponsor should keep you posted on these changes, but they are usually reported in most newspapers as well.

Observation: If the amendment is significant, you should request an updated determination letter from the IRS. Amendments should only be made with the assistance of a qualified expert.

Terminating the Plan

Terminating a plan means that the employer stops making contributions and generally all benefits are immediately distributed to members. An employer may terminate or close down a plan for business reasons—for example, if the plan is too expensive, the employer goes out of business or an important employee dies. As an alternative, a plan can be "frozen," which means that no further contributions are made and benefits are paid out when a member retires or leaves.

ERISA regulations prohibit any termination that unduly favors owners and high-paid employees. The PBGC must approve any pension plan termination and most employers also seek formal IRS approval, although it is not required.

The advice of a qualified expert should always be sought before a plan is terminated or frozen.

SIMPLIFIED EMPLOYEE PENSION

A Simplified Employee Pension, or SEP, is a combination retirement plan and IRA. As its name suggests, a SEP offers a simplified alternative to employers in order to provide retirement benefits to employees. But in most ways, a SEP really is more akin to a profit-sharing plan than a pension plan.

As with a profit-sharing plan, contributions to a SEP are based on an employee's compensation. But instead of making the contributions to a trust or a custodial account, payments to a SEP are made to a special IRA for each member.

SEPs are much less flexible than profit-sharing plans. For example, all contributions are immediately

100 percent vested, and all employees—not just 70 percent—who are at least age 21 and have worked for the employer for three years must be members. (The usual exceptions for union employees and foreign workers apply.) Unlike a profit-sharing plan, members cannot be required to be employed on the last day of the plan year to earn a contribution for that year.

Starting a SEP

A SEP must be established for a specific tax year before the due date for filing the employer's tax return. They can be set up through a financial institution that handles IRAs, such as a bank, brokerage firm or insurance company. The institution will have a fill-in-the-blanks SEP form that is very similar to a prototype retirement plan. However, because SEPs are more restrictive than other retirement plans, you won't have as many choices to make.

As with any retirement plan, it's a good precaution to get a letter from the IRS stating that your SEP meets the requirements of the law. Top-heavy rules also apply to SEPs.

Distributions from SEPs

The same rules that apply to IRA distributions also apply to payments from a SEP. SEP payments are ordinary income and are fully taxed in the year they are received. There is a 10 percent penalty for distributions to a person who is not disabled or is not yet age 59½. Like an IRA, there also is a 50 percent penalty imposed if the minimum distribution is not made after a person reaches age 70½.

A single-sum distribution of a member's entire account in a SEP may be transferred to an IRA tax free within sixty days of payment. The money may also be rolled over to another SEP. But the special income-averaging income tax treatment which applies to lump-sum payments is not available.

Q. Will Tax Reform affect the operation of my Keogh?

A. Not much. Most Keoghs were already so heavily regulated by Uncle Sam before Tax Reform that the new rules will have little impact. Congress did tighten the integration rules and indications are that there won't be any inflationary increases in the $30,000 contribution limit for quite a while. The rest of the changes are highly technical and you'll need to consult your tax advisor.

Q. Any changes on payouts from a Keogh?

A. Yes, similar to regular company plans. Those changes are discussed in Chapter 11.

PART III

EVERYTHING YOU NEED TO KNOW ABOUT INSURANCE, HOME OWNERSHIP AND INVESTMENTS

No retirement strategy is complete without an understanding of the three pillars of financial planning: insurance, home ownership and investments.

Choosing life insurance can be confusing and the uninitiated can easily get suckered into buying the wrong policy. Chapter 7 will tell you what you need to know to be a wise consumer—including whether you really need life insurance and why, with the new Tax Reform Act, it no longer works as a tax-sheltered investment.

Chapter 8 analyzes the American dream turned necessity, home ownership. For most people owning a home is a first step toward a secure retirement and their biggest lifetime investment. Choosing the right mortgage can mean the difference between financial ruin and financial security—and cashing in on that asset could be your most important financial decision.

Stocks, bonds, mutual funds, as well as the more speculative investments are discussed in Chapter 9. To retire rich it's crucial to invest your savings wisely. You'll learn six common sense tips for investing your assets profitably and keeping track of them. And you'll find out how to decide whether you need a broker and how to deal with one if you do.

CHAPTER 7

LIFE, DISABILITY AND HEALTH INSURANCE

The railroad and shipping tycoon Cornelius Vanderbilt didn't believe in insurance of any kind. His philosophy was simple: never buy anything you can't afford to lose. That's fine for a multimillionaire, but the rest of us have too many things we cannot afford to replace without this financial security blanket.

When it comes to life insurance, there are four questions to ask to see if it fits into your retirement and financial planning: Do you need life insurance, how much, what kind and where should you buy it?

LIFE INSURANCE–DO YOU NEED IT?

You need life insurance only if your death—and the loss of your paycheck—would bring financial hardship to someone. In other words, your need for life insurance protection depends entirely upon your station in life. A single person with no other mouths to feed generally does not need any life insurance, although he might want some coverage for funeral expenses, debts and medical expenses if his own savings wouldn't be enough to pay for these items. The same is true for a working couple with no children, assuming each spouse earns enough to support his or herself. Or such a working couple might buy just enough insurance to help pay off a portion of their mortgage, since it might be difficult for the surviving spouse to afford alone.

On the other hand, if you have small children, little or no savings and a large mortgage, you need life insurance and probably plenty of it. You may also need insurance for a nonworking spouse who now takes care of the kids and house, to cover the expense—after his or her death—of day care or a housekeeper.

OBSERVATION: It is generally a waste of money to buy life insurance for a minor child.

HOW MUCH LIFE INSURANCE DO YOU NEED?

Your basic goal should be to have enough money available to your family after your death to maintain a lifestyle close to their current standard of living, educate your children, pay off your debts and establish a retirement nest egg. There are lots of shorthand formulas available to figure out how much insurance you need; one conventional piece of wisdom holds that you need life insurance equal to six times your salary. But the fact is, you cannot figure out how much you need from a formula or computer program. There are too many variables involved that make each person's situation unique.

To start, you must consider how much cash your family will need for large expected—and unexpected—expenses. These might include a fund for postdeath expenses (funeral, uninsured medical expenses, attorneys' fees), debts, an emergency nest egg or just some extra money to help them through those difficult first months. You may want to provide an education fund for your children or spouse and money to pay off the mortgage. After adding up the amount of cash you'll want to be available for these expenses, subtract your current savings, generally excluding items such as your home and the IRA that you would not want to liquidate.

You must also take into account how much your spouse earns or could earn if he or she went back to work; the likelihood that your spouse would remarry; whether there are any rich relations willing to help out; whether there would be other sources of income such as investments or company pensions and whether your family would want a more costly or less expensive lifestyle after you're gone.

Generally, between 60 percent and 70 percent of the deceased person's income is needed to maintain the family's former lifestyle. But if your survivors will have enough money to pay off your home mortgage or your children's education, then remember they'll need less income. They also may receive social security death benefits (*see* Chapter 2), although some people intentionally ignore that source in figuring out how much money their survivors will need. That way, they rely on social security only as an additional resource to help compensate for inflation or emergencies.

OBSERVATION: You should review your insurance needs every year or two to keep pace with changes in your life and the inroads of inflation.

Once you know how much income you need to replace, the next step is figuring out how much money you need to invest to earn that amount. A relatively conservative calculation is to divide the income you want to replace by a projected rate of interest, such as 7 percent. For example, to earn about $30,000 in annual income, you'd need to invest about $428,000 at 7 percent interest. That assumes you would spend only your income and never dip into the $428,000 principal. If you plan to spend both your income and some principal, use a higher rate of interest, say 10 percent or 11 percent, as your rate. That would reduce your minimum nest egg to about $300,000.

EXAMPLE: Greg and Gail Greenshade (from Chapter 3) have two small children whom the Greenshades hope will attend college someday. Greg earns $25,000 a year and Gail earns $10,000 a year in a part-time job. Here's how they could figure out how much life insurance Greg would need, assuming Gail continued working part time after his death and would work full time when the children got older. Their present balance sheet looks like this:

Greg and Gail Greenshade
Balance Sheet
As of December 31, 1987

Assets	*Amount*	
Checking account	$ 300	
Savings account	1,200	
IRA: X bank C.D. (pays 11%, due 1991)	5,000	
Money market	2,200	
Acme Company stock (100 shares)	5,800	
Acme Company bond	2,010	
Tax refund due from IRS	350	
House at 111 Tree Lane Blvd.	58,000	($120,000 real value)
Total	$74,860	

Debt		
Pledge to charity	$ 600	
30-year 7% mortgage–20 years to go	45,000	
3-year car loan–1 year to go	2,000	
Total	$47,600	

Equity	$27,260	

Greg and Gail first figure that if Greg died the family would need a fund of $127,600 to meet certain expenses, pay off the mortgage and start a college fund for their children as follows:

Expense Funds	
Immediate cash fund	$ 5,000
Pay off debt	2,600
Pay off mortgage	45,000
Emergency fund	25,000
Education fund	50,000
Total	$127,600
Less available assets	(11,860)
Expense funds	$115,740

Greg and Gail next figure that they'll want to replace only 60 percent of Greg's income because after the mortgage is paid off, the family will have a much lower budget. In doing their calculations, Greg and Gail decide to ignore social security and their existing investment income (which they want to save for emergencies).

Income Replacement	
Greg's income	$ 25,000
Replacement percentage	60%
Income needed	15,000
Social security	-ignore-

	15,000
(divide by 10%)	÷ 10%
Investment fund to replace needed income	150,000
Immediate expense funds needed	115,740
Total life insurance needed	$265,740

OBSERVATION: The Greenshades can use the less conservative 10 percent interest rate in figuring out their needed nest egg, because Gail would be likely to remarry or start working full time as the kids get older.

WHAT KIND OF LIFE INSURANCE DO I NEED?

The mind-boggling variety of life insurance policies on the market all boil down to two types: term and cash value.

Term life insurance is pure life insurance protection; if you die while the policy is in effect, the insurance company pays your beneficiary the amount of the policy. Since it's pure life insurance, the policy has no cash value; if you give up the policy while you're still alive you'll have received nothing except some peace of mind. On the other hand, cash value life insurance is partly term life insurance and partly a mediocre savings and investment plan. A share of the premiums you pay on cash value life insurance provides you with term life insurance protection (if you die, they pay) and the remainder is put aside and invested by the insurance company. That investment portion, which increases in value over the life of the policy, is called cash value and can be part of your retirement nest egg.

Term Insurance: When You Really Need Protection

While each type of life insurance has its benefits, term life insurance is much cheaper and offers a bigger benefit for your dollar.

Term insurance provides financial protection if you die within the "term," a stated period of usually one year. Generally, as long as you pay your premiums you can renew the policy annually although each time you renew, the premiums usually increase. The important thing is that term rates are relatively inexpensive at the start—when you are young, need insurance the most and can afford it the least.

Most term insurance policies are automatically canceled when age 65 or 70 is reached. That's not much of a problem, because by then your family will be grown—and out of the house—and you'll need less or no life insurance protection. It's a fact of life that few retirees need life insurance. However, some policies also give the insurance company the right to refuse renewal even earlier if your health takes a turn for the worse—stay away from those and buy only "noncancelable" term insurance.

Some term insurance policies are convertible, which means that you can trade in your term policy for a cash value type of policy even if you are not in good health. There is also something called "increasing term" insurance, which means your benefit (and premiums) increase periodically, usually once a year, based on a set formula such as the rate of inflation. These are a bad idea—you, and not a formula, should figure out when you need more insurance.

Cash Value Insurance

Cash value insurance is much more costly and more profitable for the insurance company than term insurance. One reason is that only part of your premiums pay for the insurance itself, while the rest goes toward a cash value nest egg. Another reason is that part of the premium consists of profit for the insurance company and a commission for the salesperson. Typical commissions can easily exceed your entire first year's premium. Thirdly, the investment return (after deducting the fees) on cash value insurance is lower than for similar noninsurance investments, such as bank money market accounts, CDs and money market mutual funds. Finally, most policies exact a high penalty if you cash in the policy within the first few years.

So why would anyone buy cash value life insurance? Largely because many life insurance companies are incredibly deceptive. Unlike any other investment, life insurance is sold by salespeople in your home. They use complicated formulas, incomprehensible language and sophisticated psychological techniques to convince you that you *need* some form of cash value insurance. They come armed with glossy presentations that claim to prove beyond any doubt that the policy they offer is the best available and far superior to term insurance.

According to most consumer groups, though, those numbers lie. The charts and statistics are often based on unlikely assumptions and ignore the possibility that you could buy much cheaper term life insurance and invest your savings on your own, avoiding the insurance companies' high commissions and fees. Cash value insurance *was* sometimes a good deal for people in a high tax bracket, but since under Tax Reform nobody is in a high bracket anymore, those tax breaks don't matter much. For instance, the policy's investment income—like an IRA—is tax-free until withdrawn. If the policy is held until death, the death benefit, including the built-up income, generally is tax-free. But with today's lower rates, that advantage has been eroded. You also can usually borrow money from the cash value part of your policy, without paying tax on the withdrawal, at a favorable rate. That interest used to be deductible if you itemized on your tax, but in most cases is no longer deductible under Tax Reform.

There are three basic kinds of cash value policies: whole life, universal life and variable life.

Whole Life Insurance

This is the old dinosaur of insurance, in which you pay a fixed premium until the policy is "paid up," usually when you reach age 65. A portion of your premiums is used to pay for life insurance protection. The rest is invested by the insurance company, usually in bonds and mortgages. Whole life policies tend to have poor earnings, in the 5 or 5.5 percent range. Generally, premiums in whole life insurance are five or more times higher than for term insurance but are stable over the life of the policy. The investment income (if there is enough) also can be used to pay the premiums.

Some policies give the insurance company the right to cancel your insurance and refund your cash value if you don't make the required payments, or allow you to cancel the policy yourself and get back the cash value. (After the policy is cashed in, of course, you no longer have life insurance.) You also can borrow the cash value of your policy from the insurance company at fixed interest rates that on older policies can be as low as 4 percent or 5 percent.

With whole life, as with any other cash value insurance, it's difficult to tell a good policy from a bad one because the rate of return on the savings portion of the policy is not broken down for you. You should demand that the insurance company give you the "interest-adjusted cost index" of the policy, which compares earnings over a period of about ten and twenty years, taking into account the premiums paid, the dividends, the cash value of the policy and the interest that would be lost by not putting all the money in a bank account. Generally, the lower the number, the better the buy.

If you have a whole life insurance policy earning a poor rate of return, consider cashing it out and investing it in a better-paying investment. But if you need the insurance, make sure you buy a term policy before cashing out your whole life policy.

Universal Life Insurance

Because the low interest rates offered by whole life insurance make it a bad investment, the insurance industry recently began touting a "new" product: universal life insurance. Actually, universal life was first introduced in 1866. Universal life is a bit more flexible than whole life and is really a "package deal": you're buying term insurance and investing money in a money market type investment. Unlike whole life, the two items are "distinct," so it's easier to tell how much of your premium is paying for insurance and fees and how much is being set aside for investment. The interest rate can be based on a particular index (such as a U.S. Treasury bill rate) or be adjusted periodically by the insurance company. Either way, the rates generally are at money market levels. If you don't pay your full premium, the insurance company will deduct it from your investment account.

You may be able to increase or decrease the amount of your insurance without making a new application, regardless of your health at the time. You can also borrow your policy's cash value (but usually at interest rates a bit higher than whole life) or withdraw just part of it.

Variable Life

Variable life is similar to universal life in that the investment portion is distinct from the insurance portion. But instead of just one type of investment, you can choose among several investments, typically including a common stock mutual fund, a bond mutual fund and a money market mutual fund. The amount of your cash value and death benefit depends upon how well your investments do, although there is a guaranteed minimum benefit.

You generally cannot increase the amount of variable life insurance without applying for an entirely new policy—and perhaps taking another medical exam. However, some companies now offer "flexible premium variable life policies" that allow you to reduce your annual premiums and make up the difference from the investment portion. Variable life also generally lets you borrow from your account.

Term versus Cash Value

Generally, term insurance is far and away the best deal. Cash value is for people who also want to use their life insurance policy as a tax-favored way of saving for retirement. But because the fees and commissions are so high, you are much better off buying term insurance and investing any leftover money on your own. No matter what your agent tells you, it's almost impossible to come out ahead with cash value insurance.

SHOPPING FOR LIFE INSURANCE

Selecting an insurance policy and company can be very difficult. Of the basic types of insurance—term, whole life, universal life, and variable—there are many thousands of variations. To make matters worse, life insurance has its own weird vocabulary and insurance agents tend to bandy about complicated terms and charts that intimidate a lot of customers. If you don't understand what your agent is saying, don't be afraid to ask questions until you're totally clear—some agents try to hide an inferior product behind complicated jargon.

It's often difficult to evaluate different policies, too. With term insurance, you can compare price simply by finding out how much they charge for each $1,000 of death benefits. You should look not only at current prices, but also consider the premiums that will be charged as you get older.

For universal and variable life (if you're still considering them), you also can compare the cost of the term insurance portion but, as with any other investment, it's impossible to assess the future investment return. You can examine the policy's investment performance over the last few years, but don't be impressed by a guaranteed return in the first year—over the many years you'll hold the policy it won't matter much. Also examine the annual fees very closely—if a policy pays 11 percent interest, but has a 4 percent annual charge, your real return is only a meager 7 percent. And also check to see if there are any surrender charges when you cash in the policy.

If you're considering universal life insurance, a group called the National Insurance Consumer Organization will analyze a policy's net rate of return for you at a cost of $25 per policy. Just send them a copy of the policy at the address listed in the back of this book; the analysis takes about two weeks.

Choosing a Life Insurance Agent

Life insurance agents either work for a particular company—in which case they might sell only that company's policies or may sell for other companies as well—or work as independent agents, in which case they sell for several different companies. Since costs and policy terms vary widely from company to company, speak to several agents and check out a number of different companies before you decide.

A good agent will appraise your situation, help you decide whether you need insurance, and, if so, recommend how much and what type of insurance to get. A good agent should put your interests above the immediate goal of earning commissions from the insurance companies. (Many agents automatically recommend cash value insurance because it earns them the biggest commission.) Your agent should be understanding, not pushy, and should also be aware of all the different insurance products available and have the skill to match them to your needs. Also of key importance, your agent should be able and willing to shop the market, getting you the best deal available.

To find an agent, ask for recommendations from friends, business associates, your accountant or lawyer and interview at least three candidates. Avoid anyone who "blindly" calls you on the telephone or writes you offering to sell insurance to you; these agents are likely to be inexperienced charlatans.

Ask about what sort of training the agent has had, such as the courses or seminars he's attended. Also ask whether he's a CLU (Chartered Life Underwriter). A CLU must pass a series of ten exams and must have been practicing for at least three years. The title of CLU is no guarantee of the agent's competency or honesty, but it may make your choice easier. Your agent should also be a full-time career agent, not someone who is moonlighting. Finally, be skeptical about an agent calling himself a "financial planner." This falsely suggests that the person will objectively advise you regarding your overall financial needs, when actually he or she will more likely push insurance products that pay the highest sales commissions.

Rating Your Insurance Company

The financial strength of the insurance company you choose is another important consideration. A well-known insurance company—the Baldwin-United Corporation—recently went broke and its policyholders lost money. To protect yourself, buy insurance only from a company that has an "A+" or "A" rating from the A.M. Best rating guide. The Best guide rates the soundness of just about every insurance company in the country and is available from your public library or insurance agent.

Riders

A rider is an addition to an insurance policy that allows you to purchase additional coverage over and above the regular policy. Two common riders are double indemnity and a waiver of premium—neither of which is particularly worthwhile.

Double indemnity means that if you die in an accident, your death benefit is doubled. You pay an added premium for this feature. With one exception there is no reason why you should need more insurance benefits simply because you die in a plane crash instead of in your sleep. The exception is if you're relatively young and cannot afford to buy all the insurance you need. Being young you're more likely to die in an accident than from natural causes so the double indemnity helps you get the protection you need.

A waiver of premium means that if you become disabled, the company will waive the payment of your insurance premiums. This type of coverage also is usually not worth it—the price of the rider is generally too high compared to the premium you would save.

DISABILITY INSURANCE

Statistically speaking, people between the ages of 35 and 65 are more likely to become disabled than to die. Without protection, the disability of the family breadwinner can mean havoc in your retirement planning, because the paychecks stop but your expenses probably increase. Most experts agree you need enough disability insurance to replace between 65 percent to 70 percent of your normal paycheck. Chances are you already have some disability coverage from your job and also would receive social security disability benefits (*see* Chapter 2). But, as with life insurance, you may want to ignore social security in planning how much insurance you need to buy, and instead count on it only as an extra hedge against inflation.

Choose a policy that covers you if your injury makes you unable to perform your specific occupation—not just any similar type of work. That way, you won't lose benefits if you can't do your job but could do another job that wouldn't feel comfortable in. Your policy should pay benefits through at least age 65 and should also be noncancelable.

One way to reduce the cost of disability insurance is to select a policy that requires that you be disabled for six months before monthly payments start. Assuming your savings can cover you for that period, you'll save a lot on premiums.

Disability benefits are generally tax free if you paid the insurance premiums yourself. But if your employer paid the premiums, then you must pay the tax on any benefits—and in that case, you may need to buy extra protection on your own.

SPECIAL HEALTH INSURANCE

You might think that you have all the health insurance you need—probably through your job. But your current policy may not offer much, if any, help if you quit or retire. Nationwide surveys show that for many retirees, the possibility of a long illness is their greatest financial worry.

Under a new law, in most cases you must be allowed to continue your company health insurance protection as an individual when you leave your job. The coverage must last for eighteen months after you leave your job. But if you die while employed or get divorced, your beneficiaries, including your ex-spouse, can choose to be covered for a full three years. Of course this insurance isn't free, but by the new law your company can only charge 2 percent more than the low group rates it pays for your insurance, at least until you get health insurance through a plan at a new job. Although this new law is a big help to people who lose their company health benefits, eventually you'll have to get your own coverage. You will find it difficult to purchase the necessary additional protection on your own if you're deemed "uninsurable" because you've developed a medical problem such as diabetes or a serious back ailment. And, even if you're healthy, the older you are, the more expensive the cost of any new insurance policy will be. By the time you reach 65, the cost of premiums will be prohibitive—if you can get insurance at all. To protect yourself now and when you retire you should consider purchasing an outside medical insurance policy that supplements your existing insurance. The policy should:

1. be guaranteed renewable for the rest of your and your spouse's lives, so that it can't be canceled by the insurance company after an illness or because you're too old
2. pay unlimited benefits for most, if not all, covered expenses, so that no matter how high medical costs become over the years, you'll be fully protected
3. provide worldwide coverage so that no matter where you become ill you'll be protected
4. provide comprehensive coverage for all types of illness, including doctor's fees, all hospital charges, home care, drugs and medical services.

Supplemental policies usually offer you a choice of very high deductibles—say from $2,000 to $10,000—which means you or your "regular" insurance plan must pay that amount before coverage starts. The high deductible is a tradeoff for lower premiums. For example, the annual cost of a policy for a 30-year-old married person with no children would run about $650 if the deductible was $2,000. But if the deductible was $10,000, the premium would shrink to about $300. However, once you're eligible for Medicare, the premiums go *down* because the policy only has to pay the bills that Medicare doesn't cover.

Despite all the advantages of these policies, they're hard to find. At the moment, Equitable Life is one of the few companies offering this coverage.

Q. Does Tax Reform have any impact on insurance?

A. Although it was much debated, in the end Tax Reform pretty much left unchanged the rules on insurance. However, the rules for deducting your interest expense *were* tightened considerably and this will hurt people who want to borrow from their cash value life insurance policies. Basically, the interest on such loans is no longer deductible.

Q. After Tax Reform, does it make sense to buy cash value life insurance?

A. No. But even before Tax Reform, it only made economic sense if you were in a high tax bracket. Now, with the loss of the tax deduction on interest payments and new lower tax rates, term insurance is the cheapest and best deal for all.

CHAPTER 8

HOME OWNERSHIP

For many people, owning their own home remains the American dream. It's an eminently sensible retirement strategy, too: home ownership can be a terrific long-term way to build up your savings, reduce your tax bite and protect yourself against inflation, a retiree's biggest enemy. Many experts rate home ownership among the best investments around.

In many ways, a home is like a savings account: the money you invest—unlike rent—is usually recouped when you sell. Putting aside money for a down payment alone is a perfect incentive for people who lack the willpower to save just for the sake of saving. Chances are your home will increase in value, because housing costs historically have escalated faster than the rate of inflation. Although housing prices have somewhat stabilized lately and in some depressed areas have actually gone down, the extensive tax breaks that are *still* available to home owners makes it a better deal than renting for most people. And once you've comfortably settled into home ownership, you may want to consider investing in a second property.

OBSERVATION: There is a good chance that Tax Reform will push housing prices down because lower tax rates mean the value of tax deductions from home ownership are also lower. Most experts believe that this downward trend will be small and only last a year or two.

But, the house, condominium or co-op you choose, the price and the type of mortgage you pick can make the difference between realizing your retirement dreams or risking a financial crisis.

USING YOUR HOME AS A PIGGY BANK

Housing is one of the largest and most important items on your budget. If you're like most homeowners, you will borrow money to pay for your home, using your house as collateral. The long-term loan you get is called a mortgage and is paid off in monthly installments until you either sell your home or fully own it. A mortgage really is a compulsory savings plan: your house becomes a piggy bank of increasing value as you pay the mortgage.

Each monthly mortgage payment is divided into two parts: principal and interest on the principal. The principal is simply what you owe the bank. Each mortgage check you write reduces the total principal and increases your equity, which is your financial stake in your home. The process of paying back the principal on a loan is called amortization, or sometimes equity savings, because you increase your financial investment (instead of a landlord's) without actually putting cash aside in a savings account.

Mortgage payments usually are structured so that your monthly payments over the first few years consist mostly of interest and very little of principal. As a result, you increase your equity slowly. Over the years, the proportion of each mortgage check that goes toward repaying the principal gradually increases, so that your last mortgage payment consists of practically all principal. For that reason, a homeowner saves the most money if he or she owns the same home for a substantial length of time. By the time you retire, your home can be a hefty source of financial security.

Using a mortgage to buy a home lets you take advantage of "leveraging," which is a financial technique often used in corporate takeovers. Basically, leveraging means using someone else's money—in this case a bank's—to make money for yourself. Let's say you've bought a $100,000 house, using a $10,000 down payment and assuming a $90,000 mortgage. After five years, when you decide to sell, your house has increased in value to $150,000. That's a $50,000 profit for which you had to put up only $10,000 of your own money plus your monthly mortgage payments. That $50,000 profit can be used in purchasing your next home, giving you some protection against rising prices.

OBSERVATION: Leveraging is a two-edged sword. If the value of your home drops below the price you paid, you'll still have to pay the bank the full amount you borrowed.

YOUR HOME CAN STILL BE A TAX SHELTER, TOO

Most taxpayers who don't itemize—which means specifically list—their federal income tax deductions can automatically claim a minimum "standard" tax deduction. As we saw in Chapter 4, the new standard deduction for 1987 is $3,800 for married couples filing a joint return and $2,570 for singles. For 1988 it'll be $5,000 for marrieds, and $3,000 for singles, but these amounts will be adjusted annually for inflation, starting in 1989.

But if your own tax deductions exceed that standard deduction, your home can shelter you from taxes as well as the elements. The reason is that interest on your mortgage and all real estate taxes on your home are deductible on your federal income tax return, if you itemize. This offers the biggest break when you first buy your home and most of your mortgage payments consist of interest rather than principal.

For example, if a married couple in 1988 pays $10,000 in interest and real estate taxes on their home and pays $3,000 in state and local income taxes, their itemized deductions would total $13,000. Their much larger itemized deduction will give them an extra $8,000 in deductions over the $5,000 standard deduction. Itemized deductions are listed on Schedule A of your federal tax return.

Think of itemized deductions as Uncle Sam's way of sharing in the cost of buying your home. If you are in the 28 percent tax bracket and your home gives you $10,000 in itemized deductions, you'll save $2,800 in taxes. Remember, if you rented your home, your landlord would get that tax break instead.

Nevertheless, before buying a house, you can and should do a few basic calculations to be sure you really will reduce your tax load—and by how much.

It's easy to predict the extra tax deduction you would get if you bought a home. First, check the new tax rates in Chapter 4. Now estimate how much you would expect to pay in interest and taxes if you bought a house. If you already had enough to itemize, then these new deductions would simply add to your tax savings. If you didn't itemize, check if those new expenses would put you over the standard deduction. If so, multiply the extra deductions by your expected tax bracket: that's how much Uncle Sam would contribute toward the purchase of your home.

EXAMPLE: Stan and Sara are married and rent an apartment for $600 a month. Last year they were in the 28 percent tax bracket. They are thinking of buying a house that would cost them $750 a month, of which $740 is deductible expenses for interest on the mortgage and real estate taxes and $10 is nondeductible. Here's how their final costs work out:

	Rent	*Own*
Annual payment	$7,700	$9,000
Deductible expenses	None	8,880
Tax bracket	28%	28%
Tax savings	None	2,486
After-tax cost	$7,700	$6,514

Even though at first glance it would seem to cost Stan and Sara more money per year to buy a house than to rent, after taxes they come out ahead as homeowners.

OBSERVATION: Potential homeowners also should take into account additional home expenses like heat, hot water, gardening, repairs and maintenance—all nondeductible—that they probably do not pay as renters.

MORE TAX BREAKS WHEN YOU SELL YOUR HOME

The tax breaks don't end when you sell your home. Any profit on the sale of your home is taxed as a "capital asset," such as stocks or bonds or a boat. As we've seen, after Tax Reform all income is created equal and the capital gain is simply added to all your other income. But you may be entitled to a special tax break if the house you sell was your "principal residence." If you have just one house where you live all year round, that is your principal residence. If you own more than one house, your principal residence is generally considered to be the place where you spend most of your time.

OBSERVATION: If you sell your home at a lower price than you paid for it, you cannot count that loss as a tax deduction.

Normally, any profit on the sale of a "principal residence" is taxable. But you must postpone paying that tax if you use the profit to buy and move into a new principal residence within two years before or after selling your old home. You also must own your new home for at least two years, otherwise you will have to pay tax on the entire gain of the new home.

OBSERVATION: If you sold your home at a capital gain in 1986, consider delaying your next home purchase for two years so that you can pay capital gains taxes in 1986. Because the 1986 capital gains taxes are generally lower now than under the new tax reform system, this could save you some money. Check with your tax advisor before you take any action.

This cycle of postponing taxes continues as long as you keep selling and buying new homes that are as—or more—expensive. Uncle Sam catches up with you only if you sell your home, and don't reinvest the proceeds in a new home. At that point, you must pay tax on the gains you postponed.

OBSERVATION: If the new home is less expensive than your old house, you must pay tax on the difference between the selling price of your old house and the lower cost of your new home.

Special Break for Older Homeowners

If you or your spouse is age 55 or older, the government allows you a one-time-only opportunity to avoid paying any federal income tax on up to $125,000 of profit on the sale of a principal residence, even if you don't use the profit to buy a new home. That's a big plus if your retirement is approaching.

To qualify for this break, the home you sold must have been your principal residence for at least three of the last five years before the sale. To avoid paying the tax, report your sale to the IRS and fill out Form 2119 with your regular Form 1040. There are several special rules to watch out for in filling out Form 2119, and taxpayers should get professional advice or use one of the income tax guides available.

Observation: A husband and wife are allowed only one $125,000 exemption between them.

OWNING VERSUS RENTING

The question usually is not should you buy, but can you afford to buy a home and if so, how much to spend and what type of mortgage to get.

Generally speaking, it costs less on a monthly basis to rent a home than to pay a mortgage, real estate taxes, heat, repairs and maintenance on that same home. But in the long run—after tax deductions—owning usually works out costing about the same or less than renting. And if you consider equity savings and the increasing value of most homes, the retirement picture of almost everyone is improved by home ownership.

On the other hand, renting is better for people who do not expect to stay in a particular home for more than a few years. Tax Reform or a housing glut in your community could also make renting a bargain and owning a house risky. Older individuals for whom owning a house might be too much work might be better off investing their money elsewhere.

HOW MUCH CAN YOU AFFORD?

How much you should spend on your home depends mainly on how much money you have saved, your annual income and current mortgage rates.

Generally, the minimum down payment required on a house is 10 percent (in some areas it's 20 percent) of the total purchase price. So, if you've saved $5,000, the most you can spend on your home is $50,000; if you've saved $10,000, then you can spend up to $100,000.

Never borrow money for a down payment unless you're expecting a large bonus, inheritance or other windfall. If you cannot manage to save enough money for the down payment, then you probably need to reexamine your finances and saving habits, and postpone buying the home.

It would be equally foolish to spend your last penny of cash on a down payment and not leave yourself an emergency fund as well as money for other costs such as lawyers' and bank fees, moving expenses and expert appraisals. Once you move in, you'll probably discover 1,001 more expenses you never anticipated, from buying new garbage cans to fixing the boiler. The realistic home buyer allows a big cushion for the expenses of buying, moving, and setting up a home as well as for the possibility of job loss, illness or major home repairs.

There are two good rules of thumb used by financial experts and bank loan officers to figure out how much of the family budget should be spent to pay for a house.

First, your mortgage payment, taxes and insurance should not exceed 30 percent of your family's monthly income. (To appreciate the rise in housing costs, consider that until the early 1970s, it was generally recommended that housing costs not exceed 25 percent of the family income.)

Second, your family's total debt payments, including student loans, car payments and housing costs, should not exceed 38 percent of your annual income. Remember, these are just general rules. You have to assess your own special circumstances—marriage, a new baby, education costs and your personal spending habits. Otherwise, you might borrow more money than you can really afford and end up scrimping to support your new house.

SHARING THE BURDEN: HELP FROM YOUR FAMILY

If you're just starting out, you might not have enough money to buy a home and your income may be too low to make much use of the tax deductions available with home ownership. But by sharing home ownership with someone else—such as your parents—both sides may be able to enjoy substantial tax savings. And you'd be on your way to sound retirement planning. Here's an example of how it works.

The parents, who are in a higher tax bracket, share the cost of the down payment and mortgage with their son or daughter. Let's say the parent pays 75 percent and the child 25 percent. The child then lives in the house and pays the parents 75 percent of the fair market rental value of the house as well as 25 percent of the monthly mortgage payments.

The child can deduct his 25 percent share of interest and taxes on his federal tax return if he itemizes. The parents are treated as landlords for tax purposes and can deduct their share of interest, taxes and something called depreciation of the house. Although the rules are complicated, generally depreciation works out to an annual tax deduction equal to 27.5 per cent of their interest in the house. The new tax rules for landlords are discussed in more detail later in this chapter.

As the child matures financially, he can purchase the parents' share. Although this home-sharing arrangement doesn't have to be between relatives, at least one owner must live in the house and the rent charged must be a percentage of its fair market value. For example, if similar houses in the neighborhood are renting for $500 a month, the child would pay 75 percent of the $500 fair market rental value, or $375.

FINDING THE RIGHT MORTGAGE

The type of mortgage you choose and the interest rates you pay are critical considerations in home ownership. You should no more overpay for a mortgage than you would for your home. For example, with a thirty-year, $80,000 mortgage at 9 percent interest, your monthly payments would be $643.72. But at 11 percent interest—only two percentage points more—that same $80,000 mortgage would cost you $760.07 a month, or almost 20 percent more.

The thirty or forty types of mortgages on the market all fall into two categories: fixed and adjustable.

Fixed mortgages are the "traditional" kind, in which a home owner makes an identical mortgage payment each month, paying a fixed rate of interest until the mortgage is paid back, usually twenty-five or thirty years later.

The main attraction of a fixed-rate mortgage is stability: if interest rates skyrocket, you're locked into your original, lower interest rate. If interest rates go down and you want to take advantage of the lower rates, you can repay your old mortgage and take out a new mortgage at the lower rates. If your bank allows early repayment without an additional charge, your only major expense in refinancing will be the points and fees charged on the new mortgage. Generally, it doesn't pay to refinance unless interest rates have dropped dramatically

Fixed mortgages also used to offer the advantage of "assumability." This meant that the person who bought your house could simply take over your old mortgage at the same interest rate. When interest rates are on the rise, that option enhances the value of your home. But because banks have found they tend to lose money on assumable mortgages, they have become relatively hard to find.

With an adjustable-rate mortgage (ARM), your interest rate is periodically adjusted as market interest rates go up or down. With each interest rate adjustment, the amount of your monthly mortgage payment changes. The best ARMs have limits on both how high the interest rates can go and how much the monthly payments can be increased each year over the life of the loan.

OBSERVATION: ARMs can often start out two to five percentage points lower than fixed-rate mortgages.

Here's how one $80,000, thirty-year adjustable-rate mortgage might work. The starting interest rate is 10.5 percent and is adjusted each year within a range of two percentage points, but cannot vary more than five percentage points up or down over the life of the loan. In the first year, at 10.5 percent interest, your monthly payments will be $731.79 a month. In the second year, let's say interest rates jump 3 percent.

The interest charged on your mortgage then increases the maximum 2 percent, to 12.5 percent, and your monthly mortgage payment increases to $847.10 a month. Such adjustments, up and down, would be made annually for the life of that mortgage.

All ARMs are not alike. The starting interest rate, how often they adjust (every six months, every year, every five years, etc.), whether and how much of an interest-rate ceiling they have and the formula used for adjusting the interest rate make a big difference in your final costs. For example, some banks base their adjustable-interest rates on a poll of mortgage rates from across the nation that is published by the federal government. Other banks base their adjustments on the interest rates for six-month or one-year U.S. Treasury bills, plus a certain premium. The government rates tend to be more stable, which is good for you when rates are going up and bad when they're going down.

Fixed versus ARM—What to Look For

Generally, fixed-rate mortgages are best for people who plan to live in their new home for at least four years and who think that interest rates are going up. If you intend to live in your house only for a few years, then an adjustable-rate mortgage that adjusts once every three years offers almost the same security as a fixed-rate mortgage.

An ARM also is a good choice if you expect your

income to increase substantially over the next few years—for example, if your spouse intends to start working. In that way you can take advantage of lower-interest rates today—while you have less money—and if rates go up in the future, your increased family income will help offset the increase. This might enable you to buy a more expensive house than you could otherwise afford at your present salary.

But beware of taking out an ARM if you realistically will not be able to afford higher monthly payments in the future. Again, the bank lending you the money probably won't take into account your ability to make ends meet if interest rates and your mortgage payments should go up in the future.

Beware too of misleading mortgage offers. Many banks entice you to take out a mortgage by charging a below-market rate of interest at the start of the loan. If interest rates are 11 percent, they might be willing to lend you money on a one-year ARM at 9 percent interest. But you must also find out how much that interest rate would go up with your first adjustment. If the mortgage has an adjustment ceiling, find out whether the cap is figured on your starting interest rate of 9 percent, or the actual 11 percent market rate that was prevailing when you took out the loan.

An ARM that does not have any interest-rate cap or has a cap of more than 2 percent above the prevailing rate on fixed mortgages may be a bad choice if you intend to stay in your home a long time. That's because if interest rates skyrocket, the higher-cost mortgage could eat up your entire family budget. But if you intend to live in your new house only a few years, an

ARM that adjusts every three years would be safe without any cap.

Negative Amortization

There also are adjustable-rate mortgages in which your monthly payments are fixed, but the amount of the *mortgage* changes as interest rates increase or decrease. So, instead of increasing the equity in your home and saving money, you end up owing more money on your mortgage if interest rates go up. This uphill treadmill is called "negative amortization" and though you may be offered a relatively low-interest rate, you probably should stay away. Buying a home should be part of your overall savings and retirement plan and a loan that potentially can get bigger is a bad idea. And if the value of your home goes down while interest rates are rising, you could really be trapped.

What's the Point?

In addition to your monthly mortgage payments, you probably will have to pay the bank something called "points" when you first take out your mortgage. Points means that you immediately pay back to the bank a portion of what you plan to borrow. This payment is deductible like regular interest if you itemize on your federal tax return.

Each point is worth 1 percent of your total loan, so if you are charged three points on a $100,000 mortgage, it costs you $3,000 up front. You're actually borrowing only $97,000 from the bank, but your interest is charged on—and you must repay—the full $100,000 mortgage. Points are charged each time you take out a mortgage—which means that if you keep selling and buying new houses, you could end up paying almost as much in points as in regular interest.

Your Mortgage Shopping List

Get a general idea of the mortgages available before you look for a home, so you'll have an idea of how much you can afford to spend. When you've found your home, you can shop in more detail for the best mortgage for your needs.

The first step is to check the mortgage ads in local newspapers and call several banks. Even if the bank personnel lose patience with your questions—and they frequently do—keep asking until you're satisfied that you understand what they have to offer. By doing your advance homework and comparison shopping, you can save yourself a bundle.

Here is some basic information to ask for:

- how much they will lend you
- the interest rate they will charge
- the amount of the monthly payments
- the number of points to be charged
- the length of the mortgage
- whether and how much of a fee you would be charged for paying off the mortgage early
- are there any additional fees the bank will charge for lending you the money

- whether the mortgage is assumable
- the amount of the down payment required
- how long it takes to get a mortgage commitment
- how long the commitment is good for

If your mortgage is an ARM, you also should find out:

- how often interest rates are adjusted
- what is the cap, if any
- how often payments may change
- what the maximum payment would be
- the formula used for making adjustments
- if the mortgage is discounted, approximately what your monthly payment will be when the current adjusted term is up
- if there is negative amortization and what the limits are

An additional tip: many banks charge a lower interest rate on mortgages for "preferred customers." Often, you need only open a checking account, savings account or IRA with the bank to take immediate advantage of the discounted mortgage rate.

What Your Real Estate Agent May Not Want You to Know

If you buy your home through a real estate agent, you may be offered the assistance of the agent's real estate agency in getting a mortgage without having to go to the bank yourself. This added convenience can cost you.

If you're offered mortgage services by your agent, ask whether and how much of a commission the agent and the agency would receive from the lender. Since the commission usually is based on the amount of the mortgage, the agent may steer you to a more expensive or larger mortgage than you would have found on your own. And find out whether the lender is financially connected with the agent (such as owning the real estate agency).

As long as there's no charge it doesn't hurt to have the agent prepare a mortgage proposal for you while you do your own shopping. Then, choose whichever mortgage is really cheapest and best—don't let the agent pressure you.

WHAT TO DO BEFORE YOU BUY

When you've found your dream house, agreed on a price and the terms of your deal and "shaken hands" with the seller, usually either the seller's lawyer or the real estate agent will prepare the purchase contract. Have your own lawyer review the contract to make sure it offers you adequate protection and states everything that you've agreed upon. The agent and seller are mainly interested in making the sale and won't look out for your best interests.

OBSERVATION: Most banks will not finalize a loan until you give them a copy of the purchase contract.

After you and the seller sign the purchase contract, you'll hand over the down payment, which is usually 10 percent of the purchase price. The down payment is held in "escrow," which means that it is given to a reliable third party (usually the seller's lawyer) until the sale is finalized, or "closed."

If you change your mind about buying, you may lose your down payment. However, your purchase contract should state that if for any reason you cannot get a mortgage at an interest rate you can afford, or if the sale doesn't go through on account of the seller, then your down payment will be refunded.

OBSERVATION: Before signing a purchase contract, review with your lawyer any factors that could cause you to lose your down payment.

It's important to have the house you are buying inspected by qualified experts. Your purchase contract should include a section stating that if your expert finds something substantially wrong with the house—it needs a new roof, the boiler is in bad shape, it has termites, etc.—you can cancel the deal and get your deposit back.

Your lawyer also should arrange for title insurance, which protects you financially in case the seller's ownership of the house ever comes into question. If you buy a house but it turns out that the "owner" didn't have clear title—for example, because the house was owned jointly with a spouse and they're getting divorced—you could lose both your new home and the money you paid for it.

WHAT TO DO WITH THE EQUITY IN YOUR HOME

If you bought your home years ago, you probably have a very low-interest mortgage and have seen the value of your home go up substantially. In other words, you have a lot of equity in your house that should be treated as part of your overall retirement savings. You can use that equity as collateral, without selling your home, when you borrow money from a bank. The three principal ways of tapping the equity in your home are explained below.

OBSERVATION: Remember that except in an emergency, borrowing your home equity is really just another way of spending your savings.

REFINANCING

With refinancing, you pay off an existing mortgage and take out a new, larger mortgage based upon the higher selling value of your home today. Although the new mortgage will carry higher interest rates, you can use the extra money for other purposes.

Most banks will allow a homeowner to refinance no more than 80 percent of the "appraised" value of his home. That value is what an expert appraiser says your house is worth.

Second Mortgages

A second mortgage is just what it sounds like, an additional mortgage for someone who already has a mortgage. If you default on both your mortgages, the bank with the first mortgage is entitled to be repaid before the bank with the second mortgage. As a result, interest rates for second mortgages are usually at least two, three or more percentage points higher than for regular first mortgages. The term of a second mortgage is usually less than fifteen years.

A second mortgage is simply another debt, as big or even bigger than your first mortgage, and should not be taken on without very serious consideration. Unfortunately, some banks are perfectly willing to take a chance as long as there is enough equity in the house. As a result, many people have lost their homes after defaulting on a second mortgage that was more than they could handle.

Home-Equity Account

The newest way to whittle away the equity in your home is a special line of credit based on the built-up value in your home. A home-equity account is more or less just a second mortgage in a fancy package.

Basically, the lender gives you an open line of credit, up to about 75 percent of the total value of the house. For example, if you have a $20,000 mortgage on a house which is now worth $100,000, you could get a credit line of $55,000 (75 percent of $100,000, minus the $20,000 mortgage).

Home-equity accounts are available from banks, as well as from "financial supermarkets" such as Merrill Lynch, Shearson/American Express and Prudential-Bache.

Usually, the interest charged is two to four percentage points higher than the prime rate, which is the interest rate that banks charge their most preferred corporate customers. You pay interest only on what you actually borrow from your account, not on the entire line of credit.

Home-equity loans are most popular among people in the 35 to 50 age group, who often use the money for a new boat, an expensive car, a vacation abroad or a speculative investment.

This is a foolish way of living beyond your means and jeopardizes your retirement security as well. Again, avoid tapping the equity in your house for any but the most pressing of reasons—something of lasting importance that you could not otherwise pay for, such as college tuition, medical expenses or starting your own business.

Observation: The lender will usually have a rule prohibiting you from using a home-equity account to invest in the stock market or other speculative ventures, although such restrictions are difficult to enforce.

New Tax Rules on Equity Mortgages

Under the new tax rules, you can only deduct interest on home loans up to the amount you originally paid for your home plus any improvements. The interest on the rest of the loan is not deductible. For someone whose home has gone up a lot in value and is able to get a big equity loan, this limit means they will not be able to deduct most of the interest on the loan.

EXAMPLE: Laurie and Steven bought their home 10 years ago for $50,000 and have spent $5,000 on home improvements. Their original mortgage was $40,000. The house is now worth $150,000 and Steven wants to take out a big second mortgage. But under the new rules, Laurie and Steven can deduct the interest on only $15,000 of principal on any second mortgage, figured like this:

Original cost of home	$50,000
Improvements	5,000
Less existing mortgage	(40,000)
New mortgage that's deductible	$15,000

There are two exceptions to this new limit on home mortgage interest deduction. First, you can deduct interest on a mortgage equal to up to the full current value of your home if you use the money for education or medical expenses.

The second exception only applies to home loans made on or before August 16, 1986, which are generally not covered by these rules.

OBSERVATION: As we saw in Chapter 4, consumer interest is no longer deductible. So if you're planning to borrow to buy a car, boat, etc., consider borrowing the money on your home and using it to buy the car or whatever, and taking the tax deduction. Of course, this only makes sense if you'll be able to deduct the interest and if you can't finance your purchase through your savings.

OBSERVATION: Make sure to keep all records of any home improvements in case you are asked to prove to the IRS how much you spent.

The new tax rules also allow you to deduct mortgage interest only on your principal home and on one other home. If you should happen to own three homes, the interest is deductible on your principal home and one of the other two (you choose which).

OBSERVATION: These new interest rules are being gradually phased in. In 1987, you can still take an itemized deduction for up to 65 percent of mortgage interest that would otherwise not be deductible under the new rules. In 1988 it's 40 percent; in 1989, 20 percent; in 1990, 10 percent; and after that, nothing.

SECOND HOMES: PART VACATION, PART TAX SHELTER

If you have the financial resources to easily pay for your first home, you may want to consider buying another home as an investment.

Aside from the pleasure of a vacation or weekend retreat, a second home can provide an added hedge against inflation and an additional tool in your plans to retire rich. If you rent it out, it could also qualify as a great tax shelter and, in the end, virtually pay for itself.

As with your first home, the mortgage interest and real estate taxes on your second home are tax deductible if you itemize. (As a general rule, interest on any other homes is not deductible under the new rules.) Since each mortgage payment helps repay the principal of the loan, a second home is a great savings tool. And if the value of the house increases, you also increase your equity.

If you rent out your second home and limit your own use to fourteen days a year or 10 percent of the days it was rented—whichever is more—it can provide even more tax savings. If you qualify, you can deduct expenses for repairs and maintenance. You also can take a deduction for the "wear and tear" that your second home undergoes while being rented—that's called depreciation. This is a big financial plus, especially because the house will probably be increasing in value at the same time.

Because the tax rules have been changed so often, how you depreciate your property depends on when you bought or first started renting it out. Any real estate purchased between 1981 and March 14, 1984, can be depreciated over fifteen years. Property purchased between March 15, 1984 and December 31, 1986, generally must be depreciated over a period of at least eighteen years. Generally, real estate bought (or first rented by you) after 1986 must be depreciated over twenty-seven and a half years. The owner has a choice of "straight-line" depreciation, which would mean fifteen or eighteen equal expense deductions, or the "accelerated cost recovery system," in which more depreciation is taken in the first few years and less in later years. If you bought the home after 1986 you can only use the straight-line method. Remember that you cannot depreciate your house for the time that you use it yourself.

For example, if you bought a second home in 1987 under straight-line depreciation, you can deduct 27.5 percent of the cost of the house (but not the land) every year for twenty-seven and a half years.

If you decide to rent your vacation home, then the option of taking a depreciation deduction or claiming a loss for the house depends upon how many days you use the house yourself, how many days the house is rented out and much total income you have. If you rent your house for fourteen days or less each year, you cannot use the depreciation deduction—but, on the plus side, you do not have to report the rental income. If you rent your home anywhere from 15 to 149 days a year, you can take the depreciation deduction as well as a deduction for any other expenses you may incur—but you can use the second home yourself for no more than fourteen days a year. If you rent your house for 150 days or more a year, then you're allowed to stay there one day for every ten days that you rent the house. For instance, if the place is rented for 200 days a year, you can use it yourself for 20 days.

Under the new tax rules, you can claim a loss from renting your property if your expenses (mortgage interest, depreciation, real estate taxes, maintenance, etc.)

totalled more than your rental income for the year. If you actively manage the property (intead of turning it over to a manager or real estate agency) and your Adjusted Gross Income is under $100,000, you can deduct up to $25,000 of those losses each year. If you earn between $100,000 and $150,000, you can deduct progressively smaller amounts of these losses. Above $150,000, you cannot deduct any losses. However, expenses can still be deducted against the rental income, so that if they're equal you don't pay taxes on the income.

Most experts recommend that before buying a second home primarily as an investment, you make sure that the rental income and income tax savings will cover your mortgage payment, insurance, real estate taxes and maintenance costs. The new Tax Reform rules are so complicated the you should definitely consult an accountant or other expert for help.

OWNING A HOME MEANS RETIREMENT SECURITY

You should plan on having your mortgage paid off before—hopefully, well before—you retire. This will help you in four important ways. First, during the end of your working career when you'll be making your final push to save, having no mortgage payments will allow you to put aside even more. Second, not having to make mortgage payments will help your retirement budget considerably. Third, owning your home will make your housing costs almost inflation proof. And, finally, when and if the need arises, you can cash in on the equity in your home by selling and buying a less expensive place or simply renting. No plan to retire rich is really complete unless it includes home ownership.

Q. Is mortgage interest still deductible?
A. Yes. You can still use the interest on your principal home and one other home as an itemized deduction.
Q. Any limits on the interest deduction?
A. Yes. To be fully deductible the loan must be for no more than what you paid for the home plus the cost of any improvements. If you have more than one loan on a house (such as a first and second mortgage), they're added together. You cannot deduct any interest on the portion of the loans that exceeds the limit.
Q. Any exceptions to the new rules?
A. Yes. First, certain loans existing on August 16, 1986, are protected. Second, loans to pay for education or medical expenses are not covered by the new limits on the size of the loan. Finally, the new rules are being phased in. In 1987, you can still take up to 65 percent of mortgage interest that would otherwise not be deductible under the new rules as an itemized deduction. In 1988 the limit is 40 percent; in 1989, 20 percent; in 1990 10 percent; and nothing after that.

Q. Do the new rules apply to investment homes such as rental property?

A. Yes, and you'll need to see your tax advisor for help. Basically, your depreciation will be slower and you won't be able to deduct any losses from real estate, unless (1) you actively manage the property and (2) your Adjusted Gross Income is under $150,000. And even then, your deduction will be limited to $25,000.

CHAPTER 9

STOCKS, BONDS, BULLS AND BEARS

WHAT ARE BONDS?

Bonds are the long-term IOUs of corporations, bought and sold through a broker or mutual fund. They are sold and interest is paid in denominations of $1,000, which is called "par." For instance, a bond with a 10 percent rate of interest will pay $100 a year or, 10 percent of the $1,000 par. Interest is usually paid twice a year.

The money invested in bonds must be paid back by the company when they mature, which is usually 30 years after they were issued. The amount you get paid back at maturity is par (e.g., $1,000), regardless of whether you paid $200 or $1,200 for your bond.

The price you pay for a bond depends on the interest rate it pays and the financial strength of the company that issued it. General Motors bonds from

1960 that pay 4.4 percent interest and mature in 1990 now sell for well below their $1,000 par, to make up for their relatively low interest rate.

Many bonds are "callable," which means the company can require you to sell them back before they mature. The call price (what the company has to pay you) is par ($1,000), plus a premium. As you might expect, bonds are called only when it will save the company money. For instance, if interest rates have gone down since the bond was issued, it may be cheaper for the company to buy back the bond even with the added premium, and sell new bonds at lower interest rates. This is great for the company and not so great for you, since you have to turn around and buy a new bond offering lower interest rates.

The trick to avoid getting burned on a call is to buy bonds only in situations where it will cost the company a lot more money than you paid to buy it back—either because it has a high call premium or because you bought the bond at a big discount.

Convertible Bonds

Convertible bonds are company bonds that can be exchanged for stock in the same company. You pay a premium for the conversion feature, in the form of lower interest rates.

Convertible bonds usually work like this: you can exchange your bonds for the company's stock at a fixed ratio (e.g., one bond for ten shares of stock) which is figured so that the stock's price has to go up substantially in value before it makes financial sense for you to trade in your bonds. In other words, if your bond is worth $1,000 and the stock sells at $20 a share, you wouldn't want to exchange your bond for ten shares of stock worth $200. But if the stock climbed to $200 a share, then you would gladly turn in your $1,000 bond for ten shares worth $2,000.

In a way, convertible bonds are like having your cake and eating it too. You get the security of a bond but if the company does exceptionally well, you can switch over to stock and take advantage of the company's prosperity.

Preferred Stocks

Preferred stocks are a unique form of a company's IOU: they *never* get paid back. As with regular bonds, the company pays an annual fixed dividend. But usually the company can skip a payment if it wants to (generally because of financial difficulties) as long as it doesn't pay any dividends on its common stock. That skipped dividend is lost to you forever unless the preferred stock is "cumulative." Cumulative preferred stock means that any skipped dividends "cumulate" and before the company pays a dividend to its common stockholders, it has to pay off all the accumulated preferred dividends.

If the company ever goes broke, the preferred stockholders get paid off before the common stockholders. But because all stockholders must wait until the company's creditors—including bondholders—get paid, that preference isn't worth much.

The time to buy preferred stock is when you think interest rates are going to go down and want to lock in a currently high rate of return "forever." But be sure to always check whether your preferred stock is callable. Stay away unless the call price is well above what you are paying for the stock, because if the stock is ever called, your loan simply gets paid back and you could as easily buy a bond instead.

Municipal Bonds

The bonds of a city, state or public agency are called municipal bonds, or "munis." Because the interest paid on most munis is tax free, interest rates are much lower than for other investments.

That can make munis a good choice for someone in a high tax bracket. For example, if you're in the 33 percent bracket, a muni paying 9 percent puts the same amount of after-tax income in your pocket as a regular bond paying about 13.5 percent. On the other hand, munis are a poor investment choice for an IRA or Keogh, which are both tax free anyway.

Zero Coupon Bonds

Zero coupon bonds, or "zeros," are a special type of company, bank or government bond that don't pay any interest until maturity. The bonds are sold well below their face amount but, when the bond is paid back, you get the full face value. For example, you might pay $500 for a seven-year $1,000 zero coupon bond. At the end of seven years you get back $1,000—

$500 of which is your interest. For about $80,000, you can buy a zero that will pay you back a million dollars in twenty years!

The disadvantage of zeros is that you must pay federal tax on your interest each year, even though you don't actually get paid until the bond matures. For people in a high tax bracket, that can be a problem. It's of no concern if you're using a zero for an IRA or Keogh, which are tax free until retirement.

Another disadvantage is that zeros are difficult to sell before maturity. Unlike regular bonds, "used" zeros are not considered an attractive buy. And because zeros don't provide regular interest payments, their prices decline more sharply than other bonds when interest rates go up. In an extreme case reported by *Money* magazine, a group of investors is suing Merrill Lynch for investment malpractice because the TIGRs (Merrill Lynch zero) declined in value by 36 percent.

Nevertheless, zeros can be a good investment if you expect interest rates to go down, because your earnings are reinvested at a fixed rate of interest. Zeros also are sold in a wide range of amounts and maturities, which makes them suitable for many types of investors.

Fannie Mae and Freddie Mac and Their Children

Recently a new type of investment has become popular: "mortgage-backed securities." These funds consist of millions of home mortgages that an institution pools from local banks across the country and then sells in the form of bonds. The interest rate on the bonds is tied to the rate paid on the pool of home mortgages. The institution collects the mortgage payments and in turn distributes the interest to the bondholders. If the home mortgages are paid back early—for example, if people sell their houses—part of each bond gets paid back early as well. The price of mortgage-backed securities drops as interest rates rise—*only ultimate payment is guaranteed by Uncle Sam*, not your resale price before then.

Most mortgage-backed securities are sold by two agencies: the Federal National Mortgage Association (Fannie Mae) and the Federal Home Loan Mortgage Corporation (Freddie Mac). As these investments become increasingly popular, they also are being offered by Merrill Lynch and other large financial institutions.

THE RISK OF BONDS

There are two things that can go wrong when you buy bonds: (1) you'll lose your money altogether; or (2) you'll get stuck with a low interest rate.

The chances that you won't get paid back depend on who the borrower is and for how long they're borrowing your money. If you buy U.S. Treasury bills or savings bonds from the federal government, you can be 100 percent sure of being paid back.

On the other hand, when you buy a bond issued

by a corporation there is always the possibility that the corporation might run into financial trouble. The greater the risk that a company might fail to pay you back, the higher the interest rate paid. With "blue-chip" bonds, this risk usually is small and interest rates on the bonds are moderate.

You can spend hours trying to analyze which bonds are a good risk, but you needn't bother. Two private investment rating services do it for you: Moody's and Standard & Poor's. Bonds are rated from triple A (the safest) to C or D (a spin of the roulette wheel). Your stockbroker can give you bond-rating information.

The second risk with bonds is getting stuck with a low interest rate. With rare exceptions, the longer you're willing to lend your money for, the higher the interest rate. The reason is that the longer you have to wait to get repaid, the more risk you take that things will go wrong, and so the greater the reward if things go right. And if interest rates decline after you've loaned the money, then you're comfortably assured of a higher rate than everyone else or a gain if you sell the bond. The interest rate for bank money market accounts, where your money is readily available, will be somewhat lower than for a twelve-month bank CD where there is a penalty for early withdrawal. The difference is even greater between a bank money market account and a bond that matures in thirty years.

Many investors overlook the fact that the value of a bond can move up and down just like a share of stock. For instance, let's say that in 1960 you bought a 30-year $1,000 bond issued by General Motors at

4.4 percent interest. Back in 1960, when the rate of inflation was around 1.5 percent, that 4.4 percent interest rate was a great deal. But today, interest rates average over twice that and you would take a huge loss if you sold that 4.4 percent bond.

Here's another example: let's say that you buy a $1,000 bond paying 10 percent interest annually, which comes to $100 a year. If interest rates increase to 11 percent, the selling price of your bond will drop to about $900—that's so a new buyer can still earn an "effective interest rate" of 11 percent. ($100 interest on a bond that costs $900 works out to about 11 percent a year.)

WHAT ARE STOCKS?

Each share of common stock you own in a company is a fractional portion of that business—a piece of the action. If there are 100,000 shares of Eastman Kodak stock in investors' hands and you own ten shares, you have a 10/100,000th or a 0.0001 share in the company.

Owning common stock entitles you to vote for the company's top management and to approve or disapprove some major business decisions. When it's time to elect the board of directors of the company, you'll get a "proxy statement" in the mail and a nice letter from the company's chief executive officer telling you how wonderful he or she and the rest of his or her staff is. The letter will ask you to vote for them by mailing in the proxy, generally giving management the right to vote your share as they see fit. Usually, there's only one candidate for each spot on the board.

Most small investors throw out their proxy statements. This is not a good idea, especially if there is a proxy war, which is a fight for control of the company in which shareholders are given a real choice. A proxy war starts when an outsider, usually backed by a couple of large shareholders, decides he can run things much better than the current management and seeks election to the company's board of directors. If there is a proxy war, read what each candidate for control has to say (keeping in mind that the candidates are fighting for a prestigious, high-paying job) and then, for objectivity, read the *Wall Street Journal*. And vote!

Where Does Stock Come From?

If a company is "public," it means its stock is bought, sold and traded by the general public on the open market. The biggest companies are usually found on the biggest stock exchange, which is the New York Stock Exchange.

If the company is private, then only certain private investors are offered stock. For example, when the Ford Motor Company was first started it was private—owned mostly by the Ford family and some of it by the Dodge family. Eventually the Ford Motor Company "went public" and now anyone can buy its stock. (Incidentally, the Ford and Dodge families got along like the Hatfields and the McCoys; eventually the

Dodges sold their stock back to the Ford family and formed their own auto company.)

The actual shares of stock are rectangular pieces of paper with the company's name and other information in fancy letters and a picture of a locomotive, airplane or an impressive-looking building. Your stockbroker should hold the actual stock certificates for you, to save you the hassle of having to find them when you want to sell.

OBSERVATION: If you lose your stock certificates, ask the broker you bought them from for help. He may be able to prove your ownership, in which case you can be issued new shares and probably any lost dividends.

There are three kinds of stock. Stock in investor's hands is "issued and outstanding." "Issued and authorized" company stock has been printed, but is not yet being sold. And "treasury stock" is stock that the company has bought back and is now holding. Any stock being held by the company—issued and outstanding or treasury stock—doesn't count for voting, dividend or any other purposes. It just lies dormant in the company's vault.

When a company sells a lot of its dormant stock to the public, to existing shareholders or to employees, it tends to deflate the stock's price. But if the company makes good use of the money it raises from the sale, then the value of each share eventually should go back up, even though there are more shares on the market.

Until you sell the stock, the only income you receive from your investment is dividends, which are generally based on the company's earnings for that year but are specifically set by the board of directors. Most large, financially sound companies pay a regular dividend four times a year. Companies that are growing or are hurting financially usually need all the money they can get and don't pay stockholders much of a dividend—if any at all. This is not necessarily bad for the stockholder if the company retains that dividend and puts it to good use.

THE RISK OF STOCKS

Whenever you invest in the stock of a company, even if it's well established, you take a chance. A new competitor, a product failure, or changing market conditions could suddenly cut into profits. Who would have predicted the Arab oil embargo or OPEC's later price war, Union Carbide's chemical-plant disaster in India, the Tylenol scares or the cost overruns that have plagued new nuclear power plants?

Only rarely is a stock a "sure thing." If you get an ironclad tip that a small oil company has just struck oil, then you have a terrific investment opportunity—with one reservation. What you know—that no one else knows—probably makes you an "insider," and it is illegal under federal law to use "inside information" for profit. In that case, you could be forced to surrender any profit you made, fined by the government or even sent to jail.

BONDS VERSUS STOCKS

Generally, it's much safer to lend money than to own a piece of the action. When you buy bonds you earn interest regardless of the economy or company profits. With bonds, your risk that the company will go bankrupt also is offset a bit by federal bankruptcy laws which require lenders be paid back before the owners get a dime.

But in terms of retiring rich there is more to think about than just getting paid back. In the half-century since the Great Depression, the average stock has earned about twice as much as the average debt investment. To illustrate, let's look at the performance of U.S. Treasury bills from the years 1947 through 1981. Over those 35 years, the average interest rate on T-bills was 4.2 percent, while the average blue-chip company bond paid 5.8 percent and stocks averaged a yield of 10.8 percent.

An important point to remember is that bondholders don't share in the good fortunes of a company. Unlike common stock, bonds don't increase much—if at all—in value even if the company has a great year. The value of a bond does go up as interest rates go down and, as the 4.4 percent 1960 General Motors bonds show, declines as interest rates increase.

However, you should also note that there were some periods between 1947 and 1981 when you would have been much better off with Treasury bills and bonds than stock. And, of course, in October 1987 a five-year-long bull market came crashing down, and many people who had hoped to make a killing lost a chunk of their profits—and some lost their shirts as well.

AFTER THE CRASH

As even a Tibetan monk must know by now, on Friday morning, October 16, 1987, the stock market started a wild two-day 26 percent drop in value. (Or, as one headline put it, "Wall Street Lays an Egg.") There were so many stock transactions that the Wall Street computers keeping track of it all nearly crashed as well. Some experts speculated that the market crashed because of our country's high budget and trade deficits. Others called the crash a much-needed "correction" that merely cut overvalued stocks down to size. Still others blamed it on investor panic.

The bottom line is that no one knows why it happened—or whether it will happen again. Are we on the verge of another great depression? I think not. Although there are some similarities between conditions now and those in 1929 (i.e., a market crash after a long period of gain, numerous bank failures and relatively low return on investment by business) the differences are more striking. Today, citizens are protected, at least in part, by federal deposit insurance, unemployment insurance and the Social Security system. Furthermore, there seems to be a general feeling in Washington that our elected officials may be able to put aside purely political concerns and focus on real solutions to our national economic woes. Even so, we could be on the road to some hard times—possibly a further decline in the stock market and relatively high unemployment.

What to do? First, anyone who cannot afford to risk a further loss in the stock market should get out and stay out. Forget trying to recoup past losses. One thing that the experts do agree on is that stocks will be unpredictable for a while.

But even if you can afford the risk, it's still a good idea to put most of your money in a virtually can't-lose investment—plain old cash. That doesn't mean a stack of bills under your mattress; it means safe money market accounts, bank deposits, CD's and treasury bonds. It may not sound sexy, but that's where a lot of sophisticated money will be invested for a while. Meanwhile, you can wait for a further big decline in stock prices or simply for a sustained stabilization of the market. You'll be safe, while earning a reasonable, if unspectacular, return.

WHAT EVERY INVESTOR NEEDS TO KNOW

Supply and Demand

You can learn a lot about the investment world from the price of roses. Roses are never cheap, but in the summertime they cost the least. Why? Because the supply is relatively high and to sell extra stock, florists lower their prices. During the winter, when the supply goes way down, the price goes way up. And on Valentine's Day the price goes through the roof—because suddenly everybody wants to buy roses at the same time.

That's the law of supply and demand. When there's a high demand for something the price goes up and when there's an oversupply, the price goes down.

The same goes for money. When a lot of people want to borrow money interest rates go up, and as interest rates increase more people are willing to lend money. In that way, a balance is struck between the borrowers and the lenders.

Predicting interest rates would be relatively simple if it wasn't for the federal government. The problem is that the president and the Congress each year spend more money—billions of dollars more—than the government takes in from taxes. The government has two ways to make up for its overspending. It can borrow the extra cash, which creates a huge demand on the loan market and drives up interest rates. Or, the folks in Washington can simply print more money—which tends to lower interest rates because the supply of money is increased. But the government, by printing money, also tends to increase inflation—which ends up increasing interest rates. Usually, the government borrows and prints more money at the same time—so nobody is ever entirely sure of what's happening.

Stocks are the same way. As more people want to buy a stock, the price goes up. When more people want to sell, the price goes down. According to the law of supply and demand, the price of a stock will strike a balance between the people who want to buy the stock and the people who want to sell: as the price goes up more people want to sell and less people want to buy.

The demand for stocks also depends on interest rates, since people want the highest-paying investment they can get. When interest rates are very high, people tend to sell their stocks and put their money into CDs, bank money market accounts, bonds and other debt investments. As more people sell stocks, the prices of stocks fall. Eventually, stock prices drop so low that they become attractive again and people go back to buying stocks. And so on and so forth.

If you've felt like we've just come together in a giant circle, you're right. Many economists think the stock market, interest rates and even business profits follow a continuing cycle—except that no one ever knows at exactly what point in the cycle we are.

A Word of Caution

As a general rule, forget any visions of grandeur you may have. The truth is that nobody really understands precisely why the stock market, or bond market, or interest rates go up or down—neither can anyone predict what's in store for the future. That goes for anyone who offers "sure-fire" investment tips, including your stockbroker, neighbor or rich uncle. Your goal is a good long-term strategy for retiring rich—not getting rich quick.

Investment books love to tell a tale about how a

monkey throwing darts at a list of stocks did a better job at picking winners than the shrewdest Wall Street adviser. The point of the story is that sometimes even an expert with his charts, graphs and computer printouts may not be able to make more money in the stock market than the most ignorant amateur. But don't let that stop you from learning the basics.

The remainder of this chapter will explain the basics of investing in bonds and stocks, including what makes a "good" investment, how to talk to a stockbroker, how to keep track of your investments and what effect Tax Reform can have on stocks.

WHAT TO THINK ABOUT BEFORE YOU CHOOSE A STOCK

There are six simple but often overlooked principles to remember before you plunge into the stock market:

1. Buy cheap.
2. Sell early.
3. Run when you hear good news.
4. Don't worry about small losses.
5. Diversify.
6. Be a coward.

1. *Buy cheap.*

The time to buy a stock is before it becomes popular. Remember, the laws of supply and demand are in charge—when a lot of people want to buy a stock, its price goes up and when everybody's selling, the price goes down. Generally, you should buy when the stock market is down and prices are cheap and sell when the market is up.

This may sound obvious, but in reality most people get into the market too late. They hear or read that a stock is doing great and decide to buy—but by then the stock's price already has gone up. The trick is to buy the stock when it isn't popular, and sell when things are so good that everybody wants to buy it. When people hear that car sales are down, they tend to sell their General Motors and Chrysler stock, sending the price of those stocks down and making it a good time to buy.

How do you tell if a stock is cheap? First check the newspaper for the stock's "high" and its "low"—that simply means the highest and lowest price somebody paid for it over the past year. If today's price is close to the low, then the stock may be relatively cheap.

Next, look at the stock's recent performance—has the price generally been going up or down? If the stock's price is relatively low but is on a downslide, you may want to wait to see if it goes down more. On the other hand, if the price has started to go back up again, it may be the time to buy.

But cheap is not always good. A stock may be cheap because the company is chronically mismanaged and its prospects for the future are dim—in which case the price might just sink lower. If you buy a stock simply because it seems cheap, you can outsmart yourself and not the market.

You can protect yourself against sudden price swings by buying shares of a given stock over a period of time, instead of all at the same time. That way, if the stock is still on a downtrend, the average price you pay still will be a little lower than if you bought the shares all at once at the higher price. Even if the stock goes up, you will have gotten at least some of your shares at a cheaper price.

Unfortunately, if you're buying under 200 shares at a time, it may be too expensive to buy in more than one lot. Stock brokerage commissions are always higher when you buy an "odd lot" of less than 100 shares. The extra commissions you would pay by buying over time might cost you more than you might gain from any increase in the price of the stock.

Another clue to knowing when to buy is the stock's "price-earnings ratio." That is the ratio of the company's earnings for the previous year to yesterday's stock price. For instance, if a company made a $10 profit last year for every share of its stock, and the price of a share of stock yesterday was $20, the price-earnings ratio is two to one ($2 of stock price for every dollar of earnings). What constitutes a good price-earnings ratio depends on the particular industry and company. But keep in mind that price-earnings ratios are based on year-old earnings figures, and might not be a useful figure if the company's fortunes have turned around recently.

2. *Sell early.*

A famous tycoon once said that he made his fortune by always selling "too early." Or put another way, you can make money in the stock market as a bull or as a bear, but not as a pig.

Don't wait for a stock to reach its highest price before you sell—chances are you won't recognize the moment when the stock has peaked and will get caught in the downturn. *Remember you can't make money on a stock until you sell it!* If you can make a nice profit, take your money and use the earnings to buy a new cheap stock—or stash it in a money market account and just let it grow.

I once had a stockbroker who often called me up to tell me how much money I'd "made" in the market that day because my stocks had gone up. Naturally, I'd always be pleased, but, being a nervous person, I'd always ask if it was time to sell. "No!" my ex-broker would yell, "it's going to go up more." Famous last words. When the price started to drop again, my broker would advise me not to sell until it came back up. Usually, it never did, with the result that I ended up with a loss, instead of a gain, and a new broker.

The moral is that picking stocks that are winners is only part of smart investing. The hard part is knowing when to sell.

3. *Run when you hear good news.*

When you hear good news about a company—they've invented a new product or were awarded a big government contract—it's probably too late to buy its stock. Figure it this way: if you've heard the news, then the big shots at Merrill Lynch, etc. probably knew about it hours, days or even months earlier. The price of the stock has probably peaked already.

The same goes for tips from your broker or anyone else who urges you to buy or sell a particular stock on the basis of their information. Do you reasonably believe they were one of the first to find out? And are you the first one they'd call? If the answer to either of these questions is no, then tell the would-be tipster the same.

In short, when things are great, it looks like stock prices will keep soaring, and everybody is lining up to buy, SELL.

4. *Don't worry about small losses.*

You bought a stock cheap when all the signs indicated it was about to go up. You've been patient, you did everything right, but you've guessed wrong and the stock's price has actually gone down a bit. Swallow your pride and sell at a small loss. Then forget it ever happened.

Most people hate to admit that they made a mistake with a stock. They'll hold on, waiting for a silver lining, and end up turning a small mistake into an expensive one. If you've given your stock a reasonable amount of time and nothing positive has happened, dump it. This is especially true if the stock goes down just slightly. Avoid the temptation to wait "just a few more days" until you can make your loss back; if the stock has lost its original appeal to you, it's time to sell. You can always buy it again.

5. *Diversify.*

That means don't put all your dollars in one basket. Spread your risk by buying several different types of stock. If you want to invest in one industry—let's say airlines—buy stock in at least two different companies. That way if airlines in general do well, but one of the companies you choose falters, you're covered. Better yet, don't sink all your money into airline stocks—cover yourself by investing in other industries, too.

6. *Be a coward.*

Too often, someone who's made a well-thought-out decision to keep away from stocks gets sucked into investing at the worst possible time. The scenario goes like this: the stock market's down and you decide you weren't cut out for stocks so you invest in a nice safe money market account. Then the stock market picks up again and all you hear about is how much money everybody is making. Finally, you succumb and plunge into the market—at precisely the wrong time, when prices are up and you should be selling. Remember "buy cheap," "sell early" and "run when you hear good news?" You did the exact opposite, and will probably pay for it.

The moral of the story is stick with your instincts about what is right for you. And if you do decide to plunge into the stock market, be patient and wait for the right time.

A final note: whatever else happens, make sure your investment income is never idle. Your money should always earn interest while you're planning your next investment. The bank or brokerage firm should automatically "sweep" all your interest and dividends plus idle money into a money market mutual fund so that it will earn interest. The same should happen when you sell a stock or bond.

HOW TO BUY BONDS AND STOCKS

There are two ways to invest in bonds and stocks. One is to have a self-directed account at a stock brokerage firm or bank that allows you to manage and select your own investments. The other way, for people who don't have the time, training or temperament, is to invest in a mutual fund.

Brokers and Other Strangers

Stock brokerage firms and larger banks offer more or less the same basic services: buying and selling stocks for you for a commission, holding the stock certificate for you, collecting your dividends and interest and compiling statements stating what you own and how much it's worth.

A successful relationship with your broker requires that you realize two things. First, your broker doesn't know for sure what stocks will go up any more than you do; if he did, he wouldn't need you. Second, your broker is a salesman who makes a commission every time you buy and sell a stock, whether that stock goes up or down. His incentive to make you money is that if he gives you good advice you'll give him more business—and if he gives bad advice, you'll get another broker.

A recent help-wanted ad placed by a leading brokerage firm emphasizes this point. They were looking for candidates for an intensive training program leading to a job as a broker. The successful candidates, the ad stated, would have "a consistent record of success in *sales*." Qualifications such as a strong financial background or special business skills weren't mentioned.

But a truly good broker acts as more of an adviser than a salesman. He understands your investment philosophy and needs. If you're conservative, he will steer you toward less risky investments. If you're a gambler, he should help you avoid taking too many risks.

A good broker also keeps a careful eye on your investments. If one of your stocks has gone up or down steadily, he should let you know promptly and update your investment strategy. That spares you the trouble and aggravation of having to monitor your stocks every day.

At many banks that offer brokerage services, you pay commissions to the bank, not to the individual broker. This is good because the brokers don't have a direct stake in how often you buy and sell stocks. On the other hand, a broker who doesn't get commissions may not have as much of an incentive to keep as close an eye on the performance of your stocks—as he would otherwise.

Learning to Say No to Your Broker

Stockbrokers tend to be very friendly people. They're easy to talk to and they always remember to ask about your family. There's nothing wrong with that, except that it is naturally more difficult to say "no" to a nice person.

Example: Let's say your broker calls and, after making some small talk, recommends that you buy a certain stock. He gives you several reasons why he thinks the stock is a good investment, but you're not entirely convinced. But you don't want to reject him either. So you quickly search for an excuse: "I don't have the money, I have to ask my spouse." Wrong move. This is first and foremost a business relationship, not a friendship. You should always feel free to question and reject your broker's advice. Ask what the downside is. What could go wrong? Then *you* evaluate the stock and what your broker has told you. Take a few days to think about it if you want. If the stock is a great investment today, in most cases it'll still be so tomorrow. And above all else feel free to tell your broker: "No, thank you." It's your retirement dollars at stake, not his.

Discount Brokers

The financial sections of most newspapers are filled with ads for discount brokers, who in fact offer many services at commissions that are dramatically less than those charged by full-service brokers. For example, commissions on a sale of 300 shares could range from $25 to $200 depending on the broker.

Do some comparison shopping. Most stockbrokers' fees are based on how many shares of one stock you buy at a time and the total dollars involved, with a minimum fee charged for purchases of 100 shares and less. It won't do you any good if a broker has the lowest commissions on purchases of 1,000 shares or $10,000 orders if you plan on investing much less. If you're interested in other brokerage services, such as financial information about a particular company, check to see if it's offered. Discount brokers usually provide fewer services—such as investment advice—than regular brokers.

Some Simple Pointers

A conservative way to increase your income from stock investments is to sell "options" on the stocks you own. An option means that someone pays you money for the right to buy your stock at a future time at a fixed price. Wall Street calls that the "striking price." The striking price is usually well above the current price of the stock. Options expire after a set period of time—after that they are worthless. For example, say you've got 100 shares of XYZ stock in your IRA for which the current price is $62 a share. You could sell a six-month option to sell those shares at $70 a share. Whoever buys the option will pay you about $160.

What's happening is that the option buyer is betting you that the price of your XYZ stock will go above $70 within the next six months. If he's right, you'll have to sell him your 100 shares for $70 per share, even though they will be worth more than that. If not, then he won't buy, the option expires. Either way you keep the $160 he paid for the option.

Selling options gives you immediate extra income. And even if the option buyer wins the bet, you still get the striking price of $70 for your stock. You also get to keep the dividends paid on your stock until the option is exercised.

To sell options, just call your broker. He'll do the rest. But note that you may not be able to sell options in every stock you own.

Dividend reinvestment plans can be another good way to earn extra money from your stock. Some larger companies offer their shareholders additional shares instead of a regular cash dividend. That option enables you to avoid paying brokerage commissions to buy the extra stock. Further, the company may offer you bonus stock—up to 5 percent more—for choosing stock instead of the cash dividend. Of course, if you don't want any more of that stock, take the cash.

MUTUAL FUNDS: THE ALTERNATIVE

The stock market can be a particularly dangerous place for the small investor. If you have enough money to invest in only one or two stocks, obviously your risk is greater than if you buy twenty different stocks. It doesn't do you any good if the stock market is going up, when your two stocks keep going down. Strike one against the little guy.

As we just saw, it's also cheaper to buy and sell a lot of shares of stocks or bonds because the more money you have to invest the bigger the discount your broker is going to offer you on commissions. Strike two.

For some people, the way to get more investment clout is by investing in a mutual fund which pools the money of thousands of investors. Mutual funds are sold in shares, just like stock. Each share entitles you to a portion of the dividends, gains or losses on the stocks and bonds that the fund buys.

A mutual fund can diversify its investments in a way the individual investor cannot. They are also very convenient: the fund's professional money managers handle most of the details of individual investment decisions. You just have to concentrate on the performance of the mutual fund itself.

Observation: To make investing in a mutual fund practical, you should have at least $2,000 in your account. Anything less really belongs in a bank money market account or CD.

Choosing a Mutual Fund

Because you don't have direct control over how your money is invested, it's important to choose a mutual fund as carefully as you would select any other investment.

Each mutual fund has its own goals. There are high-risk funds that invest mostly in speculative stocks with the potential to earn big profits. Those more aggressive growth funds tend to do very well in a bullish stock market and very poorly in a bad market. At the other extreme, more conservative mutual funds look for investments that pay steady dividends and are unlikely to vary drastically in value. And there are many funds in between, such as a medium growth or medium growth and income combined. The prospectus for each fund explains its goals and gives a detailed list of its investments.

There are also mutual funds called "sector funds," which invest in only one industry. The trouble here is that there are no standardized categories. For example, two "high technology" funds could invest in completely different industries: one could focus on computers and the other on radioactive waste disposal. Again, the only way to know for sure is to check the prospectus.

Observation: Sector funds are very volatile; their prices can fluctuate considerably.

When you shop for a mutual fund, check into its performance over the past three years or so. Also check on how the fund fared in years when the stock market was really down: 1973–74, 1977, 1981, early 1982. A few times a year, *Barron's* and *Forbes* publish surveys on the performance of various mutual funds. Also, every issue of *Money* magazine includes a "Fund Watch" that gives useful information on quite a few funds. The most recent copy of these magazines (which you can read for free at your local library) can be a big help. But keep in mind that a mutual fund's past performance is no guarantee of how well it will do in the future.

Remember the story of the monkey with the darts picking stocks? Well it's also true of some mutual fund managers. Although some have done incredibly well, the average performance of all professional money managers over the past 20 years or so has been mediocre. In fact, studies have shown that if they had simply bought shares in every stock sold on the New York Stock Exchange, they would have been much better off. For that reason it's a good idea to divide your investments among more than one mutual fund company.

Family of Funds

Some financial institutions have packaged several of their mutual funds into a "family of funds" that could include 20 or more different mutual funds, including a money market, a fixed-income fund and an aggressive growth fund.

A family of funds makes it easy for you to conveniently switch your investments from stocks to bonds or even a money market. For example, if you expect stocks to do well, you can put most of your money in one or two common stock mutual funds. Then, if you anticipate that interest rates are going to go up, you can switch over to a bond mutual fund. And if you're not sure of what's going to happen, you can stow your money in the family's money market fund until you decide.

OBSERVATION: A lot of people have tried to make money by switching back and forth from stock funds to bond funds to money market funds at "just" the right moment. Most of those people fail to achieve their objective with this switching activity. Generally, you're better off with a steady hand at the helm.

To Load or Not to Load

A mutual fund can be a "load" or a "no-load" fund. Load means that every time you buy shares in the fund you are charged a fee or commission—sometimes more than 8 percent of your investment. No-load means that there are no fees or commissions charged. Since many load funds have no-load counterparts, you should always look for no-load funds. (But be careful: some funds that charge a commission only when you *sell* shares call themselves no-load funds.) Don't be misled into thinking that commissions will inspire the fund managers to do a better job—those fees go to your stockbroker.

Mutual funds can also be "open end" or "closed end." Open end means that an investor can buy shares directly from the fund company itself. When it's time to sell, the investor simply sells his shares directly back to the fund. Some open-end funds can also be bought through any broker, but others are available only through the brokerage firm or mutual fund company that sponsors the fund. For example, to buy certain Merrill Lynch funds you must have an account at Merrill Lynch.

Closed-end mutual funds are just the opposite: you have to buy the shares in the open market from other investors just as you would shares of stock. Closed-end mutual funds can be bought through any self-directed account.

From time to time, shares of closed-end funds can be bought at a discount. For instance, if a closed-end fund has 100,000 outstanding shares with a total market value of $1,000,000, it means that one share is valued at $10 on that particular date; on that same day you might be able to buy shares of the fund at $8—with a guaranteed $2 per share discount.

Your broker can tell you which mutual funds sell at a discount (it happens only with the closed-end variety). Discounted funds allow you to increase your investment return because the share that cost you $8 is earning income based on its "real" value of $10. The one drawback is that you may have to sell your shares in a closed-end fund at a discount, too. Of course, prices can go the other way—sometimes a fund will sell at a premium *above* its value. You should not automatically avoid a fund selling at a premium—it may still be a good investment.

In sum, check into investment performance over the past three or five years, the investment goals and whether it's a load or no-load fund. Also try to avoid families of funds that charge a fee each time you transfer money from one fund to another.

KEEPING A HANDLE ON YOUR INVESTMENTS

Every time you buy or sell an investment—a CD, a stock, etc.—you'll receive a "transaction slip" that records the date, name of the security, price and any commissions that were paid. These receipts should be part of your permanent records. If you have not received such a slip within a short time after any purchase or sale of an investment, call your broker or your bank. Sometimes, because of administrative errors, they may have failed to record your investment.

Periodically, you'll also receive a statement from the bank or brokerage firm with a list of your investments, their current value and the interest and dividends you've earned to date. But since summary statements usually do not indicate the original cost of your investments, you won't be able to tell if you've made a profit on your stocks or bonds—unless your personal records divulge such costs.

Periodic Review

Every so often you should examine your investments to see if you're meeting your retirement goals. Examine the income you've earned, including interest, dividends and any loss or gain from the sale of stocks or bonds. Then figure out the current market value of your portfolio, which is the amount of money you would receive if you sold everything at current prices.

Now evaluate the performance of your investments. Are you satisfied with your investment return? If you own stocks or bonds, are they still good investments? Use the principles outlined earlier in this chapter; and remember, get rid of any investment that has failed to perform in a reasonable period of time.

How often you review your portfolio depends on your choice of investments. There is no reason to review a fixed-rate CD until it is ready to mature—the market value is simply what you've put in, plus interest. Stocks or bonds should be evaluated at least twice a year, and more often if stock prices or interest rates have been fluctuating a lot or there is high inflation.

OBSERVATION: When economic conditions are changing rapidly, investors should keep a closer watch on their money.

WHO IS DOW JONES?

The Dow Jones industrial average is a yardstick that is supposed to measure the overall performance of the stock market throughout the day. The average is based on the share prices of 30 large companies selected by Dow Jones & Co. (the owner of the *Wall Street Journal*). The companies change from time to time but currently include such giants as AT&T, American Express, Exxon, U.S. Steel and General Motors.

It's a good yardstick, but somewhat skewed. First, it ignores the thousands of other companies whose stocks are traded, especially the stocks of new industries. And a big change in the price of one can throw off the whole average. For example, if most of the 30 stocks go down, but AT&T goes up a lot, the Dow Jones industrial average might show an increase though the market on the whole actually is doing poorly.

How to Read the Financial Section of Your Newspaper

To the uninitiated, the stock pages seem a cross between Egyptian hieroglyphics and a computer printout. Not so! The print may be very small, but with the help of this book, a ruler, and perhaps a magnifying glass, you'll be a pro in minutes.

Stocks are grouped according to the "exchange" on which they're bought and sold. If a stock is traded on the New York Stock Exchange, it'll be listed alphabetically with all the other New York Stock Exchange stocks.

Because there are so many stocks, the names of companies are abbreviated. Some abbreviations are easy to figure out; for example, International Business Machines is "IBM." Some are a bit tricky, but not to worry, your broker will be happy to translate.

Once you know the abbreviation, you can locate your stock in what at first appears to be a dozen meaningless columns of numbers. Let's take a look at how Exxon's common stock, which is traded on the New York Stock Exchange, would be shown in a typical newspaper. Each column is abbreviated at the top of the page—for convenience, I've numbered the columns although the newspaper probably won't.

1	2	3	4	5	6	7	8	9	10	11
12 Month				Yld	PE	Sales				Net
High	Low	Stock	Div	%	Ratio	hds	High	Low	Last	Chg
40	28½	Exxon	3.20	6.9	7	18160	40	39	39¼	+⅛

First, look at column 3. You'll see the abbreviation of the stock, which in this case is Exxon. Column 1, the 52-week high, lists the highest price paid for Exxon common stock over the past 12 months, in this case $40 a share. Column 2 is the lowest price paid in the same period, $28½ (or $28.50 per share). The "½" means half a dollar or 50¢. Column 4 is the total dividend paid for each share of stock for the year (or $3.20 per share).

Column 5 is the annual return on each share of Exxon stock, based on the current stock price and the amount of dividends for the year. For Exxon, it's figured by dividing the $3.20 total dividend by the 39¼ (or $39.25 per share price), which comes to about 8.2 percent.

Column 6 is the price-earnings ratio. Remember, it's a comparison of last year's earnings and the latest price, which for Exxon comes out to 7. For shorthand, a stockbroker would say Exxon is selling "7 times earnings."

Column 7 is the number of shares of Exxon stock bought and sold that day, in hundreds of shares. So on that day 18160 means that 1,816,000 shares were bought and sold.

Columns 8 and 9 are simply the highest and lowest price that anyone paid for a share of Exxon stock that day, $40 and $39 respectively.

Column 10 is the latest price or $39.25 per share.

Column 11 shows the net change in the price of Exxon stock from yesterday to today. Exxon stock went up "⅛ of a point," which means ⅛th of one dollar, or 12½¢ per share. Sunday's paper usually will show the net price change for the stock for the previous week.

Now that you've translated the paper into plain English, what have you learned about Exxon stock? First, you know that today's price is 39.25 per share, which is very close to its twelve-month high of $40. Further, at some point during the last year Exxon was selling at $28.50 a share, so the price has gone up substantially. Also, over 1,816,000 shares of Exxon were bought and sold in one day, which is a lot of trading. This might mean that there is a big demand for Exxon stock or that the people who bought Exxon when it was $28 a share are selling "early" to secure their profits.

The same basic rules apply to newspaper bond listings. Here is the information from a typical paper for the same day for a bond of American Telephone and Telegraph, which is listed as ATT:

1	2	3	4	5	6	7	8	9
12 Month		Bond	Cur	Sales in				Net
High	Low	ATT	Yld	$1000	High	Low	Last	Chg
100⅞	91	10⅜ 90	11.01	406	95⅞	94¼	94⅝	+⅛

Keep in mind that most companies have many different bonds out in the market at the same time. That's because they keep selling new bonds before they've paid back all of the old ones. Column 3 tells you that we're dealing with an ATT bond which has a "coupon" interest of 10⅜ percent and that matures in the year 1990 (that's what the "90" stands for). For each bond, ATT promises to pay you back $1,000 upon maturity. In plain English, that means for each bond you buy ATT will pay you $103.75 interest annually until the year 1990, when they'll pay you back $1,000.

Columns 1 and 2 are the high and the low price paid for that bond over the last 12 months. Remember with bonds we're talking in terms of $1,000, so 100⅞ means the highest price was $1,008.75. To figure it out, just multiply 100⅞ (or 100.875) by ten.

Column 4 is the current yield or the actual interest rate you would get if you bought a bond at today's price. In our case, it's 11.01 percent. How can that be if that bond pays only 10⅜ percent. Because the bond is selling at a discounted price of $946.25 per bond. ATT still has to pay you $103.75 in interest a year. That works out—based on today's price—to an interest rate of just over 11 percent.

Column 5 "Sales in $1,000" simply explains how

many bonds were bought and sold on that day, in this case 406 bonds.

Columns 6 and 7 tell you today's highest and lowest prices, $948.75 and $942.50.

Column 8 is the final price of the day, or $946.25.

Finally, Column 9 tells you that since yesterday, the ATT Bond has gone up ⅛ of a point which, for a bond means $1.25. That's ⅛ of a dollar times ten.

Sometimes, when there's something unusual going on, the paper will put an "E" or a "B" or some other letter next to a bond or stock. Each letter refers you to a code on the bottom of the page. For example, an "E" next to a stock could mean the company has just announced an extra dividend. Each newspaper has its own code.

EVERYTHING YOU NEED TO KNOW ABOUT CERTAIN RISKY INVESTMENTS

There are three golden rules for investing in risky, glamorous investments such as:

1. commodities futures
2. foreign currency
3. racehorses, stamps, antiques and coins
4. oil, gas and other natural resources
5. most, if not all, real estate limited partnerships
6. penny stocks

Rule 1: Do Not Invest

If you're at the level this book was written for, then these investments are much too risky and require more time and expertise than you have.

Rule 2: Do Not Invest

Even if you are willing to risk it and know something about the oil or racehorse business, do not invest. There are experts who know a lot more, who can react quickly to new developments and who have the time and money to do it right. The odds are stacked in their favor, not yours, so forget the get-rich-quick scheme.

Rule 3: Do Not Invest

Even if you know an expert who's willing to tell you what to do, forget it. What if you have an argument or your expert dies, are you going to know how or when to sell your Louis XV chair? Or, more likely, what if your expert is wrong: is he or she going to make good your losses?

TAX REFORM AND STOCKS

The effects of Tax Reform are already being felt on the stock market. Corporate tax rates have been slashed from 46 percent to 34 percent while many pet business deductions—such as those for new equipment and new factories—have been significantly curtailed. The net result is that corporate America will pay over an extra $120 billion in taxes in the next few years.

That tax increase will be felt hardest by companies that benefited from the old system of generous tax deductions: namely the auto and steel industries, railroads, airlines, telecommunications, manufacturers and oil and gas. On the other hand, companies in the "service" industries, which have fewer deductible expenses, will generally do better under the new tax system. These include advertising agencies, retailers, insurance brokers, stock brokers and newspapers.

As an example of what a change in tax rates can do, let's say that before Tax Reform a service company in the highest tax bracket paid 46¢ in taxes for every $1 it earned, leaving 54¢ in after-tax profits. Now it will only pay 36¢ for every $1 of earnings, boosting after-tax profits to 64¢ per $1 of income—an increase of over 22 percent, without any increase in business.

But before you call your broker to buy service industry stocks, remember these points:

1. Stock experts probably have already bought these stocks, so the price may be too high. (Remember: run when you hear good news.)

2. It's difficult to analyze exactly how the new tax laws will affect profits, because a company might be in several different businesses, some benefiting and others hurt by the changes.

3. The new laws are so complicated and all-encompassing that it's also difficult to predict how they'll affect the national economy. For example, a car manufacturer's taxes may go up, but consumers may use their own tax savings to buy more new cars.

Another likely outcome of Tax Reform is that individual investors will probably shift some of their investments from growth stocks into income investments. Growth stocks are shares in more risky companies that are expected to grow a lot but that don't have the cash yet to pay much, if any, dividends. Some investors choose growth stocks because under the old tax law, long-term capital gains (the "growth" in growth stocks) were 60 percent tax free, whereas interest and dividend income was fully taxable. Now that all three are taxed equally and the break for capital gains is gone, investors may prefer safer income investments. Based on the law of supply and demand this should make growth stocks less likely to go up in price and income investments more likely to.

Of course, there is still one tax benefit to capital gains: you don't pay any tax on your gains until you sell the investment. Also remember that many of the largest investors (e.g., insurance companies and corporate and government pension plans) don't pay any taxes and won't choose their investments based on tax concerns.

Another investment likely to do well under Tax Reform is municipal bonds. Because their interest is completely exempt from federal taxes, they're one of the few real tax shelters left. For many people, munis are the chief competitor with IRAs for investment dollars. But keep in mind that IRAs only let you *postpone* taxes on your investment income (and for many, make deductible contributions too) but that the tax savings on munis are permanent. For many people, an investment in both munis and IRAs will be a sound choice.

The bottom line is that you should reexamine all your investments now, and as the effects of Tax Reform settle in, move to slowly shift into new investments to fit your needs.

Q. How are capital gains taxed?

A. Basically, all income is now created equal. There is no longer favorable tax treatment for long-term capital gains. However, capital losses can still be deducted against capital gains and up to $3,000 of ordinary income each year.

Q. What happened to the $100 dividend exclusion?

A. It's gone with the wind.

Q. What about margin interest?

A. The new rules are tricky, but basically it's deductible against your interest, dividend and other investment income. It's no longer an "automatic" itemized deduction.

PART IV

FACTS OF LIFE

The time to start thinking about your estate and retirement planning is not when "younger types" regularly offer you a seat on the bus or you're eligible for senior citizen discounts, but while your career still is under way. Since nobody knows when they'll die, it's critical no matter what your age to have a will and well-organized records that will let the family track down the assets left behind. This is especially so for married couples or people with children.

Getting ready to retire is obviously most important for someone about to do just that. It means getting a precise estimate of what your social security and retirement benefits will be, taking stock of your assets and developing an investment strategy to maximize income and safety while providing some protection against inflation.

It also means thinking about how much money you'll need to live on for the rest of your life. And that's scary. If you wait until you're about to retire, it may be too late to do much about it—and that makes it even scarier. If your self-examination starts when you're still working, you'll have a much better chance at the kind of financial future you want.

CHAPTER 10
GETTING YOUR FINANCIAL HOUSE IN ORDER

WHO NEEDS A WILL?

Plainly and simply, anyone who has minor children or who owns anything worth having. You don't need to be rich. That's because a well-thought-out will, prepared by a good lawyer, ensures that when you die your property will be disposed of exactly the way you intended. If you have minor children, it can in most cases guarantee that you determine who their guardian will be. A well-made will also can help you avoid estate taxes, ensure the continuation of a family business or allow you to set up trusts for any heirs who you fear otherwise might squander your lifetime fortune.

Despite all the good reasons for having a will, many otherwise sensible people don't—Presidents Lincoln, Grant and Garfield all died without one. So did Pablo Picasso, although he had an estate worth over a quarter of a billion dollars in cash and paintings.

Superstition is one reason: people don't like to deal with their own mortality. Yet, making out a will might actually improve your health, from the comfort of knowing your finances are in order.

If you die without a will, which is called being "intestate," state law automatically takes over. Your assets are divided among your nearest relatives according to a rigid legal formula. Each state has its own formula, but chances are that in most cases your property will not be handled precisely the way you would have wanted. Not enough money may go to your spouse, while a relative whom you never liked may end up with a share of your wealth. Nor does state law make any provision for distributions to friends or charities. And your family will have to go through extra legal hassles and expense.

Who Should Prepare Your Will?

Several best-selling books promise ways to avoid probate and lawyers by writing your own will. If you've bought one of these books, do yourself and your family a favor: throw it out. Having an invalid will is the same as having no will at all.

Every state has its own complicated way of doing things and it is easy for a do-it-yourselfer to unknowingly write an invalid will simply because not enough witnesses signed it, someone signed on the wrong line, or one of a thousand other technical mistakes was made.

A competent lawyer, familiar with local laws, can ensure that your will is legally sound. A lawyer can also help you fully think through how you want to distribute your property and whether certain members of your family may need special help—because of age, health or financial immaturity—in managing their inheritance. In the latter case, again, a trust or well-chosen administrator may be a good idea.

Picking a Lawyer: What to Look For

In choosing a lawyer, as with everything else—including a bank, IRA or insurance company—you should shop around. Ask your friends, business associates or local bar association to recommend several lawyers and then meet with each one personally. He or she should be experienced in preparing wills and willing to spend all the time necessary with you. If a prospective lawyer comes across as pushy, makes you uncomfortable or your instincts simply tell you "no," keep looking.

Don't be afraid to ask about price. But beware of a lawyer whose prices are exceptionally low—he may have an "assembly-line" law practice that devotes little individual attention to clients.

Drawing Up a Will: What to Watch Out For

The original signed copy of your will is the one that "counts" after your death. It belongs in a bank vault. It doesn't belong at home or in your lawyer's office—the latter because it would force your family to go to the lawyer when you die and they might be pressured into using that lawyer's services.

However, both you and your lawyer should keep unsigned copies of your will at home or office. Periodically review your copy to make sure it is up to date. If changes are needed, say because you've acquired more assets or your children have grown, go back to your lawyer for a new will. And do not procrastinate.

Your will should name one or more people to be the administrator of your estate. The administrator is in charge of "probating" your will, which is a relatively simple task of getting a court's okay that your will is indeed your last will and testament. The administrator also files estate tax returns, collects insurance money and takes care of other financial details.

If your administrator is a bank, lawyer or accountant, your survivors usually will be charged a certain percentage of the total value of all your assets for their services. To avoid that expense, you can designate a close friend or relative as administrator, assuming they won't charge a fee and that you ask their permission first. He or she can always consult your lawyer or accountant if they need professional help. In that case, the lawyer or accountant should charge only his regular fees, not a percentage of your entire estate.

However, a professional administrator might be necessary if your family is hopelessly incompetent at these things or prone to bickering. That way, you know an objective outsider will be in charge.

Observation: Choose your administrator carefully, because unless he or she resigns or is determined by a court to be grossly incompetent, your family is stuck with him or her.

If you're relatively wealthy, then avoiding federal, state and local estate taxes will be a critical goal in designing your will. Uncle Sam's estate tax rules are rather generous: basically anything inherited by a spouse is not taxed. After deducting certain expenses, the rest of your property is taxed only if it exceeds a certain minimum amount. In 1986 that minimum was $500,000 and for 1987 and after it is $600,000. Some states tax much smaller amounts. In general, if you're rich enough to worry about estate taxes, you should hire an expert to work out an estate plan for you.

DURABLE POWER OF ATTORNEY: FINANCIAL RELIEF PITCHER

If at some point in your life you become mentally incompetent or incapacitated, you would be legally prevented from handling your affairs, including writing checks, selling assets or spending money. Your family would have to go to court to have someone appointed "conservator" of your assets, who would then be in charge of your affairs. This can be a trying, costly, and time-consuming experience; and the conservator might not have been your choice, especially since some state laws require that a stranger be appointed conservator.

There's a way out. You can give someone you trust a durable power of attorney to act on your behalf with the understanding that the power won't be exercised unless you become incompetent. Such a document must be written by an attorney. You should choose the person to whom you give the power very carefully, since he or she will be able to dispose of your property without your consent. Under some states' laws you can give durable power of attorney only to a close relative, such as an adult child.

KEEPING ACCURATE RECORDS

A magazine article recently appeared about a widow whose husband left her several hundred thousand dollars worth of rare stamps and coins—but left no record of where the safe-deposit boxes holding this fortune were located. As a result, the widow can only wait (and hope) that the bank sends out a bill for the safe-deposit box rental; until then she's almost penniless.

The moral is the absolute necessity to keep accurate financial records and to be sure your heirs know where they are. Although the safe-deposit example was extreme, in any case accurate records make it easier for your heirs to figure out what they have, whether to sell assets if necessary to raise cash or react to market changes and most importantly to save a lot of unnecessary grief and frustration.

Your list of records should be divided into at least three categories: people, places and things. The "people" are everyone your family might need to contact for information or assistance after your death, including the name, address and telephone number of your:

1. accountant
2. lawyer
3. stockbroker
4. insurance agent
5. company retirement and death benefits representative
6. financial adviser
7. real estate agent
8. trusted business advisers

Your "places" list should include:

1. the bank, the location and number of all safe-deposit boxes; the keys; and an inventory of what's stored in them
2. the location of your will
3. the location of all insurance policies
4. all tax records (e.g., returns, canceled checks and backup information)

Finally, your "things" list should include a detailed list of all your investments, including bank accounts, bank money market accounts, stocks, bonds, mutual funds, real estate, IRAs and Keoghs and their account numbers or other information necessary to track down where they're held. If you keep a balance sheet, all this information should already be on it.

OBSERVATION: These records should be updated as things change but—in any event—at least once a year.

CHECK LIST

The following check list will help you make sure your financial house is in order:

1. Have you prepared a balance sheet within the last year?
2. Have you established short- and long-term financial goals?
3. Do you have an up-to-date will?
4. Do you have a durable power of attorney?
5. Have you prepared a list of your people, places and things?
6. Have you safeguarded your personal papers, such as a will and insurance policies?
7. Do you have sufficient life and disability insurance?
8. Are all your beneficiary designations (for life insurance, company retirement benefits, etc.) up to date?

The time to do everything on this check list is NOW.

Q. Will Tax Reform affect my estate plan?
A. Perhaps. The new law makes some very technical changes that will mainly impact on wealthy individuals. If you've got a sophisticated estate plan mapped out see your tax advisor to find out if anything needs to be done.

CHAPTER 11

WHEN YOU'RE ALMOST READY TO RETIRE

The time to start thinking about long-term saving is when you start your career, so that every one of your major financial decisions can be made with the goal of being financially secure by the time you stop working. While it's difficult to assess what your income needs will be decades away, you should be aware of the crucial decisions you'll be facing and how you can best position yourself to achieve the life-style you want in retirement.

Then, about five years before you want to actually retire, you should fine-tune your plans. Decide what you want from your retirement years and how much income it will take to achieve these goals. Compare where you are to where you want to be. You can then adjust your budget and investments to get you there.

The following sections will show how to map out your retirement strategy, including how to plan for your expected social security and company retirement benefits, evaluate your personal balance sheet, prepare your retirement budget and work out your overall financial and investment program.

TAKING STOCK

Social Security

As we saw in Chapter 1, today nearly all employees and self-employed persons are included in the social security system.

To receive social security benefits, you must apply for them. Except for certain disability and survivor benefits, there is no catch-up payment for people who were entitled to benefits and failed to apply. That means if you're ever in doubt of your eligibility, apply.

Your social security benefit basically is based upon your lifetime earnings record and how old you are when payments begin. Computing your exact social security benefit is complicated and requires detailed information about your year-by-year social security earnings record. Chapter 1 showed some shortcut methods for estimating your social security benefits. But when your retirement is close at hand, you need to know more precisely what to expect.

Rather than hire a team of accountants and actuaries, you can write the Social Security Administration's Data Operations Center for a free benefits estimate. Or if you prefer, you can just stop by your local social security office. The closer you are to collecting benefits, the more accurate their estimates will be (remember, your benefit is based on your entire earnings history). It takes social security about six to eight weeks to respond. Here's a sample letter requesting an estimate. (The address and telephone number are listed at the back of this book.)

Dear Sir:

Please send my wife/husband and me a free estimate of our family social security benefits. The relevant information is

Name	*Age*	*Social Security Number*
John Smith	64	111-11-1111
Susan Smith (Maiden name: Jones)	63	122-22-2222

Remember that a benefit also is paid to a worker's dependent child or to a nonworking spouse who is of retirement age. Their benefit is generally one-half of the working spouse's benefit, but increases to 75 percent if the worker dies. There also are retirement benefits for dependent parents and grandchildren, as well as disability benefits for you and your dependent. If you think you might be eligible for any of these benefits, check with your local social security office.

Observation: Many divorced "dependent spouses" also qualify for social security benefits.

When Do Payments Begin?

It depends on your age. Workers born before 1937 are eligible to receive full social security benefits as soon as they turn 65. Younger workers have a longer wait because in 1982—in order to avoid the bankruptcy of the social security system—Congress began to phase in an increase in the retirement age. If you were born between 1938 and 1959, you can start collecting social security somewhere between ages 65 and 67—the exact age depends literally on the month you were born. For workers born on or after 1960, the minimum retirement age will be 67.

The following chart shows the current retirement schedule—but chances are Congress will change it yet again before the current crop of younger workers retires.

Year born	*Retirement Age*
1937 or earlier	65
1938	65, 2 months
1939	65, 4 months
1940	65, 6 months
1941	65, 8 months
1942	65, 10 months
1943–1954	66
1955	66, 2 months
1956	66, 4 months
1957	66, 6 months
1958	66, 8 months
1959	66, 10 months
1960 or later	67

The early retirement age has not been changed. Workers and their spouses can start collecting social security benefits under early retirement at age 62, and spouses of deceased workers can collect after age 60. Of course, early retirement benefits are smaller, because they are made over a longer period of time. Basically, an early retirement benefit is permanently reduced by 5/9 of 1 percent for each month you retire before your "regular" retirement age. For example, if a worker retires at exactly age 62 when his normal retirement age is 65—36 months early—his benefits would be reduced by 20 percent (5/9 of 1 percent × 36).

OBSERVATION: As the regular retirement age gradually increases under the new law, the reduction in early retirement benefits will get even larger.

What If I Want to Work Past Retirement Age?

If you want to work past retirement age, the social security system offers you two options. You can start receiving benefits immediately, but the benefits will be reduced if your wages exceed a certain limit. Or, you can delay collecting benefits until you stop working, in which case your social security benefits are increased for every month you postpone collecting benefits—until age 70. The older the worker, the greater the increase.

This is roughly how it works out if you delay retirement and also delay collecting benefits:

If you were born in	*Your annual benefits increase will be*
1916 or before	1% per year past retirement
1917–1924	3% per year past retirement
1925–1942	3½% per year past retirement
1943 or later	8% per year past retirement

Let's say Susan, who was born in 1946, retires two years and six months past her normal retirement age of 66. If she had retired at 66, her monthly benefit would have been $700. Instead, her monthly check will be increased to $840—8 percent for each year she delayed retirement or 20 percent (two and a half years × 8 percent).

OBSERVATION: If Susan was born in 1916 and had delayed retirement for two and a half years, her benefit of $700 a month would be increased by only 2.5 percent to $717.50 per month.

OBSERVATION: Your final benefits may go up an additional amount if your earnings continue to increase during the years you work past retirement.

Why Delay Receiving Benefits Past Retirement Age?

As a general rule, it's best not to delay receiving social security benefits merely to take advantage of the additional credit. Even at 8 percent a year, the increase in benefits still may not compensate you for the several years of benefits you lose entirely.

Let's go back to Susan. By delaying retirement by two and a half years, she missed out on thirty monthly social security payments of $700, or a total of $21,000 (before taxes). If Susan instead put that $21,000 in an investment paying 10 percent interest, after two and a half years she would have a total of about $27,000 (before taxes). That extra $27,000 could earn her investment income of about $225 a month (before taxes) for the rest of her life on top of her $700 monthly social security benefit—for a total of $925 a month. If she delayed receiving social security benefits, her $700-a-month check would increase only $140, to $840 per month. Depending on her tax bracket and investment return, she ends up with more monthly income by not delaying her benefits—plus she has an extra nest egg of $27,000 to rely upon.

The situation changes if you want to continue working past social security retirement age. Presently, the benefit to someone under age 70 who works past normal retirement age and earns at least $8,160 ($6,000 if under 65) annually is reduced by $1 for every $2 in earnings. Starting in 1990, $1 in benefits will be deducted for every $3 in earnings.

Back to Susan. If she was working at a job that paid $30,000 a year and opted at age 66 to collect her social security benefit immediately, it would be reduced by $15,000 a year or $1,250 a month. Since her original benefit was only $700 a month, Susan would end up receiving absolutely zero from the social security system while she still worked. She would have to either retire or postpone collecting social security benefits until she turns age 70 in order not to lose out.

In general, workers who retire before age 70 or who earn less than $8,160 a year should not delay collecting their social security benefits. If you've reached the retirement age and are earning above $8,160, compare the delayed retirement credit with the amount you would get if payments began immediately.

OBSERVATION: If you're having trouble with the calculations, ask your local social security office for help.

How Is Social Security Adjusted for Inflation?

Social security benefits are increased every year by the government to help compensate for inflation. The increase in benefits, called a cost-of-living adjustment (COLA), is figured each September based on the increase in the Consumer Price Index over the previous twelve months. The increase is paid starting the following January.

However, the purchasing power of your social security benefits may not quite keep pace with inflation. By law, the COLA increase can be reduced if the social security system has paid out more than it has taken in that year. For example, there was no cost-of-living increase paid between March and September of 1982. If the system runs into more financial problems—which most experts predict will happen in the relatively near future—Congress may again reduce or delay cost-of-living increases.

The Tax Bite on
Social Security

Social security benefits for decades were completely tax free. But starting in 1984, up to one-half of your social security benefits are taxed as regular income if your Adjusted Gross Income, plus tax-free interest income, exceed a certain amount.

Adjusted Gross Income simply means the total income you report on your annual tax return "above the line," after deducting items such as IRA contributions and deductible moving expenses. Your Adjusted Gross Income is on line 32 of your Form 1040.

If you're married and file a joint federal income tax return, you and your spouse can earn up to $32,000 without paying any tax on your social security benefits. For unmarried individuals, the maximum tax-free income level is $25,000. If you're married, but file a separate return and live with your spouse for at least part of the year, you automatically pay tax on half your social security benefits, no matter what your income is.

The part of your social security benefits that's taxed is figured one of two ways, whichever is less:

(a) either half of your total social security benefits for the year or

(b) your Adjusted Gross Income, *plus* your tax-free interest income, *plus* half of your social security benefits for the year, *minus* your base limit of $32,000 or $25,000, depending on whether you're married or single.

The bottom line is that, at worst, 50 percent of your social security benefits will be taxed.

EXAMPLE: Joyce and Roger are both over 67. They have an Adjusted Gross Income of $34,000 and receive annual social security benefits of $10,500. Their taxable benefits are the smaller of (a) $5,250 (half of their total $10,500 social security benefit) or (b) $7,250 (their adjusted gross income of $34,000 plus half their social security benefit of $10,500 minus $32,000, their base limit). In this case, $5,250 of their social security benefits will be taxed as regular income.

There are special tax rules for people who receive a lump-sum payment from social security (to make up for an earlier year's underpayment) or whose benefits are offset by workmen's compensation insurance. Consult your tax adviser if you're in these situations.

OBSERVATION: At year end, the Social Security Administration will send you a statement of the amount of benefits you received over the year.

The Easier Way to Apply for Social Security Benefits

The Social Security Administration consists of thousands of employees, in 1,300 local offices and an enormous headquarters, who all depend on a temperamental giant of a computer to keep track of 110 million workers and 35 million retirees. In other words, it's a superbureaucracy that you must approach with patience, common sense and some advance planning. Here's how:

First, you should apply for benefits in person at your local social security office three to six months before you plan to retire. (If you're applying for early retirement benefits, the earliest you can apply is three months before your 62nd birthday.) Bring with you your social security card (and your spouse's), proof of both your ages (such as a birth certificate), a copy of your marriage certificate, last year's W–2s (and tax returns if you were self-employed), proof of any divorces and a good book to read while you're waiting.

OBSERVATION: You should bring both a copy and an original of each document. That way, once the social security office authenticates your copy you can keep the original.

Try not to show up on a Monday, a Friday or the first few days of the month, when the system's 35 million retirees are most likely to need help. And once you've applied, do as much as possible over the telephone. Try to get the name and telephone extension of any helpful employee when you apply in person so you can ask for him or her specifically when you call.

Social security checks usually arrive by the third day of every month or you can arrange for direct deposit of your checks to your bank account. If one of your checks is late, avoid going to the local social security office in person if you can help it—instead call your local office and file a claim report for a lost check.

If for any reason the Social Security Administration denies your claim for benefits you will be notified in writing. If you disagree, you have sixty days to request reconsideration and you should seek help from a lawyer.

What about Medicare?

If you are eligible for social security benefits you'll also qualify for Medicare when you reach age 65, even if you're still working. Medicare is also available for anyone who has been receiving social security disability benefits for two years or who has chronic kidney disease. A nonworking spouse is also eligible for Medicare at age 65 if the working spouse is eligible for social security benefits.

An application for Medicare is included when you apply for social security retirement benefits. If you don't apply for benefits at age 65, then you must apply separately to be covered by Medicare. To avoid hassles, sign up three months before you turn 65.

Medicare insurance comes in two parts. Part A involves no premium and pays for hospital care. There is a deductible of $492 for each hospital stay, after which Medicare will pay 100 percent of your eligible hospital bills for sixty days. After sixty days, you pay $123 a day for the next thirty days (for a total of $3,690) and $246 a day for the next sixty days (for a total of $14,726), with Medicare picking up the balance of the hospital's charges covered. If you stay in the hospital longer than that, Part A doesn't pay a dime. Once you're out of the hospital for at least sixty days, the Medicare payment cycle makes a fresh start.

If you're 65 or over and not eligible for Medicare, you can still sign up for Part A, but you will have to pay monthly premiums (currently $214). You should sign up for this voluntary program within three months of your 65th birthday.

OBSERVATION: These amounts are in effect for 1986, but are changed each January 1, based on the inflation rate for hospital care.

Part A also pays for some health services that are provided in your home, including a part-time nurse, physical therapy and certain medical supplies (but not prescription drugs) and equipment. It also covers certain hospice care for the terminally ill.

There are a few hospitals that do not participate in the Medicare program—be sure to check, otherwise you won't be reimbursed. But if you're rushed to the closest hospital in an emergency, Medicare may reimburse you even if the hospital is nonparticipating.

Participation in Part B, the second part of Medicare, is voluntary and involves a monthly premium of $15.50. (But when you enroll for Part A they'll automatically include you in Part B unless you tell them otherwise.) Part B is a good deal, because the $15.50 premium represents only about one-quarter of the actual cost to the government for the coverage.

Under this plan, you pay the first $75 of any medical expense and then Medicare pays 80 percent of the remaining "allowable" expenses.

Here are some of the medical costs covered by Part B:

- doctor's services
- X-rays and other tests
- casts, splints and similar items

- drugs you cannot take without medical assistance
- ambulance service, medical equipment, such as iron lungs, hospital beds, artificial organs, limbs and eyes

There are some items that neither Part A or B covers. These include:

- prescription drugs
- medical services outside the United States (except for some nearby Canadian areas)
- cosmetic surgery
- most dental services
- personal comfort items
- routine checkups
- most eye exams and glasses
- hearing aids
- private nurses
- private hospital rooms, unless needed for medical reasons

Observation: When in doubt, submit a bill for reimbursement. If it's rejected, you can always apply for a review.

Most Medicare claims are handled by an insurance organization such as Blue Cross and Blue Shield. Many doctors and hospitals deal with the organization directly and simply send you a bill for the uncovered balance.

If you're covered by a company medical plan, your

medical bills must be submitted for reimbursement under that plan before any claims are submitted to Medicare. This rule applies only until age 70 and covers only companies with more than 20 employees. If you're between 65 and 69 and covered by a generous company plan, it's probably best not to sign up for Part B until your company coverage ends, or at age 70, if sooner.

OBSERVATION: By law, if you work past age 65, your employer must offer you and your spouse the same medical benefits as younger employees.

WILL SOCIAL SECURITY SURVIVE?

It has often been said that America is graying. As the birth rate declines and people live longer, there are more and more people over age 65 and steadily fewer under age 65. That's bad for the social security system's "pay as you go" setup. The social security taxes paid into the system by today's workers are funneled directly out to current retirees. Money isn't put aside for the future—which means that the social security system faces a critical shortage of cash as the number of new retirees continues to grow far faster than the number of new workers paying into the system.

This prospect puts dual political pressure on the Congress: to protect the social security checks of current retirees, but not to raise social security taxes for current workers. Most likely, the solution will be a compromise. Social security taxes won't go up too much more, but at the same time benefits will not quite keep pace with inflation. And probably the standard retirement age will be raised again. The bottom line is that the social security system probably will not go bankrupt, but the value of each retiree's benefit probably will go down.

A ray of hope for the future is that America is in the midst of a mini baby boom, as the original postwar "baby boom generation" has settled down and begun to raise families. When those children enter the work force in 20 or so years, the scales may be tilted back a bit in favor of workers supporting the social security system.

What Will My Company's Retirement Benefit Be?

Just ask. Generally, you must work for a company for a minimum period of time, stated in the retirement plan, before you have an absolute or "vested" right to receive your earned retirement benefit. You will lose your benefit if you leave the company before you are vested.

By law, your company must provide you—upon your request—with a statement showing the exact amount of your benefit to date from your company's retirement plan, whether the benefit is vested and, if not, when you will be fully vested.

If you are old enough to be nearing retirement, chances are that you already are vested. If not, by law you will *automatically* become completely vested if you reach the plan's retirement age (which is usually age 65) while still employed by your company, even if you have not worked for the minimum vesting period.

It also is very important to find out when and in what form (e.g., a lifetime pension, in installments or in a single sum) your retirement benefits will be paid. Many company retirement plans allow their employees to choose both the form of payment and the date on which payments will begin. Depending on your decision, you can significantly stretch your retirement benefit dollars and save on taxes to boot.

Different Forms of Payment

Company retirement plans each have their own "normal" or standard form of payment. Some plans allow you to specifically choose another alternative. Your choices, if any, depend entirely upon the terms of the plan, which are summarized in what is called a Summary Plan Description (SPD). The SPD describes the basic features of your company's retirement plan and must be provided to you by your employer without charge, upon your request. By law your employer also must explain to you, in simple terms, what your payment options are. And, if you ask, you must be told what the amount of your payments would be under each option and how you would be affected financially by choosing one option over another.

If there are choices offered for payment of your retirement benefit, they must be of equal value or cost to the company as the standard form of payment (as figured by the company's actuary). There's an exception for certain subsidized early retirement or spousal benefits, in which payments are a bit more than usual. More on that later.

The following is a brief explanation of the most common ways for companies to pay out retirement benefits.

Life Pension or Annuity. A fixed monthly pension is paid for the rest of your life. Usually, it is not adjusted for inflation and payment stops upon your death.

Joint-and-survivor Option. In exchange for getting what usually is a somewhat smaller monthly pension during your lifetime, after your death all or a portion (usually either 100 percent or 50 percent) of that benefit is paid to your beneficiary for the rest of his or her lifetime if you should die first. The reason for the reduction is that payments are likely to be made over a longer period of time. The reduction in your own pension is based upon your age, your beneficiary's age when you retire and how much will be paid to your beneficiary. Some companies offer married employees a "subsidized" joint-and-survivor benefit, in which the monthly payments are not reduced even though payment will be made over the life of you *and* your spouse. This extra benefit is valuable, especially if your spouse is relatively young.

OBSERVATION: All pension plans and some profit-sharing plans require that a spouse give notarized consent *not* to be paid a survivor's benefit.

Period Certain and Life Option. With this method, a monthly pension is paid during your lifetime or for a fixed period (usually ten years), whichever is longer. If you die before receiving payments for the minimum period, your beneficiary receives the rest of the payments over that period. The monthly payments are usually less than with a regular pension because of the guarantee.

Installment Option. Monthly payments under this setup are guaranteed only for a fixed period of time, usually five, ten or fifteen years. If you die before the end of the installment period, payments continue to your beneficiary until the end of the period. The amount of the payments may be more or less than a lifetime pension, depending upon the age at which you retire.

Single-sum Option. Payment is made in a single sum when you retire. To avoid a big tax bite, you may be able to use income tax averaging or a tax-free rollover to an IRA. The tax treatment of the single-sum option as well as the other forms of payment are discussed below.

Forced Single-sum Payment. Some retirement plans automatically pay a pension benefit of up to $3,500 in a single sum at retirement, even if the employee prefers an optional form of payment.

How Is My Retirement Benefit Taxed?

If you receive your retirement benefit in any form other than a lump-sum distribution (described below), it will be taxed as regular income. For example, if you received a total of $7,000 in monthly pension payments for the year, you must include this amount on your income tax return as ordinary income.

Rollover to IRA. Part or all of your retirement plan payment can be transferred (rolled over) tax free into an IRA within sixty days of payment without meeting the usual requirements for contributing to an IRA. For instance, you don't have to have any earned income for that year and the usual contribution restrictions for people age 70½ don't apply. Nor is there any penalty for contributing more than $2,000 in a single year from a retirement plan payout to an IRA.

To roll over a single-sum distribution to an IRA, you simply fill out a form that is available from your IRA custodian and attach it to your rollover check. But there are two requirements: first, you must have received at least half of your retirement benefit in a single year. (This is usually the case anyway.) The second is that payment must have been made because you met certain conditions in the plan such as: your retirement, reaching age 59½ or terminating employment. Because the rules are complicated, you should always check with your company or tax accountant to make sure you're eligible.

EXAMPLE: Maureen has quit her job with a vested benefit in her company profit-sharing plan of $6,000.

She has chosen to receive the entire benefit immediately. Maureen can roll over any portion of the $6,000 to an IRA within sixty days without paying any income tax.

OBSERVATION: Again, any portion of a retirement plan payment that is really a return of your own after tax contributions (as shown on the Form 1099) isn't eligible for a rollover to an IRA.

Of course, you are taxed on any part of a retirement plan distribution that is not put in an IRA. If you receive property instead of cash from the retirement plan, you must roll over either the property or the cash proceeds from the sale of the property to an IRA to avoid paying income tax.

Once the retirement plan money is in an IRA, it is governed by regular IRA rules. This means that if you are over age 70½ when you roll over your retirement payment to an IRA, you must immediately start withdrawing money from the IRA each year. Your IRA trustee can tell you the exact amount that you must withdraw.

OBSERVATION: Don't take a chance of losing your benefits check or missing the sixty-day rollover deadline. Make your rollover the very same day you receive your lump-sum distribution.

IRAs, including how to start one and how to invest them, are fully discussed in Chapter 5.

Lump-sum Distributions. A lump-sum distribution is a form of single-sum distribution available to people who have belonged to their company plan for at least five years. A lump-sum distribution is a payment of the entire balance of a person's retirement benefit, made only *in the event of* the employee's retirement, terminating employment, death, or reaching age 59½. The difference is that a single-sum payment can be made while an employee still is working (for example, if the company's retirement plan is terminated), before the employee has been in the plan five years or because the payment is not for the entire amount of the benefit.

As discussed next, lump-sum distributions are good for certain special tax breaks that single-sum distributions are not. But as you'll see, those breaks were reduced by Tax Reform.

Minimum-distribution Allowance. Under both old and new law, if the lump-sum distribution is less than $70,000, a certain portion called the "minimum-distribution allowance" is tax free. The minimum-distribution allowance is $10,000 or one-half of the lump-sum distribution, whichever is less, minus 20 percent of the amount of the distribution over $20,000. For example, out of a distribution of $20,000, $10,000 is tax free but for a distribution of $40,000, only $6,000 is tax free.

Five-year Averaging. Basically, five-year income averaging means that you figure out your taxes as if your lump-sum distribution was being paid out over five years. (Before Tax Reform you could use ten-year averaging which was twice as good.) This means that if you received $100,000 from your company at retirement, you would be taxed as if you had been paid only $20,000 a year for five years, but you pay the total tax the year you receive the distribution. Because tax rates increase as income increases, you pay less tax on five annual $20,000 payments than on one $100,000 payment. Also, the tax on a lump-sum distribution always is figured as if you were single and had no other income.

With one exception, discussed below, a person must be over age 59½ to use this method and it can generally only be used once, even if the person receives more than one lump-sum distribution.

The following list illustrates what the tax on lump-sum distributions would be, using the five-year averaging method, based on 1988 tax rates:

Amount of Distribution	*Tax*
$ 10,000	$ 750
20,000	1,500
50,000	6,900
75,000	11,250
100,000	16,398

Form 4972 must be used for income averaging on a lump-sum distribution.

Capital Gains Treatment. Employees who joined their retirement plan before 1974 (the year ERISA went into effect) may have the added advantage of being able to treat the portion of the lump-sum distribution which was earned before 1974 as a capital gain, which will be taxed at a flat 20 percent rate. Obviously, this will only help people in the 28 or 33 percent brackets. Any part of your lump-sum distribution that was earned before 1974 will be reported on the Form W–2P or 1099R, which should be sent with your lump-sum distribution check.

However, it could work out to your advantage to figure your taxes using the income averaging method on your entire lump-sum distribution, including the pre-1974 capital gain portion. You or your tax adviser should figure the tax both ways to see which saves you the most taxes.

However, Tax Reform will slowly erode the capital gain advantage. Starting in 1989, that advantage will be phased out for your pre-1974 benefits based on the year of payment,

Year	*Portion That You Can Use Capital Gains On*
1989	95%
1990	75
1991	25
1992	None

So if you received a $75,000 lump sum distribution in 1990, of which $50,000 was earned before 1974, you could only use the special 20 percent tax rate on 75 percent of the pre-1974 earnings, which comes to $37,500.

OBSERVATION: These new Tax Reform rules apply to lump-sum distributions made in 1987 or thereafter. However, there is a special rule that if you quit or retired from a job in 1986 (or perhaps died), and got a lump-sum distribution before March 16, 1987, you can choose to be taxed under the old rules. If you're in this situation, see your tax advisor for help.

Grandfather Protection for People Over Age 50. When Congress slashed the benefits of ten-year averaging in half, members felt guilty about older people who were about to retire. So there is a special break (called "grandfather protection") for anyone who was at least 50 years old on January 1, 1986. These people can choose between using five-year averaging with the lower Tax Reform rates or ten-year averaging with the higher 1986 tax rates, whichever works out less. For example, when the lowest rates are effective in 1988, ten-year averaging would save you more money than five-year averaging on lump-sum distributions of under $350,000.

You only get one chance at choosing *either* five- or ten-year averaging for your entire lifetime. But "grandfathered" folks over age 50 don't have to wait until age 59½ to use one of the two methods.

As an added break, anyone in the grandfather category can also choose to be taxed at a flat 20 percent rate on the capital gain portion of a lump-sum distribution, even if they get it after 1992.

What To Do When You Get a Lump-Sum Distribution. Before you decide to get a lump-sum distribution of your benefits, estimate how much tax you'll owe using any of the special rules for which you qualify, namely five-year averaging, ten-year averaging and capital gains, versus just paying a flat tax on the money as if it was a regular pay check. See which comes out cheapest and by how much. If you expect to get a second lump-sum distribution from another plan sometime in the future, do these calculations for that distribution as well. Since you only get one chance to use five- or ten-year averaging, you should have that opportunity for when it will save you the most on taxes.

Added Tax on Large Benefits. Starting in 1987, you will have to pay a 15 percent tax on any payment over $112,500 from your retirement plans and IRAs combined, in addition to regular income taxes. But if you receive a lump-sum distribution and use five-year averaging, then the $112,500 cut-off is raised to $562,500. Over time, the $112,500 and $562,500 amounts will be adjusted for inflation.

Congress also felt a little guilty about this one. So as an exception to the new rule, generally any benefits that were earned before August 1, 1986 (when the extra tax was first proposed) won't be penalized. Figuring out this new tax and the exceptions is very, very tricky, so if you think your benefits may be anywhere close to the cut-off point *see your tax advisor.* And don't delay. You have to choose the special exception by the time you file your 1988 tax return, even if you don't receive any benefits before that.

Income Tax Withholding. Unlike the automatic tax withholding on regular wages, you can choose not to have income taxes withheld from your retirement checks and pay the total tax on April 15th. When it comes time for your retirement payments to begin, your company will give you IRS Form W-4P to specify whether you want any income taxes withheld, and if so, the amount of personal exemptions you want to claim. If you don't fill out the Form W-4P, your company will automatically withhold taxes.

Before you decide whether you want to postpone withholding, speak to your tax adviser. But if you're simply rolling over your distribution to an IRA tax free, you should always elect no withholding.

Which Form of Payment Should You Choose?

That depends upon your overall retirement strategy and your income tax situation. It's best to consult with an accountant before deciding.

A lifetime pension or a pension with a survivor benefit for a spouse will guarantee you the security of a steady monthly check, but won't protect you against inflation. If you receive your pension in a single sum or over a short installment period, then you can invest the money you don't need immediately. If it's a single-sum payment, you can postpone paying any taxes by rolling it over to an IRA or pay less taxes by using ten-year income averaging, if you are eligible. But you may find it harder to plan ahead enough to stretch that money and your other savings to last a lifetime.

A few simple calculations can help you decide. First, find out from your company how much your single-sum distribution would be and whether you would be eligible for income averaging and/or capital gains treatment. (Of course, if you're under age 59½ and would owe the 10 percent penalty on early distribution, don't take a single-sum distribution unless you can roll it over tax free into an IRA.) Then estimate, perhaps with the help of an accountant, how much income tax you would have to pay on that single-sum distribution. The difference between those two amounts is what you get to keep if you take a single-sum distribution. Next, figure out how much income you could earn from that single-sum distribution in a conservative investment such as a bank money market account or several blue-chip company bonds. (For purposes of this figuring, you can ignore income taxes on your investment income because you would be taxed on your pension anyway.)

You may discover that the annual income you could earn on your single-sum distribution would be about the same as the amount you would receive in a lifetime pension. In that case, you would be better off electing a single-sum distribution because in addition to being able to use the investment income, you would still get to keep your principal—the single-sum distribution itself.

Example: Anne, age 65, is about to retire. She

has a choice of receiving either a $9,000 annual lifetime pension with a $4,500-a-year benefit paid to her husband if she dies, or getting an immediate lump-sum distribution of $100,000. She figures out that she would have to pay $14,471 in taxes if she took the lump sum, leaving her with $85,529. She could earn 10 percent interest, or about $8,500 a year, on that $85,529—about $500 less a year than if she took the $9,000-a-year pension. But Anne chooses a lump sum. Why? Because she decides it's much better to have a $85,529 nest egg that she can pass on to her heirs or use in an emergency than simply a lifetime monthly pension.

If Anne does not need the interest income on the lump sum right away, she might consider putting the full $100,000 into an IRA, where it can earn tax-free income until she has to start withdrawing money from the IRA at age 70½. In that case, however, she would lose the benefit of income averaging.

Another option is to ask a few insurance companies (or your insurance agent) how much they would charge to arrange for a lifetime annuity equal to the amount of your monthly pension. If the insurance company would charge you less than the amount of your lump sum, then you could take the lump sum, arrange for the monthly annuity and still have some money left over to invest.

When Does Payment Begin?

In most company retirement plans, you receive your benefit at your plan's stated retirement age, which usually is 65, unless you continue to work past retirement age.

If you're thinking about working past retirement age, ask whether your retirement benefit will be increased for the delay. If the answer is "no," then you might consider changing jobs (although that could be hard for someone of retirement age) so that you can collect your retirement benefit immediately.

But the new Tax Reform rules require that payments start by the April 1 after you reach age 70½. Otherwise, you'll owe a 50 percent tax on what you should have been paid. (The IRS can waive the tax if the delay was due to a "reasonable error" and it's corrected when caught.) This is just like the IRA rules. These new rules apply starting in 1989, except for people who were working and over age 70½ by January 1, 1988, and people who made special elections before 1984.

Some company retirement plans provide an "early-retirement benefit" in which an employee who retires before age 65—even to take another job—can begin collecting his retirement payments immediately. In most cases, an early-retirement benefit is significantly less than a normal-retirement benefit, since the payments start much sooner. But some companies who want to encourage employees to retire early offer a "subsidized" early-retirement benefit that actually is worth more (taking into account that the payments begin sooner) than the benefit at age 65.

Keep in mind that if you retire early and do not go to work for a new company or become self-employed, the amount of your retirement income probably will be less than the amount of your working income. And if you start living on a fixed income at a much earlier date, your retirement nest egg will have to be stretched that much further.

PLANNING YOUR RETIREMENT STRATEGY

How Much Is Enough?

The American Association of Retired Persons estimates that a retirement income equal to 75 percent of current salary is enough to maintain a person's present standard of living. That's because once you retire, some of your biggest budget items will be cheaper—taxes, housing, children and savings. Your taxes will be lower because you'll be earning less income, at least half of your social security benefits will be tax free and you won't have any social security taxes taken out of your pension. Your mortgage is likely to be paid off and by the time you retire, your children are likely to be fully educated and off on their own. And you won't be putting aside as much savings toward retirement—you'll be ready to start spending it.

But rather than relying on a mechanical formula, you should also calculate for yourself how much you're now spending and how much you expect to spend after you retire. Chapter 3 gives you the details on how to prepare a current budget. The same rules apply for your retirement budget, with two major adjustments.

First, recalculate your income taxes, based on your lower retirement earnings. An easy way to do this is to take out last year's tax return and "prepare" it as if you were already retired and receiving social security benefits and a company retirement benefit. But you'll have to adjust for all the changes made by the 1986 Tax Reform Act. Chapter 4 shows you how. And don't forget to adjust for any major changes such as state and local taxes (if you move to a new state) and for the fact that you won't be making any more IRA contributions.

Second, take into account increased leisure time expenses. If you plan to spend a good part of the year on the tennis court or golf course or traveling, then your budget should reflect those costs. Be realistic—don't assume that things will always work out in the least expensive way ("I'll only play tennis during the week when fees are cheapest"). And keep in mind the expense of any other possible changes in your life-style, such as moving to a warmer climate or maintaining a vacation home.

Now compare your retirement budget with your current income. Nobody, especially when they first retire, wants to have to dip into their savings to maintain their life-style. They want to keep that nest egg handy to meet emergencies, guard against inflation and just for plain old security. That means you'll have to make some hard choices in balancing your immediate financial needs in retirement against the possibility of outliving your nest egg.

Many retirees try to preserve their savings and rely only on their income (and maybe save some of that too) for expenses. But it's unrealistic to plan on *never* spending a dime of your capital—you don't want your savings to outlive you. After you've been retired for a number of years and you find your expenses increasing, you should consider taking a set amount from your capital each year without significant anxiety about running out of money.

The following table estimates how much you could withdaw each year from your nest egg over a set period of years, assuming you earned 7 percent interest and used both income and capital (ignoring any income taxes), until the money was gone.

To figure for other amounts, just divide your savings by 1,000 and multiply that answer by the number in the years column. For example, to figure out how much you could spend if you had $10,000 over five years, simply divide 10,000 by 1,000 and then multiply the answer, 10, by $244 to get $2,440.

Figuring out how much money you need is only the first step in developing your retirement strategy. You must also consider: when (or whether) you want to retire; what to do with the equity in your home and your IRA; and how to develop a sound investment strategy to fit your needs.

When Should You Retire?

This question raises as many philosophical issues as financial ones. Much of your decision to retire is based

Nest Egg Invested at 7%	*Years of Annual Spending* *5 yrs.*
$ 1,000	244
25,000	6,100
50,000	12,200
100,000	24,400
150,000	36,580
200,000	48,800

10 yrs.	*15 yrs.*
142	110
3,560	2,750
7,120	5,490
14,240	10,980
21,360	16,470
28,480	21,960

20 yrs.	*25 yrs.*
94	86
2,360	2,140
4,720	4,290
9,440	8,580
14,160	12,870
18,880	17,160

on personal factors such as health, outlook on life and job satisfaction. In terms of economics, the longer you wait to retire, the less time you'll be living on a fixed income and the more time you'll have to build your nest egg instead of spending it. Further, your social security benefits will be increased and your company retirement benefits also may be sweetened if you postpone retirement.

Thanks to Congress, the decision is largely up to you. By law most people cannot be forced to retire. If you're not compelled to retire, seriously consider how much better financial shape you could be in by delaying retirement for a year or two. It could make the difference between just getting by and peace of mind.

What to Do with Your IRA

One of the biggest advantages to having an IRA is that all your earnings are tax free until the money is withdrawn. In general, the longer you leave your money in your IRA, the longer you can collect interest on Uncle Sam's tax money.

You cannot touch your IRA without penalty before age 59½. Between the ages of 59½ and 70½, you can take as much money out every year as you choose. So if you're 60 years old and need an extra few thousand dollars—even if you're not yet retired—you can simply withdraw it from your IRA. And if you're still working that year, you can put up to $2,000 back into the IRA.

EXAMPLE: Peter, 62, is planning a three-month vacation from work. To help pay for it, he withdraws $12,000 from his IRA and pays regular income tax on the money. When he returns to work, he can still put up to $2,000 back in his IRA that year and take a tax deduction too.

But if you are still working and are between age 59½ and 70½, your IRA should be your last resource for cash. Otherwise, wait for the low-tax-bracket years after you've retired.

You *must* begin taking a minimum amount of money out of your IRA each year starting with the April 1 after the year you turn age 70½. This rule applies even if you have not yet retired. If you take out less than the minimum you'll face a very stiff penalty: 50 percent of what you should have taken out. For exaple, if you were required to withdraw $2,000 and didn't, you'd owe the government $1,000 (unless you prove the delay was due to a reasonable error).

The minimum you must withdraw each year after you've reached age 70½ is based on your life expectancy or, if you're married, the joint life expectancies of you and your spouse or other named beneficiary. The minimum is figured so that you could withdraw equal amounts each year of your *expected* life (or the combined life expectancies of you and your beneficiary). Your bank or other IRA custodian can figure how much you will be required to withdraw. You also can use the money in your IRA to buy an annuity that will provide payments to you (or you and your spouse or other beneficiary) for the rest of your life (or lives).

When it comes time to actually retire, if your total income from other sources is more than you need to live on, then leave as much money as you can to compound tax free in your IRA.

Should You Sell Your Home?

Your house, condominium or co-op could be your single most valuable asset in retirement. You may be tempted to cash in on that investment.

Let's look at the situation of a couple we'll call George and Martha Williams. Both retired, they paid $30,000 for their home 25 years ago and today it's worth $180,000. The Williamses figure out that they could rent a similar home in their neighborhood for about $8,500 a year, sell their house and invest the proceeds from the sale at 10 percent interest. They would earn almost $13,000 a year after taxes, assuming they're in a 28 percent tax bracket, which would put them $4,500 ahead after paying their rent. Even better for them, because they are over age 59½ they can waive income taxes on up to $125,000 in profits from the sale of their home. (*See* Chapter 8.)

But you should exercise caution before selling your house just to gain extra income, unless you're struggling for cash. Your home can be one of your biggest hedges against inflation because it is likely to keep going up in value. By owning your home you insure that your only housing expenses will be utilities, taxes and maintenance. And even if these amounts do go up over time, your rental costs would be likely to go up by much more. The longer you wait, the more your home could be worth to you. Besides, getting used to retirement is hard enough without adjusting to a new place to live.

Annuities: You'll Never Run Out of Money

An easy—but expensive—way to ensure you'll never outlive your nest egg is to buy a lifetime, guaranteed annuity from an insurance company.

With a lifetime annuity, you hand over a pot of money to a life insurance company to be paid back to you in fixed installments over the remainder of your life. You can arrange for payment over a minimum number of years, even if you die before that, or buy a survivor benefit that continues after your death to be paid to your spouse or other beneficiary for the rest of his or her life. The amount of your annuity will depend in part on your life expectancy, prevailing interest rates and whether you want benefits to continue to a beneficiary after your death. If you outlive your projected life expectancy, the insurance company will have to come up with the additional money to continue payments. If you die sooner (and don't have survivor benefits) the insurance company keeps the extra money.

The downside of annuities is the high commissions charged by most companies. Shop around and speak to a number of insurance companies or agents before buying. (*See* Chapter 7 for how to shop for insurance.) You may find that different companies charge very different amounts to pay out the same benefit. And ask for advice from your accountant or someone else who, unlike a life insurance salesperson, won't earn a large commission if you choose an annuity.

Investment Income

Once you retire, your investment income will be the most important element of your finances because you have the most control over it—it can make the difference between living well or just getting by. Your investment income includes all interest, dividends, stock market profits (less any losses), income from other sources such as property rentals and tax-free income such as interest on municipal bonds or cash value life insurance. One way to estimate this amount is to look at how much investment income you earned last year, taking into account that after you retire, your investments will be more conservative and probably earn less income. You also should disregard any recent big, one-time gains and losses that are unlikely to occur in the future.

Another way of estimating your investment income is to add up all your cash savings (e.g., bank money market account, stocks, life insurance) and assume that you could invest that sum at a very conservative rate of return such as 7 percent. That way, any extra income you earn above 7 percent can be added to your retirement nest egg to save for a rainy day.

Investing for Security

You need to rethink your investment strategy when you retire. As we've seen, social security benefits are unlikely to totally keep pace with inflation, your pension probably won't keep up at all, and when it comes to your investments—the state of our economy makes it difficult to be absolutely sure where to put your money for best results. A look at recent financial happenings reveal just how unstable the economy is.

After a tough recession combined with double-digit inflation and interest rates and soaring gold and real estate prices, our economy reversed itself in the mid-1980s and entered into the recent period of relative prosperity—low inflation, lower-interest rates, a booming stock market and declining gold prices. At the same time, unemployment remains relatively high, "real" interest rates even higher ("real" means the difference between the interest rate and the rate of inflation) and there is a mind-boggling federal deficit. Plus, the president and the Congress just "Reformed" our tax system and nobody knows what that will do to the economy. Today, economists seem more muddled than ever.

The bottom line is that if you're facing life on a fixed income, your investment earnings are crucial and your safest bet is to diversify among several prudent types of investments. You may not make a financial killing, but you should be protected no matter in which direction the economy goes. Here's what to consider in diversifying your investments.

Cash

You need to have a reservoir of cash to draw on in an emergency or for a special expense such as a child's wedding. Cash means readily available investments in a bank money market account and short-term CDs. This pool of money allows you to avoid having to cash in less-liquid investments when prices are low. About 25 percent of your investments should be in available cash.

Longer Debt

Another 25 to 35 percent of your investments should be in longer-term debt, meaning CDs of longer than one year, company and municipal bonds, U.S. Treasury bills and government-guaranteed mortgage pools such as Ginnie Mae and Freddie Mac. Also consider investing in one or more bond mutual funds with average maturities of under ten years (the prospectus will have this information), instead of just choosing individual bonds on your own. While maturities of five to ten years are best, it's also wise to arrange for your investments to mature at different times so you can reinvest some money if interest rates go up. (Of course, this would work against you if rates are on the downswing. But remember the goal is preserving your fortune, not building another one.)

Equity

Another chunk of your wealth, say 25 to 35 percent, should be invested in solid blue-chip stocks. As we saw in Chapter 9, over time equity usually outpaces debt and is a better hedge against inflation—but, it's also riskier and usually less liquid (i.e., harder to quickly turn into cash without any loss). But hold off any investment until the stock market stabilizes. To spread your risk, consider investing in several reasonably conservative common stock mutual funds.

Real Estate

Traditionally an inflation-proof investment, owning your home, a rental unit or a vacation home has already been discussed in detail in the previous section and Chapter 8. You can also invest in real estate through one of countless limited partnerships available, but because they're highly speculative and harder to evaluate, I don't recommend them for any but the most sophisticated investor. Anywhere from 10 to 15 percent of your money, in addition to your home, is a safe amount to invest in real estate.

Gold and Silver

These precious metals don't pay interest or dividends. They just sit in the vault, getting more or less "precious," depending on the market. Generally, metals do best in times of depression, rampant inflation or a stock market panic—when people want the security of owning something "real." About 5 percent to 10 percent of your wealth in gold and/or silver bullion should be enough to cushion you in any disaster. You can buy bullion from many banks and brokerage firms that will hold onto it for you. Another way to invest in gold and silver is to own stock in mining companies—but this is riskier and requires much greater financial expertise.

Wild Speculation

If you love playing the stock market and would be bored by having nothing but safe, intelligent investments, take no more than 5 percent of your money and invest in whatever crazy stocks, racehorses or other idea strikes your fancy. Just don't go beyond that 5 percent stake.

This suggested mix of investments is only a rough guideline. Nobody but yourself can figure out which mix of investments is right for your income and safety needs.

FINAL NOTE

If you have planned well, your retirement income will exceed your expected expenses. But as time goes on, inflation may still creep up on you.

If you own your home or apartment, have built up a solid nest egg, have a reasonable amount of health insurance, and choose your investments wisely, you will have done about all you can do. Unless inflation goes crazy à la Germany in the late 1920s and early 1930s, you should do fine. You owe it to yourself and your family to plan for retirement during your working years.

Q. What will Tax Reform mean to my retirement benefits?

A. For some retirees, lower tax rates mean that they'll get to keep more of their benefits. Those people will feel like they got a raise from Uncle Sam. But people who were expecting lump-sum distributions may be disappointed, because the special advantages of ten-year averaging have been cut in half to five-year averaging. And, you must be over 59½ to use five-year averaging.

Q. Any exceptions to the loss of ten-year averaging?

A. Yes. Anyone who was at least 50 years old on January 1, 1986 can choose between using five-year averaging with the lower Tax Reform rates or ten-year averaging with the higher rates, whichever works out best. Ten-year averaging usually works out better for distributions of under $350,000. You only get one chance to pick either of these methods, but you don't have to wait until age 59½.

Q. What about the capital gains treatment for pre-1974 plan benefits?

A. Starting in 1989, you can only use this method on a portion of your pre-1974 benefits as follows:

Year	*Portion That You Can Use Capital Gains On*
1989	95%
1990	75
1991	25
1992	None

The tax rate on the capital gain is a flat 20 percent, so obviously it's not for people in the 15 percent bracket. This phase-out doesn't apply to people who were age 50 by the end of 1985.

Q. When must I start getting payments?
A. By the April 1 after you reach age 70½, even if you're still working. There are exceptions for workers who were age 70½ by January 1, 1988 or who made special elections before 1984. Otherwise, these rules apply starting in 1989.

Q. What if I violate the age 70½ rule?
A. You'll owe a 50 percent tax on what you should have taken out but didn't. The only exception is if you can prove to the IRS that the delay was caused by a "reasonable error" and you then receive what you should have received right away.

Q. What about very large benefits?
A. If you receive more than $112,500 in any year from all your retirement plans and IRAs combined, you'll generally owe an additional 15 percent tax on the excess. But there are many exceptions to this rule, so consult your tax advisor if you may be in this situation. And don't delay. There is a special exception that you must choose to apply to you by the time you file your 1988 tax return, even if you don't receive any benefits before then.

APPENDIX

HELPFUL ADDRESSES

Debtors Anonymous
316 Fifth Avenue
Room 301
New York, NY 10001
(212) 868-3330

Inquiries and
Complaints Department
New York Stock Exchange
55 Water Street
New York, NY 10041

Internal Revenue Service
1201 E Street, N. W.
Room 900
Washington, DC 20226
(202) 488-3100

International Association for Financial Planning
5775 Peachtree Dunwoody Road, Suite 120C
Atlanta, GA 30342

Institute of Certified Financial Planners
3443 S. Galena, Suite 190
Denver, CO 80231

National Foundation for Consumer Credit
8701 Georgia Avenue
Silver Springs, MD 20910
(301) 589-5600

National Insurance Consumer Organization
121 North Payne Street
Alexandria, VA 22314
(703) 549-8050

Pension Benefit Guarantee Corporation
2020 K Street, N. W.
Washington, DC 20006
(202) 956-5000

S. E. C.
Department of Consumer Affairs, Room 2115
450 Fifth Street, N. W.
Washington, DC 20549

Social Security Administration
Wilkes-Barre Data Operations Center
P. O. Box 20
Wilkes-Barre, PA 18703
(717) 826-6241

INDEX